To Denmark,
With Love

———————

To Denmark, With Love

Judy Falck-Madsen

Illustrated by
Asbjørn Gyldenlund

C3   CR

Polar Bear & Company
An imprint of the
Solon Center for Research and Publishing
Solon, Maine

Polar Bear & Company™
Solon Center for Research and Publishing
PO Box 311, Solon, ME 04979 U.S.A.
207.643.2795, polarbearandco.org, soloncenter.org

ISBN: 978-1-882190-42-3
Library of Congress Control Number: 2016934616

Cover Design by Ramona Cornell du Houx
Illustrations by Asbjørn Gyldenlund

Manufactured on durable acid-free paper in more than one country.

To Denmark—and her people—with love
And to my husband, the Viking
Our wonderful children
And their wonderful children
With love and gratitude for the support
And joy you've always given me

Contents

Introduction

I t was a bright, sunny day, an autumn blessing that can come before Denmark's harsh winter. The sky was that incredible September blue, the garden glowing with late summer flowers, with the intense colors of the second bloom, kept fresh by the heavy dew that comes with the passing of summer.

I sat on the terrace, watching the myriad of insects among the masses of flowers: honey bees and flies, moths and gnats flitting dangerously close to the glistening spider webs that miraculously appear among the stalks of flowers at that time of year. The cat stretched luxuriously by my feet, his snowy white stomach deceptively free of any signs of what poor creatures he had undoubtedly devoured on his morning hunt. His beautiful green eyes flickered with sudden interest as a flock of swallows, gathering to migrate, swarmed into the treetops, chattering cheerfully at having such fine weather for their journey southward.

I felt blissfully happy at being privileged to sit in the sun and enjoy the moment. Lazy like the cat, I postponed thoughts of chores to be done and mused over the idea of being active when the cat is — in the early morning hours when all around is still. There was plenty to do: The rowanberries were ripe and should be made into clear ruby-red jelly to serve with the game meat for winter dinner parties. The flower beds needed tending to insure a good season next year. This was also the best time of year to paint woodwork or clean the larder, and summer clothes needed storing.

The mental list was by now too long to contemplate seriously on such a fine day, and I continued to sit, with the sun on my face and a relaxed smile. The very tip of the cat's tail twitched, as if it were a part of the animal which didn't fancy lazing in the sun. He indolently sat up and batted it soundly with a white paw for a few moments before turning his gorgeous eyes towards me. With a leap that reminded one more of a mental feat than a physical effort, he landed gracefully on the folds of my skirt, made his nest and settled down, purring. I ran my fingers through his soft, warm fur and thought, happiness is like a fat cat on a sunny day. It often flees when pursued, and one has to hold it gently when it's there. I would allow myself to sit still as long as this fickle beast chose to enjoy my company. Lord knows how many small creatures I'd be saving from his claws.

I began to wonder how it had come about that nearly thirty years of living in Denmark had made me the way I am. I couldn't put my finger on the changes. They hadn't been conscious efforts, but small compromises and adjustments, easily lost in the many aspects of learning to live in a foreign land during the busy years when one's children are growing and there isn't time to make a fuss about retaining one's quirks. The strange part was that the adjustments had been to a life which was already an anachronism, a part of Denmark which seemed to be disappearing, as all around me people were realizing their dreams of becoming part of what is termed "Little America."

I thought with longing about the rewards which would have been mine had I belonged to my mother-in-law's generation. The kids having left the nest, I could have been the well-groomed matron, attending tea parties in the afternoon. But now the neighborhood was deserted during the daytime. Even the smells were different — the bygone smells of meals that took long preparation. The sounds of children playing in the streets were replaced with the drone of traffic and the chugging of machinery in the adjacent churchyard — devices purchased to replace the quiet man who used to smooth the gravel with a rake. My particular Denmark had become a curiosity, like an insect trapped in a beautiful piece of amber.

I had realized the extent of the changes that very sad day, the last day I spent with my mother-in-law in her home. She was very ill, and my father-in-law had to leave her in order to attend a meeting. Though eighty-one, he was still quite active. He called and asked me to be with her while he was gone, and the look on his face when he opened the door warned me that her condition was worse. She had fallen asleep on the sofa, and I sat down quietly in a high-backed chair by the window.

Their home had a special atmosphere, and to recall its very distinct charm is, invariably, to remember its inhabitants. The front windows had sheer white inner curtains which were arched in the middle and edged with rich lace, framing lovely porcelain crocks with flourishing pink begonias blooming in them. On that day, dazzling spring sunlight was filtered through the curtains, softening it to match the antique richness of the room. I sat gazing out the window at the Chinese magnolia tree and the delicate pink petals it had scattered on the bright green lawn, thinking how unfair it seemed that Mums should be dying during the springtime, after having endured the discomforts of a long winter. A blackbird with a freakish white head lighted on the branches of the tree, striking an unpleasant note in the reassuringly predictable beauty of the season. I turned and looked at Mums, asleep on the green sofa, her frail hands pale against the old Scotch plaid I had covered her with. Her emerald ring with the circlet of diamonds caught the light and blazed for a moment before she fidgeted with her hands, moving them out of the hold the sunbeam had.

Within the stillness of the room, one heard the melodious song of the blackbird and cooing of pigeons. A gilded clock with bright gold figures frozen in an attitude of elegance stood on top of a magnificent bureau. Its steady ticking and regular chiming was like a reassuring presence. It had always seemed odd, when we came by to look after the house while my husband's parents were away, to enter the room and not hear the clock. As soon as they returned, it was wound, and I came to associate its sounds with the warmth and comfort of their hospitality. Now it reminded me of the passage of time on a day quite unlike all others, and I again looked at my mother-in-law to reassure myself that her breathing was even. It was hard to understand that just one month earlier I had been here to help her with a luncheon she gave for her friends, to celebrate her eighty-first birthday.

That had been a day in April, and I bicycled through the woods on the way to her house, stopping to pick a bouquet of white windflowers that were always out just in time for her birthday. When I arrived, the table was already set, and the florist's flowers had arrived, a spring bouquet with pink tulips and cherry blossoms that had been forced to bloom early. She had chosen to use the dusty rose linen that made such a good background for the delicate floral pattern in her Limoges china. The ladies were to drink a Mosel wine, and the long-stemmed glasses with hand-painted ivy were in front of each plate, the glasses that none of the rest us dared to wash up. "Papa brought them home one day. He had such good taste," she said, as she lovingly picked one up and held it to the light.

The food was being catered, but no other corners had been cut. The silver was gleaming, the napkins stiff from having been put through the old-fashioned mangle cold. Each place setting had been subjected to the scrutiny of her experienced eye. I marveled as I always did, at the demands her generation placed on themselves, even though they no longer had servants to make these demands more feasible. She was dressed in her good blue suit with a soft white blouse, her white hair still thick and pretty. I knew even then how ill she was and wondered what this effort had cost her, but as soon as the doorbell rang, she was buoyed by the pleasure she took in the role of hostess once everything had met her approval.

There were only eight of them left, women who had known each other since their youth, those golden years in Scandinavia for those who had the means to enjoy them. They had shared their child-bearing years, the years of the Occupation, and the bewildering years that began when Denmark began to take part in the prosperity of the sixties. I poured champagne and smiled at seeing how much this older generation is always capable of consuming. The conversation was lively, kept going by the fun of sprinkling it with old memories.

By the time we moved into the dining room the years had slipped off them, and they were like girls again, without the burdens of old age. Mums' green eyes were twinkling, and she was basking in the compliments she had known she would receive for having arranged everything so nicely. It was a scene so familiar to me in that home — the well-set table, the carefully chosen courses, the dessert that simply had to be that particular dessert (even though it meant someone being obliged to go into Copenhagen and get it at the confectioner's shop at Hotel d'Angleterre), coffee in the living room, served on an occasion like this in the demitasse cups once painted for the Czar of Russia, frequent laughter, the scent of flowers, cognac in large snifters, the candles burning low and the cold draught from the hallway when the first guest left.

ଓଃ   ଓଃ

The birthday party had been a supreme effort, and now, such a short time afterwards, there was only the waiting and watching for death to come. Mums stirred, and I asked her if she would like some tea. Refusing to be weak, she insisted on moving into the verandah to sit on the Christian the Eighth sofa where she could drink her tea in the afternoon sun.

I knew the ritual: It had to be the tea from the blue caddy, saved for special occasions. She wanted me to make it in the china pot with orange dragons and serve it in the thin cups that matched. When I was younger, this attention to detail had been incomprehensible to my American sense of practicality, but today I catered to it with barely a thought of my old impatience. I prepared the tray, the one on which her mother had carved an intricate decoration in the beginning of the century when it was a pastime popular among ladies of leisure. First there had to be the linen napkin, snowy white with English cut-work, the tea steeping under a tea cozy, the delicate cups that had been a wedding gift from her brother, a silver plate with thin slices of cake, and a box of matches to light the inevitable candle.

The flame looked wan in the bright sunlight, and I felt a longing for those days when we would have been outside on such a splendid day. Mums looked cheerful at the sight of the tea being poured and suggested that we make the day more festive by having a glass of cognac. "When I was a child it was something we were given as medicine, and it has taken me many years to learn to like it." And that sip of brandy took her back in time, reminding her of bits and pieces of her childhood in Norway, stories I had heard many times before, but which took on a special poignancy with the realization of how much I would miss hearing them.

Snatches of her life in this house flittered like ghosts in the room, and I thought of her as a young girl of fifteen, with mischievous eyes and long, taffy-colored curls, seeing her new home in Denmark for the first time, with its steep, red-tiled roof, the small panes of the mullioned windows, the freshly painted green shutters, and the window boxes filled with pansies, giving it a typically Danish, well-tended look — a friendly, welcoming look, which had been wasted on her. She had compared it with the grand home she and her family had left in Norway and was angry and disappointed. She had walked through the rooms with indifference, lastly stepping onto the balcony of the master bedroom to look out over the shimmering green beech trees that filled the woods down to the sea.

The sea was bright blue, broken by summer whitecaps and bobbing sails. The woman who had opened the house for them followed her out on the balcony and said in the Danish that sounded so harsh in the ears of a Norwegian, "Isn't it a lovely view? You're a very lucky girl to come to such a beautiful part of Denmark!" She looked away so that the woman wouldn't see the tears that were stinging her eyes, as she thought of the scene from her beloved home at Nordstrand, overlooking the fjord, with views in all directions. How could she be expected to be impressed with such a small view as this one, with the wall of beech trees blocking it on the one side and the flatness of Copenhagen shortening it on the other? With all the passion of a fifteen year old, she longed to return to what seemed a so much grander life than the one she was stepping into here.

It had been a comfort when their things had arrived from Norway and became part of their new daily life. They had had to pick and choose in order to fit some of their old belongings into the new, smaller surroundings. They had chosen the very best pieces, and, as the years passed, the more commonplace things that were left behind were forgotten as they were and remembered as something matching in elegance the chosen pieces. When she realized that they would not be going back, the memory house of Norway was locked and remained forever a place of sunshine and laughter, fine foods and wines and enchanting summers and winters. Everything else paled by comparison.

The Danish house was never given the opportunity to become a magical memory house, for it became her home for always and suffered the contempt or indifference which is often allotted to old friends and too familiar surroundings.

Her "Papa" never changed either. He remained the *bon vivant* entrepreneur who made his fortune in Norway and spent it grandly on excellent wines, good food, tasteful furniture, exquisite china, beautiful paintings and presents for an adoring family. He had loved the hunt, his hunting dogs, and the game that had been bagged and prepared in rich sauces. It was not surprising that he died of a heart attack at the age of fifty when en route to a health resort to try to repair the havoc wreaked by too many good meals. He became enshrined in his daughter's memory, and, like an actress with her props, she passed him on to us through the things he had owned.

Mums' mother was a more shadowy figure, receding into the neutrality of old-fashioned parenthood. Papa was described more like a beau, Mamma in dutiful terms of respect. It was considered quite natural that the youngest daughter should stay home and be a companion for her widowed mother. Dreams of returning to Norway were crowded out by the natural sequence of events in Denmark, but they flavored the atmosphere of the small house that became her permanent home.

As disappointed as my mother-in-law had been in this house on the edge of the woods, as enchanted was I when first I saw it. It was like stepping into a world quite different from any I had known, a world that appealed to the senses, with keen smells and tastes. It was entering an epoch which seems to have disappeared with her, and I began to feel an urge to try to recapture in words some of the moods of those days, while I can still close my eyes and picture the details.

1

First Impressions

Denmark is a tiny land filled with comforts. They aren't the sort of comforts that I knew in Hawaii and California, but they are the sort of comforts that reduce the rest of the globe to easily digestible bits. Sudden insights into the size of Iran or Mexico produce a temporary shock which diminishes in its impact by the time we have finished our evening coffee and eaten a second piece of Napoleon cake. We are rather like hobbits; our vexations disappear in the concentration we devote to polishing the brass fixtures on our doors and planning the day's meals. I say we, for I tend to associate myself more and more with the people who were so kind and patient in teaching me to sit still and enjoy the six eating pauses of the day, no slight accomplishment, considering an American's compunction for Doing Something.

I hadn't really wanted to come to Denmark, but, as my father used to say, "We all have our druthers," a phrase with an ominous clang, referring to the darker side of "ruther," which was a good old Okie way of saying "rather." It combines what one should do with what one rather would do. As I sat on the rooftop of an old apartment building in San Francisco, amidst the sunshine all around me lighting that sparkling city with all its allure, I knew I would rather live there than in Copenhagen. But something told me that I would never again meet anyone quite like this handsome Dane who was so earnestly trying to convince me that my future should be in Denmark, married to him.

My premonitions about Finn were at least correct: He was to prove unique — one of the last genuine Vikings. However, in those days of my youth I didn't really know what it meant to marry a Viking, and after all these years of living with him here in the North, I would be too bewildered by the real world to return to it. This is the story of Denmark as I have experienced it, with all respect to the Danes who will not recognize any aspect of it. Even in a country as small as this, there are all walks of life and space for many different lifestyles, with no one model being the "right" one.

It wasn't a life I consciously chose. One tends to make choices about the small things in life and mindlessly drift into the more important decisions. We are often unaware, until afterwards, of what is important and what will prove to be insignificant. Muddling through, the British call it, but that is usually in retrospect, when everything has come up aces.

Once Finn had talked me into going to Denmark, we booked passage on a Danish freighter sailing out of New Jersey. He had just returned from Africa where he had had too many flights with pilots who had boozed their way out of any chance of working elsewhere in the world, and he refused to fly. The expression used to be "getting there is half the fun", but I sometimes wonder. Admittedly, nineteen days on stormy seas with a Danish crew was a good introduction to the Danes. They were capable, friendly, quick to laughter, and they approached the most God-awful lunch table with an eagerness which confirmed my initial doubts as to how well I would be able to conform. I nibbled at crackers and sipped tomato juice as I sat round-eyed and watched gigantic portions of fatty, heavy food miraculously disappear.

An important part of this procedure was obviously the beer and snaps they used to wash it all down, and though the small ship pitched and tossed in the rough sea, their enthusiasm didn't diminish. As I was later to learn, it was typical of Finn's father to visit the ship before its departure from Copenhagen and give the steward enough money to warrant his son remaining afloat whether the freighter did or not. With the prospects of being able to drink his way across the Atlantic and being able to eat not only his share of the food but also mine, Finn's spirits soared. Meanwhile, he assured me that I would soon discover that such a diet was the only proper one for a cold climate.

We weren't the only passengers. There was an elderly Danish couple who loved to play the creaky gramophone in the lounge, listening to nostalgic Danish evergreens. This always put them in a very special mood, and they relished filling me with long, detailed accounts of hardships suffered during the German occupation, gloomily recalling the unraveling of old sweaters to make socks, or vice versa, and wearing their babies' wet diapers around their midriffs in order to dry them during the months when there was no heat in their house. Being from Hawaii, I was naturally distressed to have to add the possibility of uncomfortable world wars to my list of reasons-for-not-wanting-to-live-in-Denmark, a list which, up 'til now, consisted mainly of a large variety of fruit and vegetables which I figured I would never again taste or smell.

More cheering was George, a man in his fifties. He was seen off by a very attractive wife who had spent thirteen years keeping him away from anything alcoholic, because he had an ulcer. George bounded into his cabin like a boy taking a holiday from a strict boarding school. After dutifully looking sad at the railing as he waved farewell, once out to sea he could be seen at all times, the flaps of his tweed hat pulled down around his ears, as he faced the November weather from the vantage point of the prow, which never ceased to buck up and down as we surged through the icy waters. We liked old George, and by the first evening, he was inviting us into his cabin to have "just one wee glass of sherry before dinner."

There were a couple of other, younger fellows, but I think it significant that all these years later I can no longer recall any striking features that could be useful in describing them. Perhaps this illustrates the value of age in establishing an interesting personality.

The captain and crew were marvelous sorts who all expressed to Finn the common Danish sentiment that it was practically criminal of him to be removing me from a warm, sunny climate like California's to the Danish one. I basked in their concern, confident that after a few interesting years in wonderful Copenhagen, Finn himself would choose to return to the land of plenty.

We sailed into Thorshavn in the Faroe Islands, and the ship was boarded by local people who were well-versed in getting a good supply of liquor despite the Faroese prohibition. Although far from Denmark, these islands remain a part of the Danish kingdom. The proud inhabitants are so fiercely independent that I think they prefer to be part of something far away, rather than a close neighbor. We were approached by a handsome giant with a cap on his head and a warm, woolly sweater typical of the region. Finn, who is very big himself, was like a small boy alongside this fellow, whose open, honest face we both liked immediately. He asked Finn if he would be willing to get some whiskey for him, and they hit it off so well while making the arrangements that we were both invited to the man's home.

We knew that the islanders don't really cotton to the Danes who are from outside their fold, and we felt privileged to get a chance to meet his family. We followed him along dark streets, arriving at a small, wooden house where we entered a warm kitchen. We were surprised when he introduced his wife, for she was a beautiful woman, but obviously seventy years old at least. Then we turned and saw that he had removed his cap, and, above his very youthful face was a bald head with a fringe of white hair.

He was a carpenter and proudly showed us the house which he had built and furnished with his own hands, pointing out, in a most natural way, the large double bed as the most important piece of furniture. Meanwhile, his wife and a daughter busily prepared a good cup of coffee and served it in the kitchen which was scrubbed so clean that one could imagine finding them at work there any hour of the night or day. They were shy and pleasant and warm, with a quiet strength of character. The old couple had had thirteen children, but they had lost many of them in World War II and the sea had taken others.

While in Thorshavn, we were invited to join the captain for dinner in his cabin. Behind a round, placid face, he hid a more complicated character. Like many a seaman, he had a wife and family at home, but being away to sea so much of the time, he could harbor more philosophic thoughts than a man might be able to do when daily distracted by a busy household. He was well-educated and very articulate. Finn has always liked me best when I'm not talking, but this was just my cup of tea, and the captain and I were soon launched into a hefty discussion about the virtues of Plato and intrinsic values.

While we rattled on, Finn occupied himself with the virtues of the captain's cognac. He has a gut instinct for the correct conclusion of a discussion and can become quite bored with the rest of us as we savor the process of arriving there. Suddenly, however, he was wide awake over something I said which he chose to misunderstand. Before the evening was out, we were absolutely furious with each other, and my mind was clear — I was going home.

At the crack of dawn, I stomped off the ship and wandered off towards the countryside — not a difficult task, Torshavn being so small in those days. With enough fresh air and exercise, my mind cleared, and I realized that the Faroe Islands weren't the best place to be if you wanted to walk out on someone. It seemed a rather desolate place to stay while waiting for money from home and passageway out. At that point, Finn solved all my problems. He caught up with me, scolded me affectionately for not having awakened him to join me for my walk, told me my cheeks were rosy, and looked most self-satisfied after he gave me a big kiss. It was quite obvious that he didn't remember a thing about last night's row, and by now it didn't seem very important to me either.

This mostly pleasant interlude on the Faroe Islands was followed by more days of being battered by the stormy sea, until we sailed into the lovely fjord to Stavanger in Norway. Our next stop was Bergen where we arrived just as the fjord turned the color of lapis. Not a breeze stirred the deep waters; we soon had docked and left the ship to climb the hillside above the harbor. We reached the top just as the low afternoon sun turned the slopes of long grass to burnished gold, and we stood in its glow until it set, as the blue of the evening sky deepened to set off the first bright stars.

When we returned to the ship, we greeted the others with mixed feelings. The beauty of Bergen made us impatient to get to Denmark where Finn had so much he wanted to share with me, but after so many days at sea, we had developed a comradeship so close with a few of the passengers and most of the crew, that it was sad to think of parting with them. This is a feeling one invariably gets after days of being confined with a group of people. Even those you have had to tolerate will be missed.

George retired rather early after dinner; the single glass of sherry had by now developed into a rather boisterous *l'heure bleue*, and he was sleeping soundly at nights. We decided that we should make use of our last opportunity to play a practical joke on him. He knew we would be sailing early in the morning, and although at this time of the year it would still be dark, he was very keen on being at his post as figurehead as we sailed out of the fjord.

With his heavy snoring to cover the sound of our movements, we were able to sneak into his cabin and take his trousers from the chair alongside his bed. It was my job to sew the bottoms of the legs together with long basting stitches, and for Finn to replace them on the chair while an accomplice rushed off to fetch the gong that was sounded each morning before breakfast. With the sound of the gong, George bounded out of bed like a shot. Finding it difficult to get his legs into his trousers and not wanting to miss a single moment of our setting out to sea, he came hopping out of his cabin, one leg inside a trouser leg and the other frantically trying to push its way through, and in his excitement and confusion, he seemed quite indifferent to the difficulties his leg was having or the spectacle he offered.

Just them, the lugubrious couple whose fondest memories were from the years of the Occupation, came out in the corridor to see what the commotion was. Those of us who had instigated the joke were laughing too hard to explain, and George merely confirmed their suspicions about all of us when he took a pause in his exertions and hailed them with a hearty, "Good morning!"

We sailed into Copenhagen late the following evening, and we were met by Finn's parents and sister and one of his friends. They had evidently made up their minds to accept me, no matter what, for they had planned a wonderful welcome, with an orchid when they greeted me and champagne upon our arrival home. With the confidence of youth, my only concern had been as to whether or not I would like them; it wasn't until years later that I would realize how many things an American can do to alienate a close-knit family which is steeped in traditions. Of course, knowing Finn's sense of humor, he might very well have written such awful things about me that the warmth with which they greeted me may have been inspired by a sense of relief, rather than genuine approval.

At any rate, this was my first real encounter with the magic which a Danish family can weave into an occasion they want to remember. The house had been cleaned within an inch of its life. Even the facade had been given fresh paint. Finn's mother and sister had made open-face sandwiches that were works of art, and it didn't take a cold climate to make them appetizing. After a very merry late-night supper, I was installed in a cozy room and blissfully crept into a bed with fine old linen with exquisite lace inserts, covering an eiderdown duvet. When I came downstairs for breakfast, I found a silver napkin ring with my name on it, a thoughtful touch that made me feel even more welcome. It was the beginning of a long, loving relationship with Finn's family.

Finn's sister was a very special person, with the family's marvelous sense of humor. She lived in Norway but had rushed home to surprise us upon our arrival. Her English was impeccable, but for Finn's parents, speaking it was more of a chore. They belonged to the generation which had learned German as the first language in school, and their English was certainly adequate, but required a concentrated effort. The first few days, they politely wracked their brains to converse with me, and they managed so well that I decided right then and there that there was really no need for me to learn Danish. However, I soon discovered that in the heat of any really interesting discussion or a good joke, they apologized and reverted to Danish. My mother-in-law, being Norwegian, proved to be even more single-minded. She simply spoke Norwegian to me from the third day on, even though her ear for languages made it possible for her to utter an occasional perfectly true intonation of, "Hands up, buddy, or you're a dead man in a minute!"

Being convinced that we wouldn't be staying in Copenhagen long, I decided to learn to do needlework instead of learning the language. This way I could sit and amuse myself while surrounded by interesting, albeit incomprehensible talk. Finn didn't object to this plan, for as I have pointed out, he likes me best when I'm quiet. Somehow, nonetheless, the language seeped in, and I learned it much the way a child must absorb a language, not at all academically and with little regard for grammar.

It is proof of Danish tolerance that I have gone on chattering away all these years, murdering their language with an increasingly wider range. This tolerance may also be due to the average Dane's critical attitude towards his own language. They apologetically claim that it sounds more like a throat disease than a language. However, contrary to what they like to say, I find its guttural softness soothing. It is an excellent language which deserves more respect. It contains an earthy element which left English after Chaucer, and with Danish, one can eat with more gusto, express feelings more tersely, and swear with more vehemence. I love to get angry in French, to be pedantic in English, but Danish is best for having fun.

The Danish language is an excellent vehicle for humor, most of which cannot be translated. Like most Americans, I used to turn my nose up at anything too "corny" and snobbishly prefer what could pass as more sophisticated humor. Here in Denmark, one laughs at nearly everything, for whether or not it was meant to be funny, it often becomes so in the telling. This sense of humor colors everything from politics to religion, leaving us laughing many of our waking hours, but underneath this humor is basically a very sound way of putting things into a reasonable context, giving many Danes a healthy outlook on life. As a famous Danish humorist, Storm Petersen, once made one of his cartoon figures say, "What do you think of the world situation?" "I don't know," replied the other one seriously, "I have something in my eye." I guess I can say that after all these years I have Danish in my ear.

As for whether or not it is important to learn a language which is spoken by such a small amount of the world's population, I've realized that it is only through thoroughly understanding the language of a country that one can understand its people. And, with each language, a new world is opened up. If ever there were an argument for trying to master telepathy, this would be it, for the most brilliant linguist cannot master all the world's languages, let alone the countless dialects.

Words precisely understood are vehicles for comprehension, but when translated, the very emotions they convey are often distorted or inaccurate, thereby making words barriers when they should have been links. I've known Danes who speak absolutely perfect English to be entirely different personalities when they speak Danish. To understand and accept this fact is to understand the scope of problems faced by those who hope to merge all the countries of Europe, much less all the nations of the world.

In learning to appreciate a new country, it is easier to trust one's senses than one's intellect, and without having to communicate, I discovered Denmark's beauty. Life here is colored by the seasons, and they intensify the enjoyment of each day. Spring comes softly with fragile carpets of yellow winter aconite and pert white snowdrops. The bare trees offer no resistance to the penetrating northern light, and everything begins to stir under its white glare. Soon the crocuses are in bloom, great splashes of color on a sunny day or richly glowing against the black earth in a silent spring rain. The swans beat their great wings and swoop and glide over the blue lakes on days when the joy of the season is in the air, and before long, the countryside is lushly covered with green fields and borders of bluebells, hyacinth, early tulips and daffodils.

Everything accelerates, and still the cool hand of springtime retains the early blooms until they are joined by the later ones. We walk in the woods with masses of white windflowers underfoot and wait for the day when the beech trees will unfurl their large, silky leaves, brilliantly green and translucent in their newness. The sun warms the earth, the wisteria, lilacs, mock orange and honeysuckle make the air heady with their fragrance, and the fields in the countryside are the color that a child smears in his coloring book, not realizing that a green as green as that isn't possible. Every tree and bush seems to harbor a songbird or a flock of chirping sparrows, and the lark warbles the song of summer as he flutters over the checkerboard fields of green grain and bright yellow rapeseed.

The warm air thickens the leaves of the beech trees and turns them dark green, but their springtime magic is replaced by billowing white clouds on a summer blue sky. Roses bloom in every garden and spill out into the streets, and elderberry bushes spread their lacey blossoms like ghostly fans in the late evening twilight. The sun rises at four in the morning, and with it comes a riot of bird song. On sunny days, Danes flock to the beaches and come home aglow from the sun and salty air. When the rose hips along the beaches are bright red, and the grain is ripe, the days grow shorter, and warm days are heralded by the ground fogs which were the source of legends about witches and trolls making their brew.

By September, the sun wanes, and dense early morning dew sparkles like diamonds on the veils of spider web, constructed the night before. The white-breasted squirrel with his bushy red tail busily scampers about in the hazelnut trees, pilfering what he can and reminding us to store things for the long winter. Soon the evenings are chilly, and we seek the cheer of a fire in the hearth, candlelight glowing in a dark room, a bouquet of heather gracing a coffee table, while the wind and rain dash against the windows. Autumn days are often splendid against a pure blue sky; the gardens are still bright with dahlias and chrysanthemums, late roses and goldenrod, but the rains come to drench the fiery trees and strip them of all but a few golden pennants to accentuate the sodden black trunks. The barren trees are beautiful in their starkness, and the bright green moss that is brushed on the northern side of the trunk matches the green of the grass.

This dark season is the time of year that Finn brought me to Denmark, the one most people call dismal, and the season that fascinates me as much as all the rest. And here I have stayed, watching the morning sun dapple the leaves of a walnut tree outside a small window in an upstairs hallway in the month of June and seeing the winter moon beyond the bare dark branches of that same tree in November. We became a part of the old house where we came to live and of the garden and the seasons, always here, with movement and change all around us.

2

Settling Down

My father-in-law, who was a large, handsome man commanding a great deal of respect, looked at me over the brim of his glasses and rumbled in his deep voice, as a passing remark, that "in our family there has never been a divorce," never getting a special emphasis by virtue of his accent.

Startled, I replied that in my family nearly everyone divorced. I fondly recalled my Great Aunt Flossie who had informed me early on that anyone who puts up with a difficult man is nothing short of a twit. She was married eight times but retained a genuine affection for all her ex-husbands, having left them at the first sign of annoyance. A look at the alarm on dear Paps' face, and I decided to spare him the details.

A free spirit is so frightened of being confined that it is constantly on guard when faced with even the trappings of security. Had Finn's very stable family been American, I could more easily have recognized the dangers of being ensnared in a permanent lifestyle, but their ways were so new to me that I was intrigued rather than repelled. If I could have foreseen that I would be settling down in a family house, in a quiet neighborhood, in such a calm little country, I would have panicked and fled. But the days after my arrival rushed by with new impressions and pleasant surprises.

It takes many years of living in a country to become prejudiced and stiff in one's appraisals. I was blessed in those days with a genuine interest in every Dane I met and no pre-conceived fears of what interactions their life patterns would have with mine. And by the time I had learned enough to make judgments, they no longer seemed important. All that really matters is loving those you are surrounded by and enjoying each day. And for that one has only one's self to blame if failing. I soon found that I had developed a rather relaxed criteria for liking people, the only demand being that they like me.

However, at the time I met Finn, I had just come back to California after a year and a half of traveling around in Europe and Africa, and I had learned two things: I never wanted to own more than I could quickly pack into a suitcase and be off on a new adventure, and, even more decidedly, I never wanted to marry a European, Scandinavian or Englishman. They were lots of fun, but far too spoiled. They took for granted traits which an American husband would be eternally grateful to find in his spouse. But here I am — a walking testimonial to my lack of character. I'm married to a Dane, and we spent years filling an old house with decidedly immobile things.

All this was made easy for me by the fact that we started a family so soon after we got married. I don't know how modern couples manage when they give themselves so much time for second thoughts. First we had a baby girl whom we named Lani, a nostalgic reference to my birthplace, Hawaii. She was a big, healthy, beautiful baby, the sort one could pick up at night to show off to company and smugly observe their amazement when we put her back to bed, wreathed in smiles and without a murmur of discontent. Nursing her was a peaceful interlude in a tranquil day, and we took her wherever we went — knowing that she could be relied upon to sleep when she was supposed to and never be cross while awake.

Naturally, we assumed this was due to our superiority as parents, so it served us right when next I gave birth to a red-headed cannon ball. We named him Bjørn, which means bear and is as unpronounceable in English as Lani is in Danish. He weighed more than eight pounds at birth, and a good deal of that weight was in folds around his neck, which made one think the only thing missing was a big cigar sticking out of his mouth. Nursing him was a wrestling match where he seemed to have the idea that what counted was getting the most possible in the shortest amount of time. Within three months he was so fat that I had to dismiss the public nurse, her having made so many unkind remarks about his weight whenever she came on her rounds. (There was a theory then that fat babies become fat adults. Our old doctor snorted his disapproval and claimed that mother's milk could do no wrong, and I'm inclined to think he was right. Our son has been slim ever since he started running.)

Despite the comparison to his sister, I have to admit that he was also an also extremely easy baby, good-natured and playful, hardly ever crying. But then he started to crawl . . . much too soon, despite his size. Poor little Lani, who by now was a young lady of two, could hardly believe her eyes as she watched Bjørn do all sorts of things she would never have considered doing. He was perpetual motion, built like a Sumo wrestler, barreling around the house with the plug from Lani's toy iron stuck in his mouth and the iron banging and bouncing behind him. Disciplining Lani was unnecessary, disciplining Bjørn was impossible. When caught red-handed in making some huge mess (like the time he dipped his teddy bear in a pail of white-wash to help me paint the kitchen) he beamed at me and said, "Fun, Mommy!" And I had to admit it did look like fun.

Those were such wonderful, happy years. Chubby arms around one's neck, rubbing one's nose in soft, fluffy hair after the evening bath when cuddled up for a good-night story, pride in seeing the rapid progress of two healthy kids, and the feeling that alongside their well-being nothing else really mattered. My staying at home with them meant that we had to do without a lot of material goods, but I can't really remember what they might have been, as I look back on the fun we had. With the luck of the Irish, I had found a man who could make me feel that what I was doing was important enough to justify every minute of my pleasant day, and I didn't give much thought to how settled we were.

But I'm getting ahead of myself. First, we did marry.

3

Anchor Bo

We had a storybook wedding in a very old church we found in a tiny village far north of Copenhagen. By the pond which lay in front of the church, was the nest of a graceful pair of swans which glided in and out under a weeping willow tree with its bare, yellow branches trailing in the dark water. The vicar and his wife were a stately old couple who looked kind, and they became quite excited about the prospect of wedding an officer in the Royal Guard, who was planning on wearing his full-dress uniform, and, furthermore, marrying an American. Every detail of the ceremony was meticulously planned over tea and home-baked cookies in the parish, with the vicar's ninety-year-old father, who had also been a vicar, attending and adding his opinions.

We were a small gathering that spring morning, Danish weddings having been mostly a family affair in those years. Nonetheless, we did it up in style with the guests in formal attire and Finn looking like a fairy book figure in his red gala uniform. Sun sparkled on raindrops as I walked the path to the church. Sudden gusts of wind whipped the snowy white plumes of Finn's hat and the sun glinted on his silver sword. The church dated back to the days prior to the Reformation and, therefore, had an atmosphere quite unlike an American Protestant church. The pulpit was adorned with figures carved out of wood and painted in bright colors. These figures depicted various saints, but they looked more like gaily garbed characters from a Middle Age feast.

There is no building prettier than a Danish church with its tasteful mixture of simplicity and elegance and its bright embellishments. On that day, this little church in the country was especially charming with bunches of yellow daffodils lighting the way up the aisle. The kind, old vicar seemed to be giving us his personal blessings, and his wife put all her efforts into pumping out strains of Bach on the old organ, Mendelssohn's Wedding March being more than it could manage.

Churches are plentiful, but apartments were almost impossible to acquire. Having been away for nearly two years, Finn did not qualify for a waiting list. We had given up on any hopes of finding even a small rental and had no choice but to move into the upstairs of Finn's father's childhood home. It was named Anchor Bo, in English, the anchorage, a friendly old house on the outskirts of Copenhagen. People often stopped and gazed down the drive on a spring day, enjoying the richness of flowers in a long bed with bulb plants which multiplied steadily since they were planted there by Finn's grandmother at the beginning of the century. The fir tree towered above everything else on the street, as if to protect the garden behind it, and the petals from ancient fruit trees disappeared in the dense green of crocuses through blooming and the bright splashes of bluebells and forget-me-nots.

The giant wisteria that cascaded from the balcony was planted one spring day by Grandfather Julius, long since gone, when he himself was a young man. The richly scented roses unfolded their wealth for more than eighty years, and blended with them were the countless flowers and shrubs that had come since, on birthdays or anniversaries, or simply on lovely spring or autumn days when someone in the family wanted to add one more dimension to the treasures of the unfolding seasons.

The white house had a steep roof covered with black glazed tiles, and the large windows were composed of hundreds of small panes. On warm days the door to the verandah was open onto the steps leading down to a small terrace, and one could hear the hum of bees swarming around a wall of honeysuckle and climbing rose. On the other side of a brick wall, loomed the great crowns of copper beech trees, blue-green cedars, and the lacy branches of birch trees, with nothing else to obstruct the sweep of the sky or the flight of a bird. The wall was covered with shiny green ivy and Virginia creeper, a backdrop to the deep bed of perennials and summer flowers.

The rose bed was more dignified, with its bird bath and formal lineup of peonies, viburnum, gigantic lilac bushes, mock orange and trumpet flower shrubs. Under the windows of the house were more flower beds and fruit trees, seeking warmth and shelter. The tranquility of this scene was ensured by the churchyard which enclosed the garden on two sides and was dense with trees and shrubs all the way to the ancient church, nestled in among giant oaks. It wasn't a desolate, ghostly sort of graveyard, but a typically Danish burial place where each plot is a miniature garden, and one wouldn't be surprised to encounter a ghost sipping tea from a blue and white porcelain cup.

The house had been inherited by Finn's aunt, and she lived on the ground floor. I called her Faster Eli, as did everyone else, *faster* meaning "father's sister." (Danish is very sensible in the way in which it sorts out the family, *faster* coming from one side, and *moster*, or mother's sister, labeling the aunts from the other side. This system is used throughout the list of family titles, keeping grandparents and uncles in order, too.)

Eli was a terrific old gal whose great weight and sedentary habits kept her largely confined to her favorite easy chair, smoking cigars — a habit that was, oddly enough, socially acceptable in Denmark — and listening to the radio while looking out at the garden. She had a small group of old friends over once a month to play chamber music, and the smell of cigar smoke was augmented with that of freshly brewed coffee. As the years passed and they became less competent, the amount of music they played and the amount of coffee they drank seemed to have switched in importance. They grew older, but they retained their critical senses and had decided that the coffee had become better and the music worse. Anyway, I enjoyed those sessions, because the music came up through the floorboards filtered, so to speak. Like an impressionistic painting, it had to be enjoyed at a distance.

The amazing thing about Faster Eli was that, despite a very secluded life, she had a wonderfully open mind. She was able to convey to me a view of the life that had gone on in the house in old days, without the limits one would have expected to exist from the vantage point of an old maid. She was also a perfect example of what the strict schooling of former times could do for a person who was strong enough to take it. She had learned an incredible store of knowledge by heart, and seventy years later still possessed the ability to recall it. Her English was flawless, her French adequate, and, of course, German she spoke fluently and correctly. She knew the Latin names of each plant in the garden and most wildflowers, and she was well-versed in history, literature, music and art.

As Paps put it, Eli was the bright one, the one most suited to being a scholar, but their father, who had been a benevolent tyrant, thought it unwise to over-educate a daughter. Paps was sent to the university to become a chemical engineer, but the only compromise their mother could extract on Eli's behalf was that she be allowed to attend the Conservatory of Music, where she specialized in cello and song. Thus, her achievements could be put to use at home, where her father played the viola, her mother the piano, and Paps the violin. As a monument to a dutiful daughter, we have heaps of exquisite needlework and lace, made by Eli all those hours when she could have been finding a path to the outside world.

When I met her she was sixty-one, and it must be said, in all fairness, that in a generation that placed housekeeping first on the list of feminine accomplishments, she was an incongruously messy housekeeper. I decided that this was simply youthful rebellion at the late date when Julius had died and she finally became mistress of the house.

Her home was an Eldorado for our children and other kids in the neighborhood, and they visited her for hours on end, drinking soda pop, making fantasy houses out of empty cigar boxes, banging away on her grand piano, and coming out of her place dirtier than if they had found a cave on a vacant lot. She always had time to listen to them, and she was always able to understand what they were trying to express and to open up new perspectives in the world they were discovering around them.

It would have been nice to have moved into our very own house and start our family in more spacious surroundings, but, in retrospect, I count Faster Eli as one of the blessings of the exciting years of bringing up small children.

Because she was so untidy, none of the memorabilia and prized possessions of three generations had been thrown out. As we took over more space in the house, first the attic and, later, the cellar, we were faced with the task of sorting these heaps of dusty clutter. In the process, she could tell us much of the family history, and over the years, the house became peopled with these shadowy figures, in a pleasant way. I could easily picture the life that transpired after the turn of the century, when a live-in maid lit a fire in each room at the start of her day. There had been a cook and a weekly laundry woman, a full-time gardener, and Eli and her mother set a good example by not having idle hands. The floors were always waxed, the silver and brass and copper gleaming, the air of each room free of dust, smelling of soap and furniture polish.

Purchases had been far fewer than today. One treasured the things acquired by past generations and, being of good quality, they seldom needed replacing. A family's income went largely to the pleasures of the table and the maintenance of the home. If only Faster Eli could have had the freedom to take advantage of such an efficient home base, she might have had quite a different life.

I look at her photograph now, the one I like best, of a twelve-year-old girl with long golden hair, large dreamy eyes and a soft, pretty mouth. Later photos are of an overweight, unhappy looking young woman. Except one, where wearing a full-length fur coat, she takes a jaunty stance in a photo from the thirties, taken during a brief period when she finally had found the courage to find a job and move into a flat. However, with the death of her mother, it was taken for granted that Eli should move back home and take care of her father in his large house.

We shake our heads at such sacrifices today, and I won't say I would recommend them. I will only state that Faster Eli's life wasn't wasted in those confines. Grandfather Julius was dearly loved and respected by everyone who knew him, and the memories my husband has of the many occasions spent in that house wouldn't have been possible without Eli's presence. It wasn't very long ago that a man in his seventies told me what an impression a very old Julius had made on him, and Faster Eli can be thanked for having made it possible for her father to remain so well-preserved. Without being aware of it, we can sometimes touch many lives, and if those lives are within a family, the touch is never lost. If the soul lives through fond memories, Faster Eli's soul will still be around when our children are old.

Perhaps the very best thing I can say about Faster Eli is that she had a marvelous sense of humor, and despite her personal problems, I always remember her smiling and laughing. Her good-natured temperament even allowed for regular visits from Fru Trier, the octogenarian director for the local symphony orchestra. Trisa, as she preferred to be called had earned the title of *Fru*, or Mrs., from a two-day marriage to someone who remained a mystery. She was a tiny, hunchbacked, wizened creature who propelled herself around very rapidly, apparently by moving her feet rather than her legs, always with a shopping trolley in tow.

She had a seemingly unlimited source of energy, and she expected the same of everyone else, except Faster Eli whom she seemed to regard in a category all to herself, beyond hope of improvement. Trisa looked so frail that I used to wonder how she got about in a strong wind, but the two-mile walk from her place to Faster Eli's never discouraged her from coming. They shared, of course, a common interest in music, and, with pep enough for both of them, Trisa made sure that Eli didn't shirk her evenings with the orchestra. Mainly, however, I think Trisa put Eli high on the list for the one or two times each month that she was invited for lunch.

Trisa had very definite likes and dislikes. Because of the war, she adamantly refused even to eat from German porcelain, demonstratively turning her plate over to inspect it, if she was in doubt. With the tolerance that comes from a deep well of wisdom, Faster Eli could only be amused by this peculiar little lady and was usually successful in overlooking her lack of tact. On one occasion it was, however, almost too difficult. While Faster Eli had to be very careful about her diet and still remained overweight, Trisa could tuck away unlimited amounts into an expandable pot-belly and stay skinny.

Faster Eli watched with amusement while Trisa spread her bread with what in Danish is called "tooth butter," butter so thick that a bite from the bread leaves an impression of one's teeth. Although Trisa was economic to the point of being miserly, she could easily put away a quarter of a pound of butter in one sitting when she was at Faster Eli's. Though she didn't begrudge her little friend her butter binge, Eli found it unfair that while she was scarfing it down, Trisa ran a steady commentary on Eli's weight and told her that she should try to be careful about calories. A look at the expression on Eli's face, however, and Trisa said defensively, "Well, I can allow myself these pleasures, but you, dear Eli, have such an unfortunate figure!"

It was typical for Faster Eli that not only could she laugh about this remark, but could also share the story with me. And we both continued to be fond of little Fru Trier, in spite of herself. I have often thought what good luck it is that not everyone fits into Jane Fonda's schemes. What a dull world it would be!

4

And They Ate Happily Ever After

Any study of the Danes has to begin with their eating habits, that being the axis of the things they are inclined to take most seriously. There are many words and phrases in the Danish language to define this emphasis on food, but they are not easily translated. They speak of something called "food culture", thereby placing it on a plane equivalent to Renaissance art or any number of other things an American is likely to pay respect.

I used to find it a bit silly, this lingering over a well-set breakfast table, only to follow it up with forenoon coffee, thereafter a ritualistic lunch washed down with beer and aquavit, which made one drowsy enough to have coffee once more and to appreciate a cup of afternoon tea, which was cleared aside to set a nice table for a long dinner. The crowning blow was the evening tea with "night food," something entirely superfluous, being a stimulus to sleep on.

I fought for awhile against making the universe revolve around my stomach and tried to retain a notion of a life where eating was the means rather than the purpose. I'm much older now and have come to the conclusion that this purpose is just as good as so many others. At least no one can accuse the Danes of mindlessly gorging. On the contrary, it is done with a good deal of thought and concentration. Just to illustrate how brain-washed I have become to the notion of food as a religion, I'll launch into an attempt to explain the Danish idea of "food culture."

Nowadays, there is more interest than ever before in what we eat, but very little attention paid to how we eat. Food culture is devotion to the principles of eating in such a way that we show respect for one of life's most basic requirements — food. For many Danish families, this devotion has been sacrificed to make way for pursuing a lifestyle that puts other values in the high seat. Some people are simply too busy to gather around the dinner table. This is a bewildering development for a traditionalist like Finn whose zest for the joys of the table is evident in his prediction that getting strawberries out of season would be the beginning to the end of real civilization.

To equate civilization with strawberries might seem flippant, but I have to admit that with the slipping of Danish food culture, we have witnessed a decline in the quality of family life, the keystone to civilization. The most meaningful conversations usually took place around the dinner table, and respect for the framework of the many meals prevented us from shortening a good discussion in order to pursue some other activity. Evil tongues might have it that while we thought we were expanding our minds we were really expanding our waistlines, but I think the latter would have taken place anyway with the fast food that seems to be the alternative.

All this has to do with strawberries in the same way that churches have to do with religion. They are a useful vehicle for creating an atmosphere conducive to transcending a humdrum existence. One becomes jaded to strawberries when they can be consumed anytime of the year, whereas they used to furnish the trappings for a joyful experience during the brief four weeks one could buy them, evoking memories of festive occasions and summer days — a seasonal reward for those who gave food its due respect.

In the past, when great civilizations have declined and vanished, it was often linked with a loss of respect for that civilization and its values. I presume that the seeds for a new civilization must have remained in smaller units, like the family, ready to germinate when the climate was right. Otherwise we wouldn't have had the spiral development that has been the case. The many hours we spent around the table were a pleasant framework for knowing and influencing our children, and the fact that they now carry on the tradition is proof to us that they found these sessions meaningful. It has given them a convenient vehicle for continuity in pursuing values established long ago within the family.

That is probably the most highfalutin argument that ever has been written in defense of Danish eating habits. That should, I hope, prepare you for the next step in trying to understand these important civilizing factors, silly though they may seem to an outsider looking in.

Another strong principle in Danish food traditions is a respect for "food-peace," and that is best illustrated by a story about Viggo. He was a window-cleaner with extraordinary physical strength. Finn has always prided himself on the rather questionable talent of being able to beat everyone in Indian wrestling, and when Viggo demurred upon being contested, Finn assumed that it was temerity inspired by the fact that Finn was the boss and, in Viggo's eyes, too much a gentleman for that sort of activity. He finally relented, however, and promptly lay Finn's arm flat on the table. Taken back by such quick defeat, Finn challenged him to try left arms, being sure he could beat him then. Viggo was even more reluctant, and this time Finn was certain he would be the victor; however, it turned out that Viggo's reluctance was due to the fact that he was left handed, and of course, he won that round even quicker.

Though possessing great physical strength, Viggo was a real softie and normally could be counted on to be a model citizen. Unfortunately, the rough neighborhood in which he lived and a tendency he had to go on benders made it impossible for him to avoid fights. Sometimes the police were obliged to take him in for a cooling off period in detention. They had learned, however, to respect Viggo's notion of food-peace, and if they wanted to arrest him while he was eating, they always waited politely until he was quite finished, at which point he would placidly put down his napkin and meekly follow them off to the station. The rookie who didn't know that unwritten law and disturbed him before the end of the meal would never make the same mistake twice.

If you ask a Dane, among my kind of Danes, to explain the religious or political significance of the countless national holidays in this country, he will be unlikely to be able to tell you; however, he will without hesitance inform you as to the sort of food one traditionally eats for the occasion, and he will point out that all the breweries have a special beer for that particular holiday. (At first I naively believed that "Easter beer" would be a non-alcoholic beverage, but quite the opposite, it is a brew that will never fail to knock you for a loop.)

It isn't that Danes have short memories about the roots of these holidays, but rather due to the fact that their celebrations go much farther back in history and have simply been usurped by more recent movements. Rather than keep track of trends, they tend the eating traditions. Long before there was Christianity in this part of the world, the Scandinavian farmer was brightening up his years with home brew served on the special occasions needed to give life more meaning. The only cloud on the present-day horizon is that the modern Dane is too affluent to reap the full enjoyment out of these refreshment orgies, the contrast with everyday food and festive fare being too slight. That is why I look with equanimity upon any hard times that may come. In such times, the Danish people will again be able to find the joy they used to have in simple things greatly appreciated.

My first chance to participate in the preparations for one of these food festivals was that first Christmas when I was staying at Finn's parents'. Towards the end of November, Mums set aside three days for Christmas baking, one to make the various types of dough, and two for the actual baking; tradition had it that there had to be seven types of cookies to serve with the afternoon tea on the first Sunday of Advent, when the first of four candles anchored in a pretty wreath was to be lit. Each week from then on was allotted a certain amount of tasks, in the order long ago established in such an orderly household as hers.

The final result was that by Christmas Eve every inch of the house and its inventory were shining clean. There were decorations throughout — both those freshly made and those brought out of chests and cupboards — and the larder was so filled with food that I could only imagine it all being consumed if we were to invite a whole regiment. I was soon to discover, however, that all Mums' work was to be devoured by the immediate family and a few old friends, and I was flabbergasted when I later could witness that we had succeeded. While I was engrossed in the beauty of my first Nordic Christmas, the rest of the lot concentrated on that which they considered the prime purpose of yuletide: Eating.

With all my qualms about moving to Denmark, I regarded a Christmas in this kingdom so far north as a grand compensation. Instead of the party-pink Christmas trees or neon Santa Clauses of California, this was going to be the real thing, with snow and all the trimmings. That first Christmas was like a dream out of my childhood. It actually did snow, an exception rather than the rule, and we bundled up for a sleigh ride through fairy-tale woods where deer flocked among the trees. Long walks were part of the daily routine. What I thought was a series of outings planned to inspire a Christmas spirit, actually was a program designed to work up sufficient appetite for three days of overindulgence.

Christmas Eve is the big event. Following a church service in the afternoon, the family gathered for a rather formal dinner, with a tablecloth used only on that occasion and the table set with the best china and crystal. My mother-in-law served a shrimp cocktail, followed by roast goose for the main course, fixed the traditional way, with a stuffing of apples and prunes, accompanied by pickled red cabbage and small potatoes browned in a caramel coating. The Christmas dessert is *risalamande*, a rice pudding fluffed up with whipped cream and full of chopped almonds, with one almond remaining whole. With this is served a cherry sauce. Whoever finds the whole almond in his portion has won the "almond prize" — a gift chosen to suit anyone's fancy. The fun is in managing to hide this almond until that rich dessert has been consumed by all the poor souls who hope to get the prize. Once that ritual is over with, we are more than happy to adjoin to another room and have a good, strong cup of coffee, before we light the multitude of small candles on the tree and dance around it while singing carols.

On Christmas Eve, the only alcohol consumed is the dinner wine, and when I was introduced to the traditions of the Christmas lunch the following day, a cold table that will put stars in the eyes of any normal Dane, I could understand why. After a brisk walk in the woods, the mere anticipation of this feast is intoxicating. We came in, stamping snow from our feet, bright-eyed and eager. The dining room was like a delicatessen shop, the table and buffet loaded with appetizing dishes. Mums was an expert in tempting the eye as well as the palate, and one of her specialties was a platter with various kinds of pickled herring, garnished with alternate bands of chopped, hard-boiled eggs, finely chopped pickled gherkins, chopped pickled beets and fresh green cress, arranged like the spokes of a wheel. There were bowls of Danish caviar and tiny shrimp, anchovies from Norway, large sardines garnished with lemon slices and dill, each item to be tasted in the proper order on the delicious black bread of this country.

The good mood that is invariably present with the mere thought of this feast is certainly augmented by the quantities of beer and snaps used to wash it down. One has to be wary when faced with such a wide range of choices of types of beer and snaps, the latter of which is chilled to the point that is seems deceptively smooth and easy to down. Though served in small glasses, it usually contains forty-five percent alcohol, and after the first few toasts, it is easy to forget to count how many times one's glass has been filled. The best advice I can give a novice is to be sure that the glass really is empty before allowing any more to be poured into it. Otherwise, it is impossible to keep an accurate count. Furthermore, don't, for goodness sake, empty your glass completely unless you are willing to have it refilled. A well-meaning Danish host will be convinced that your empty glass is proof that you like the stuff and that you are merely being modest in refusing a refill.

On the sideboard was a barrage of meat dishes to follow the seafood: Cold thin slices of roast beef, a pork roast with crisp crackling on top, homemade liver paté, small Danish meatballs, various sausages, and the pièce de résistance — Mums' homemade headcheese. I had learned early on that when the family showed special enthusiasm for some unique dish, it was likely to be something I would have to swallow with my mind switched off and my eyes closed. Because they were so generous, the better they liked something, the more they wanted to share it with me, and as soon as I had willed my way through a moderate helping, I would find my plate heaped with more.

The head cheese had been made with great care and ceremony. With the wisdom infused in good housewives of her generation, Mums had developed a great deal of hocus-pocus to use when making certain dishes. It is an art to be able to make something appear difficult when years of practice have actually made it easy, and she knew how to make sure that the family didn't take her for granted. To create this particular dish, a certain faïence bowl with just the right contours had to be used, a snowy white cheesecloth that also had been used by her mother was needed to line the bowl, and when all preparations had been made, Mums donned a freshly ironed apron and went about the job much like a high priestess would do in a more primitive society. (Years later she was to initiate me into the secrets of making head cheese, and by the crestfallen look on Finn's face when I told him it was easy, I could see that I had deprived him of some of the pleasure he took in eating it.)

Anyway, there it was — the meat from the head of a pig and from a calf's shank, solidified in its own aspic, shaped like a half sphere, coated with thin slices of boiled pork rind, studded with whole cloves, and garnished with bay leaves. And, everyone was clearly anticipating my delight when I took the first taste. Actually, I've grown to be very fond of *sylte*, as we call it. It is nutritious, and if coated with mustard and topped with pickled beets, it's very tasty.

Once we had eaten our way through all these delicacies, we started on the selection of cheese. A lunch of this sort takes a minimum of four hours, and as the winter sky darkens outside the windows, you find yourself encapsulated in a cozy little candlelit circle where time stands still and problems disappear. With a bit of effort, one comes to accept this sort of experience as being just as worthwhile as any other. We all felt very drowsy when we finally adjourned to the lounge to have our coffee; indeed, the family retained very fond memories of a Christmas lunch where all participants nodded off in their seats, accompanying the chiming of the clock with soft snoring.

CB   CG

Over the years, I've been amazed at how quickly Danes have adopted foods from all over the world. With characteristic zeal, they have plunged into new culinary experiences, following them up with all the dieting fads that invariably seem to come from America. Currently there is an interest in *nouvelle cuisine*, but in my opinion, much of that is a case of "the emperor's new clothes"; if made with great skill, it can be a treat, but in the hands of the average cook, it is a decorative confusion of flavors, more deserving of being hung on the wall than put in the stomach.

The purest form of Danish cookery at its best is to use the absolute prime quality of raw materials and prepare them in such a way that the true flavor is not lost. It is a very difficult kind of cooking, for one's mistakes cannot be disguised in a good sauce, and a mere recipe isn't sufficient in learning to prepare these dishes. One has to have a feeling for it. Gleaning secret recipes from experienced housewives is made difficult by the fact that no Danish housewife with self-respect will like to admit to using flour where whipping cream could be the ingredient; it took years of trying decoy recipes before Finn's old secretary initiated me into the magic formula for her Danish meatballs.

No matter what sort of food one favors, however, and in our household it might come from any corner of the world, it is a true joy to prepare a meal for most Danes. No matter how much work has gone into the table setting or the cooking, it all seems worth it for the fun of seeing their enjoyment. And this fleeting life seems a bit longer in retrospect when filled with the memory of all these well-defined meals.

5

Dining, Danish Style

A Danish dinner party is a very noisy affair. We always have a seating plan, and the gentleman to one's left is obliged to do his utmost to insure that his table lady has a good time, and vice-versa. This is an admirable system, by and large, but obviously, unless there are very few people around the table and the conversation can be coordinated, it leads to a lot of lively individual conversations which get progressively louder as the evening wears on.

The dining rituals are quite elaborate and to a foreigner they may appear to be a test of stamina; however, they have become relatively tame since I first came to Denmark. In those days, not only did one have to consume an awesome amount of food and drink, but in order to gain respect, one had to remain sober enough to eat "night food," which was served with beer and snaps, or tea for the timid. There was, on the other hand, an affectionate feeling for the chap who got so bombed that he couldn't remember having consumed night food, he being the one who had so graphically demonstrated that the host hadn't been stingy in his servings.

A well-bred Dane will be very modest about the helping he takes, and this used to be carried to an extreme whereby he was considered crude if accepting anything the first time it was offered. The dish was offered three times, and on the third he would tip his head to one side, smile shyly and say, "Well, you're making it hard to resist," and take a generous helping. If you, as a host or hostess, didn't comply to this ritual, you risked that he would comment on your party by saying, "Oh yeah, the food was alright, but the arm-twisting was lousy." (It has become a risky business, however, now that manners and customs change so rapidly. A modern host is more rational and might whisk the platter away after the first refusal, leaving you surprised and hungry.)

Night food has more or less disappeared from the scene now that most of us drive cars. In fact the very mention of such a temptation is enough to cause people to put on their coats and head for the door. The one exception is Finn who always has night food whether the guests will join him or not, and, when he is the guest, will make it for himself as soon as he's home, no matter how late it is.

Most foreigners are impressed with the amount of entertaining we do by candlelight, and, indeed, candles are very much a part of the daily life, not something lit just for the benefit of company. This might have its roots in Viking times when a fire was the midpoint for all gatherings.

Buried just as deep in the foundations of Scandinavian culture is the custom of saying skål (pronounced skole), when toasting each other. Whereas the origins of the word give frequent rise to debate, the fact of its importance as a civilizing factor in this part of the world is beyond question. The next time you visit Denmark, try keeping your eyes on your host rather than your plate. You will see that when he says "skål", he will lift his glass, look into your eyes, drink, and, before replacing the glass on the table, he will look at you once more with a smile and a nod. It is very charming and quite practical. It gives one the opportunity to keep a constant check on the degree to which the host and the other guests are getting inebriated, and, if you find yourself in doubt, you've had too much. This manner of drinking is so much part of the Danish notion of coziness that it is a shock to them the first time they encounter a person who is ignorant of the custom and merely puts his glass down, leaving the Dane with the feeling of being all alone in the world.

Speeches are also an important part of the dinner party in my Denmark, and we love to hear a good speech, especially a funny one. If I hadn't married my husband thirty years ago for his looks, I would marry him now for his speeches. Dinner speeches can, at their worst, be murder to sit through, or, at their best, something to remember for years to come. In any event, they do give one the opportunity to say thanks in a setting that makes that "thank you" more memorable and furnish us with a rare opportunity to tell those we love how much we appreciate them.

I think this love of eating and entertaining is what saves the Christmas season from giving rise to the disappointments one is bound to feel occasionally if associating it only with peace on Earth and goodwill to mankind. With heathen eagerness, we plunged into each Christmas season, helped by the fact that for three whole days nearly everything was closed down. The consumerism necessary for modern times has made it necessary recently to change this system, and stores are now open like in other parts of the world. Perhaps my description of a Danish Christmas will be quite foreign to a modern Dane.

In our family, the celebration actually starts on what Danes refer to as "Little Christmas Eve," the 23rd of December. This is the evening when the tree used to be decorated and all the last minute preparations were made for Christmas Eve, but I've turned it into a party evening in order to keep Finn in line.

Years ago, he made a show of going to work on the morning of that day, telling me as he left that he would be having the Little Christmas Eve's Day Annual Lunch with his old shipping cronies. At about three o'clock in the afternoon, he used to call to tell me he would be late for dinner. He would always come home sooner or later though, apparently from instinct, and he would be virtually glowing with holiday spirits. I usually decided on the spot that the biggest help this man could offer would be if he would go to bed. However, he felt like being supportive, seeing how busy I was, and he sat on a chair watching me with red and green Christmas eyes as I decorated the tree.

Feeling gallant, he saw it as his duty to make a red wine toddy, laced with aquavit and furnished with a generous handful of raisins, chopped almonds, cloves and lemon peel, and serve it to me so that I wouldn't be bored. His share of this life-giving elixir invariably had a spectacular rejuvenating effect on him. The spirit of Christmas had not only been rekindled, it was a roaring fire. While I tried to make preparations for the feast his family was going to have at our place the following day, he followed me around, lifting lids on pots, upsetting decorations, sitting on wrappings and getting more and more happy. Finally, he felt justified in leaving me to do the rest of the work alone. After all, he had been at the office all morning. But just as he disappeared into our bedroom, he mentioned that he had invited a friend home for breakfast — that being the only time that this friend could squeeze a visit into what must have been a very busy schedule. I gave this last bit of information little thought, seeing as Finn didn't seem to know which day of the week it was.

At around two a.m., I had wrapped a few last-minute presents, and I proudly surveyed my work. The tree was a joy, there were arrangements everywhere with fresh boughs of evergreen and holly, evergreen garlands with holly berries and red silk ribbons were draped up the stairway, and freshly made wreaths mingled their fragrance with the scent of oranges hanging from red ribbons and studded with cloves. There were heaps of brightly wrapped presents and full flowering azaleas by tall candles. Contented, I tumbled into bed like the gal in the Christmas poem and blissfully settled down for "a long winter's nap." Except Pa wasn't in his cap nor I in my kerchief. Pa was in his shoes, which he somehow forgot to remove before he collapsed in a din of snores.

The nap turned out to be just that. At six-thirty in the morning; the doorbell rang, and standing there in the cold, like a jolly little elf dressed in an over-sized coat, muffled by a woolly scarf, and sporting a hat which obviously was on the bottom of the pile when he took what appeared to have been a very muddy fall, was one of the more illustrious of my husband's shipping pals. "King Boding," as he was known in those circles, was a true genius in his profession. A propensity for pleasure had lost him the best of jobs, but he was indispensable enough to always land a new one. He could have doubled for Mickey Rooney as he whipped off his hat and bellowed out a "ripping good morning!" followed by a whole lot of nonsense in Italian, Greek, Spanish, French and Russian, as if he remembered that I was foreign, but he wasn't quite sure how foreign. One of my few virtues is that I'm not easily rattled, and I forced open my reluctant eyes, tried to look delighted, and invited him in.

It seemed that Finn had actually invited him for the evening before, but that being impossible for Boding, it was agreed that he should come for breakfast. (Finn has a definite talent for hitting upon compromises.) Boding's busy schedule obviously had consisted of making full use of the state of inebriation which he had achieved at yesterday's lunch, for he had been out all night and came direct from the last pub. Fortunately, he was so entertaining that when he left four hours later, I turned to Finn full of good will to tell him what he might do to be helpful that day, but all I saw was his back as he disappeared into our bedroom.

He was in the grips of what he claimed to be a very virulent, though short-lived, case of the flu. All day long he napped, insisting that he would help me if only he weren't so ill. My revenge was inflicted by the kids who by then were so excited that they filled the air with their gay little songs, their shrieks and their laughter as they bounced up and down on our bed.

As for Boding, he became part of our Christmas, always showing up for breakfast on the morning of Christmas Eve. The children grew up thinking he was a combination of Santa Claus and Donald Duck. The first couple of years I made a job out of baking bread and fixing bacon and eggs, until I discovered that he was more or less on a liquid diet, knowing which saved me a lot of trouble.

This was the start of our Christmas celebration in those days, followed up by a splendid Christmas Eve, then the traditional lunch at Finn's parents' on Christmas day, and another lunch with friends on the 26th. In retrospect, those days were almost tame compared to later Christmases when Mums retired from making the lunch, and our children became young adults with their activities melting in with ours. We soon started celebrating much earlier, with the rationalization that as long as I was doing so much work anyway, we might as well see more people.

Christmas is by no means the only excuse for a big celebration. Danes love celebrating for any reason at all. Thus, one year fades into the next with a continual anticipation of the next feast and a satisfied feeling following the last. Oddly enough, certain of these occasions stand out from the rest, and the tableau they form is like a man's private monument, comparable to the impressive heaps of earth made by the Vikings to mark the place where a chieftain was buried. They took a lot of hard work, but they loom grandly on a flat landscape.

Many such occasions are inspired by an anniversary or birthday. "Round" birthdays get special attention, and a person is considered to be somewhat of a cheapskate if he tries to skip out on his fiftieth, for example. It is unforgivable to let a round birthday pass by without at least inviting the family for a gala dinner party, and I willingly comply to this custom; however, being a superficial American, I used to toy with the idea of at least taking the day off on my ordinary birthdays. After all, I told myself, my family *did* have a few traditions, one of which was never to do any work on one's birthday. But here is a good example of how a weaker culture succumbs to the stronger one; I have not yet succeeded in shirking my birthday duties.

Once I almost thought I was going to be let off the hook. That was the summer when we decided to close down the house and move up to the summer place the day after my birthday. It would have been most

impractical to have guests, and, the week prior to the big day Finn said to me, "By the way — don't give a thought to your birthday. Just make sure you and the kids are all dolled up at seven in the evening." I went around on a cloud all week, thinking that at last I was getting invited out to dinner.

I didn't even get suspicious when Finn nonchalantly asked me how to make a dressing for shrimp cocktail. "Clever old stick," I thought. "He wants to make a little snack so the kids won't be too hungry if we have to wait a long time for our dinner."

By Sunday though, Finn was obviously in a bit of a panic about something. We were sitting on lounge chairs in the garden, and he looked worried. I asked him what the trouble was, and he confided in me that he was just sitting there wondering how to roast a leg of venison and whether or not, by chance, I was planning on baking a fresh batch of dinner rolls the next day.

My suspicions well-aroused, I turned a beady eye on him, and he voluntarily started babbling about having intended to surprise me with a nice homemade dinner on my birthday, but that a friend on our street who had promised to help him was called out of town. He ended this breathless statement by admitting that he also had invited another couple, the last bit of information being delivered with a winning smile that indicated what a lucky girl I was.

I tried not to show my disappointment as I told him that I had been nourishing the hope of having an easy snack from a hot dog stand, but he looked aghast at the mere suggestion of what he considered such a modest request and said, "Oh no! Not on your birthday!" He managed to look so distressed that instead of hitting him with a potted petunia, I consented to being a technical advisor, knowing full-well how it all would end.

That turned out to be a tactical error. While expected to give the appearance of a lady of leisure, graciously watching the hustle and bustle of preparations for the dinner party, I had to secretly bake bread, make a dessert, whip up a first course in aspic, and turn out a roast. To further complicate matters, I couldn't get off to an early start, for I had to lie in bed, acting like I was asleep while Finn and the kids made an elaborate breakfast.

After breakfast, I tried to size up how much I would be stuck with doing, while trying to look like I had all the confidence in the world that they could manage all on their own. This would have been easy if the occasion could have been whittled down to something manageable, but any suggestion I made to jump over where the fence was low was met with shocked disapproval. Finn and Lani and Bjørn made it abundantly clear that nothing was too good for me on my birthday.

Finn wouldn't tell me who the surprise guests were, but I think it was at this point that I asked him if his parents were invited. When he told me that they weren't, I said that since we were going to have a dinner party after all, they would be hurt not to be included. He beamed his approval, and they readily accepted when I called.

It was a splendid summer day, and while everyone else in the world was getting a gorgeous tan, not least of all Finn who had sneaked off and was sitting in the sun, I was getting flushed cheeks from slaving in a hot kitchen. About an hour before the mystery guests were scheduled to arrive, the phone rang, and it turned out to be a couple from California who knew my cousin. "Invite them to dinner," I yelled from the kitchen. "Two more won't make any difference."

At five to seven, I threw a long dress over the bikini I had worn all day long in the vain hope that I could duck outside and lie on the chaise lounge. Mums and Paps loved birthday parties, and they arrived promptly at seven, about the same time as the couple from California. We all sat in the garden, having a drink and waiting for Finn's surprise couple. After nearly an hour of pre-dinner drinks, we figured something was amiss. Danes are always on time when invited to dinner. Finn revealed who it was who was supposed to come, and we went inside to call their home and find out whether or not they had left.

Their daughter answered the phone and said, "Yes, they drove more than an hour ago." She told us they were invited out to dinner, but we didn't want to worry her by telling her that it was at our place they were expected. We all went to the table and morosely picked our way through the first course, with visions of the missing couple, lying injured in a ditch somewhere. Finally, Paps couldn't stand the suspense. He left the table and systematically called all police stations and hospitals between our friends' home and ours. That gave no result, but as soon as he put down the receiver the phone rang, and the mystery was solved.

It was our friends who had called their daughter to hear how things were going, and when she told them we had called, they realized that they had made a mistake. They had accepted another dinner invitation, thinking that Finn's was for the following night. We were so relieved that they were safe and sound that we broke out a couple of extra bottles of wine and had a real celebration.

Many hours later, when the house was quiet, and I had finished washing the last glass, I found Finn sitting on the terrace, drowsily staring into the remains of a bonfire we had lit. The smoke was whiffed away by a gentle breeze against a sky already turning light, and the smell of honeysuckle was in the air. I put my arms around his neck and told him sweetly that I had done all the dishes. "Well, that's fair enough," he said with a smile. "After all, they were all your guests."

Ꮳ   Ꮳ

Some of the most rip-roaring entertaining I have experienced was back in the late sixties, with Danish farmers. We once were invited to a shoot to be followed by a dinner dance on a farm on Lolland, one of the islands that are part of Denmark. We left home at six a.m., the car loaded down with all the gifts, proper apparel, and Finn's hunting gear. Upon arriving, the hunting party gathered in the cobblestoned courtyard, an enclosure formed by the four wings of the thatched roof farmhouse. The buildings were whitewashed to set off the dark half-timbers and the small windows glowed cheerfully in the somber November setting. We were each given a shot glass of Danish bitters, something which furnishes you with a warm glow for the first hour of the hunt to be followed by an empty feeling in the pit of your stomach which will make all your thoughts for the rest of the morning circle around the lunch break.

In was cold and misty, and I was to be one of the beaters, those who push their way through brush and brambles to startle the game. Accordingly, I was dressed in such a manner that had a Salvation Army truck passed by, I would have been chucked into the back to be sent to an underdeveloped country — old hunters' green trousers and a warm woolly sweater with a tacky, brown jacket and big, heavy Wellington boots. After several hours of marching through forests and over fields one has rosy cheeks, a red nose, frizzy hair and a tremendous appetite, and the reward was being able to join the hunters for lunch.

This is a rowdy affair with good old songs, like the one about the comfort there is in drink, when a man's wife loses her figure and he loses his vigor, and each verse is washed down with beer and snaps. The ever-present candles and a blazing hot wood stove warmed everyone's wet clothes, and with the pleasant drowsiness produced by an aura of steam, alcohol, tobacco smoke and stale beer, I wondered how ever I was going to have the stamina to go to a party that evening. The men were in such high spirits, however, that they made only polite objections to my leaving them. I found the way to the bedroom we had been assigned and crept gratefully into a warm feather bed.

The Danish farmer of those days was responding to a new sort of prosperity. They have apparently always been very clever at providing for the basic needs, but their world was widening. Especially the rich farmlands of Lolland were providing ordinary farmers and their wives with the means to emulate the fads and fashions of the city. The women were attending courses in cordon bleu cookery and their husbands were serving wine instead of just the traditional beer and snaps. However, they didn't relinquish their old customs and the mixture of old and new was definitely quite extraordinary.

The hunters who had been so boisterous a few hours prior were all spruced up and very reserved, in the company of their wives, when we met in the parlor at seven and were served a glass of sherry while everyone eyed each other stiffly. Candles were lit everywhere and condensed water formed quickly on the small-paned windows under the low, beamed ceilings. The long room was filled with an indiscriminate mélange of potted plants, knickknacks, and, unbeknownst to the owners, a good many priceless antiques. Those few who passed a remark in the stillness of the room turned out to be the local lions in a society where not only does each man know the other man's worth, he's likely to know the other man's grandfather's worth. No one seemed to be sipping his sherry, but suddenly the host announced that dinner was served, and it was down the hatch and off to the dining room.

Two long tables were set for forty people. There was an impressive display of Royal Danish porcelain's seagull pattern bearing witness to the stability of families in the country, there being far more place settings than could be collected in just one generation. We were served beer with the seafood course, a concession to the diehards, I presumed, followed by red wine with the meat course. Flushed country lasses scurried around, making sure each glass was filled, and because the old-timers preferred beer to wine, that glass was kept filled, too, and it wasn't long before the serving help had been persuaded to add a snaps glass to the battery of glasses before each person.

By now a great transformation had taken place. Even the most staid of the lot were feeling very amiable, and toasts were being made in all directions. Being a newcomer and the wife of good old Finn, I was included in most of these toasts and was obliged to respond by drinking the beverage in which they were proposed — Try mixing wine, beer and snaps for three hours and tell me if you have had a good time. Fortunately, all these glasses were removed when the tables were cleared for the dessert, but by then one lacks the good sense to say no to the drink which is offered with that course. This was a choice among port wine, Madeira and sherry, all three of which were equipped with screw caps and had been bought at the local general store.

We then adjourned to the parlor to be served home-baked cookies with coffee and an impressive selection of cognac and liqueurs. Cigars were passed around and the older generation settled comfortably into easy chairs to indulge in local gossip while the dining room was being cleared for a dance. This particular evening was always to be remembered with affection, for everyone danced with such exuberance that a heavy chandelier broke loose from the ceiling and crashed through the floor, making a large hole that we had to avoid the rest of the night.

The guests had come dressed to the nines, but with such lively dancing, the men had soon shed their jackets and their shirts clung to their backs, wet with perspiration. To refresh the dancers there was what appeared to be an unlimited supply of beer or highballs, and no one showed any sign of fatigue, except me, and I wasn't about to admit it. Night food was served around three in the morning and consisted of boiled salt-herring and rye bread. The hostess confided in me that it took days to get the smell out of the pot in which the fish had been boiled, but I would have sworn every bit of the smell was still in the fish.

While everyone devoured this feast, washing it down with beer and snaps, they were slyly eyeing us to see how we city-slickers were faring. Never let it be said that I would let a smelly old boiled fish stand between me and their esteem, but I envied Finn. He loves fish any horrible way. (The following morning he was to be mercilessly quick to inform me that it definitely wasn't the fish that made me feel so peaked.)

Much to everyone's amusement, the last guest left on a wobbly bicycle across the barren fields, his wife having taken off in their car hours before. When finally everyone had left, we squeezed in what seemed like a couple of hours of sleep before people started to return. Ostensibly, they came by to say thank you for a grand party, and this is *comme il faut* in Denmark; however, these men didn't just make do with a courtesy call. They had come for breakfast — without their wives. The women were undoubtedly at home coping with children who tend instinctively to be unlovable when their mothers are dead tired.

We all sat there, bleary-eyed, reminiscing about the night before, and the hostess kept setting another place for the latest arrival. All the men were drinking a "little one" (as they label a shot glass of snaps when trying to make it sound harmless) with their coffee and before long they had worked up such a thirst that a case of beer was brought in. It dawned on me that the party wasn't really over at all and wouldn't be until all these funny fellows all went home. It must have been the country air. They seemed to be made of other stuff than we ordinary mortals. From my first encounter, I gained enormous respect for their stamina, and, over the years, they have never disappointed me.

Even we town dwellers are seldom less than three hours around the table when guests are invited to dinner, and dinner often takes at least an hour just with the family, except in families which have opted for a modern way of life. In old days, children were usually kept away from this scene until they were old enough to endure the rigors of sitting still so long. In order to combine the American way of life with the Danish, we compromised by telling the children they had to conform to grown-up table manners but could leave the table when they got bored; however, once dismissed they weren't allowed to come back.

Our more progressive friends were shocked at the demands we put on the kids and preferred their own system, whereby the adults slackened their standards to allow for the presence of lively children at the dinner table. Finn stuck to his guns, never having allowed himself to be distracted by the opinions of child psychologists and friends, and Lani and Bjørn grew up accepting the idea that mealtimes were the grown-up scene. In the homes of those who accommodated the children the meals disintegrated into such a state of chaos that both adults and youngsters stopped bothering to come home to them. I'm happy to say that due to the wisdom of Finns methods or the loyalty of our offspring, meals remained a pleasant entertainment in our household with common grounds for all generations.

While accepting the fact that Danish hospitality required of its recipients a very strong constitution, I've always been a little uncomfortable when inflicting it on guests from other countries. The only surefire ploy to take if you're worried about your diet is to hide behind religion. An unexpected visit from a Muslim friend who was visiting our home for the first time brought that home to me. Knowing that he wouldn't eat pork and doesn't drink alcoholic beverages put Finn in a state of alarm I wouldn't have believed possible.

It being Sunday when all the stores are closed, the only thing that saved us was Finn's old army rations, where we found a can with a picture of a cow on it. The result was edible, but Finn suffered a feeling of inadequacy he hadn't experienced before. It isn't enough for a Dane just to feed his guest; he has to feel he is giving him a treat. Therefore, when we received a letter saying that the parents of two very good friends who are Jewish were coming to visit Copenhagen, Finn started planning the dinner days in advance.

He called the top rabbi in Copenhagen and asked what one could offer to Orthodox Jews. It was the end of the month, and I paled as he ticked off a list of acceptable things to serve, including fresh salmon, a good Mosel wine, and everything to be cooked in butter. All the choices were expensive, and if our guests turned out to be truly orthodox, we were informed that they wouldn't want to eat anything at all in our home. Upon their arrival in Denmark, Finn called their hotel to arrange to pick them up for dinner. Mrs. Florsheim spoke with an accent, having gone to America late in life in order to escape from Nazi Germany with her husband and children, and she said something to the effect of not putting us to any trouble. "Don't meet us," she said, and Finn eagerly agreed, assuming she had said something about not serving meat. He said he would pick them up in an hour at their hotel.

After they arrived, we sat in the study chatting, and we took an immediate liking to this aristocratic couple. We had understood from the rabbi that we shouldn't serve drinks, and we decided to serve dinner right away. On the way to the table, having mentally recalled our Muslim friend's discomfort in approaching a meal at our place, I said to Mrs. Florsheim, "By the way, we have taken care not to prepare anything which won't be all right for you to eat or drink."

She gave me a puzzled look with her keenly intelligent eyes and said, "What do you mean?" I awkwardly explained, whereupon she broke into youthful laughter and said, "My God, we're not religious, are you?!"

℃ ℂ

So whether we stay home or go out to the homes of Danish friends, the business of entertaining has probably been the most serious of our endeavors. Over the years, we have had hundreds of dinner parties, both small cozy affairs and very formal occasions. Because we have only entertained for the fun of it, never because of professional or social ambitions, I don't feel that the work involved has been in any way a sacrifice. If you like seeing friends and enjoy the process of making an evening a bit out of the ordinary, the rewards are manifold, if for nothing else than the store of memories one has at the end of the day.

6

Sunshine

The first thing most people used to ask me when they learned that I came from Hawaii and Southern California was, "How can you stand the Danish climate?" The answer is easy: I've advanced from being a sun lover to being a sun worshipper. I've learned this attitude from the Danes themselves, but in recent years, many of them have lost touch with the technique. As more and more people join the working world of the pulsating city, they are obliged to seek the sun in places like Spain, where they can be guaranteed sunshine each day of a prescribed holiday. Meanwhile, here in Denmark we have plenty of sunshine, if you don't have work to interfere with your enjoyment of it.

The first summer I spent in Denmark, I was pregnant, and the doctor advised me not to over-do it with sunbathing. I thought the man was mad. Not yet being acclimated, I found the summer just as chilly as the winter, with the added annoyance of the central heating being turned off. My idea of feeling it was summer would have been to put the heat on full blast and throw open the windows. By the second summer, however, my blood was thicker, and not only could I appreciate the fact that it was warmer than winter, I was also hooked on getting a tan, that being a major occupation of Danes.

May and June lulled me into a false sense of security, with weeks of balmy weather. Then, one day Finn called from the office and asked me why the devil I wasn't outside enjoying the sun. "I'm practically on my way," I said. "Just have to make the beds and do the dusting."

That was a flawless summer morning; an hour later, I looked contentedly at a tidy house, picked up a book to read, and stepped outside just as a giant dark cloud blotted out the sun. I had witnessed the end of summer. It rained most of July and all of August, and by the time we were blessed with an Indian summer, I was past caring. Since that memorable day, I have vowed that I only have myself to blame if I don't enjoy the sun in Denmark, and actually there is more than enough of it, if one doesn't let any less serious activities interfere with sitting in it.

In the Hawaiian Islands and California where there is sunshine all year around, one takes the weather for granted. Visitors from warm climates are often quite pale compared to us, for they would have to be a bit addle-pated to want to lie in the sun when it shows up every single day. Here, we never miss an opportunity to enjoy it.

The more industrious Danes will disagree with me when I invariably remark that it has been a marvelous summer, but there are those few who share my evaluation, and they are brown as old leather by the middle of June. They are also unemployed, or like Finn, unwilling to let work interfere with living. You see them on the beaches on the most fitful of summer days, alternately wrapping themselves in blankets, like papooses, as small clouds scurry across the sky and quickly throwing off their covers like streakers, as soon as the sun blinks at them.

Many Danes treat sunshine like a vitamin pill and resolutely take a dose each day. One such example was a priceless old lady who could be seen as late as October, taking her constitutional on Bellevue Beach. She arrived on a bus, tote bag in hand, marched down to the beach with the brisk determination of a Margaret Rutherford. She was dressed in a tailored suit with sensible walking shoes and a crocheted cloche hat. Out of her bag she took a beach towel and a bathing cap, then, while standing at attention, head tilted back, she soaked up a few minutes of afternoon sunshine, testing its strength.

In a businesslike manner, she proceeded to strip down to her version of September Morn, lastly taking off her hat which she replaced with the bathing cap. Next, she did exercises which looked like they were learned first-hand from Isadora Duncan, and, finally, she jumped resolutely into the sea. Ten minutes of splashing around in the icy water was part of her routine. When she emerged, she stood straight as a ramrod, facing the sun, while she dried off. After redressing in a no-nonsense manner, she replaced the bathing cap with her funny little hat, and marched off to her bus. What I loved about my little old lady is that I was apparently the only one who took any notice of her.

Many tourists who come to Denmark are intrigued with the number of nude bathers on the beaches, but even the most prudish Danes are more relaxed about nudity than we Americans are, a fact which caused me considerable embarrassment the first time we visited one of the most beautiful beaches on this island. Finn wanted to take us there, because he loved the wild beauty of the place when, as a child, he had played in the bewitching woods that flank it and the graceful dunes which give shelter from the wind. It was an ideal place to spend a day at the beach with children. That's what he told me, and I believe him, but I suspect that when he took us there on a hot summer day, he must have known that nowadays hardly anyone who goes there wears a stitch of clothing.

Shunning crowds, I didn't object when we reached the beach and he pointed out the most distant dune, about a kilometer down the shore, and said he thought that would be a good spot to spend the day. We spent the next half hour trudging through warm sand, our little dachshund covering twice the distance as she pursued her dream of catching a seagull on the wing. Out of the corner of my eye, I noticed that our dog was the only one of our lot who was appropriately dressed, or undressed, however you want to put it.

Finn is much too independent to worry about being different, but by wearing a bikini among so many nudes I felt like an exhibitionist trooping past staring nature-lovers. Not only were they looking at us like we were a bit weird, I imagined they judged us to be child-abusers for having put our kids in bathing suits. Even if I weren't burdened with a puritanical background, however, taking off my clothes wouldn't have helped. I would have still been wearing telltale white marks with my tan.

At long last we reached the solitude of the selected dune, and I decided it had been well worth the effort. The place was enchanting. It had been a sand-swept wasteland centuries past, until a man named Reventlow, an advisor to the king, had the nerve to plant a vast area with trees. Any halfhearted attempt to hold down the drifting sands and claim the land would have been doomed to failure, but his scheme was so sweeping in its scope that it succeeded. Once inside the forest, the wind becomes a gentle whisper, its strength being spent on the gnarled trees along the windswept beach, giving them the shapes of trolls and goblins. Cool shadows are cast on the white sand by the large dunes, and patches of wild rose and tough seagrass stubbornly cling to a magical band between the dunes of the sea and the trolls of the forest.

I lay basking in the shelter of the sunny side of our dune, grateful for the fact that nature-loving nudists apparently didn't like transistor radios, and the only sounds were from the breeze in the pines and the surf lapping on the sand. Finn and Lani and Bjørn were in the water, and I was just about to doze off when I realized our little dog had disappeared. I knew that in order to find her, all I had to do was to look for someone trying to enjoy a picnic lunch, and I soon spotted her, sitting up begging for a tidbit, with an adoring stare fixed on her victim. When she saw me coming, she shot under the nearest shelter to get out of arm's reach. Unfortunately, this just happened to be a nude man's legs.

Anyone who has ever had a dachshund knows that they do exactly as they please, and I could see from the way she was entrenched under the man's knees, her dark eyes fixed on him with a pathetic plea for help, that the only way to get her out would be to drag her bodily. To complicate matters, he and his wife happened to be speaking German, a language in which I am very limited, and while he appeared willing to understand what it was I wanted, his wife looked bent on misunderstanding. Thank God for European manners. The man was naked as a jaybird, but that didn't prevent him from jumping up to greet me properly. I could quickly stoop down and pick up Spooky before I got hit on the head with any loose appendages.

Such an encounter would be a sure cure for anyone who has trouble looking a person in the eye, I thought, as I hurried back to the safety of my dune, firmly gripping the dog. I put her on her leash and went to join Finn in the surf, but just then I saw him on his way up the beach, headed towards a crowd where one other man was wearing swimming trunks. There was a roar of laughter as Finn, with a dazzling smile on his tan face, walked up to the fellow and shook hands with him, saying, "Dr. Livingstone, I presume!"

Cʒ Cʁ

Not all Danes go in for nude sunbathing, but those who do are not exhibitionists by any means. They have simply removed the last barrier between themselves and the sun and air they love so much and which they long for all during the cold months of the year. Therefore, they can be puzzled by tourists who bring their cameras to the beach and take pictures of the locals.

Considering the fact that Danes are very practical people, I was puzzled that first summer I spent here, when I noticed that on the windows there are no screens to keep out the multitude of insects that begin to stir with the first thaw. Now I've learned to appreciate that feeling of not wanting to have any physical obstruction between oneself and the spring air. We open the doors and windows and welcome all the light and air. If there are bees and mosquitoes with it, one merely opens a window on the opposite side of the house, and they will be carried off on the crosscurrent.

Thirty years ago it wasn't common practice in Denmark to use insecticides to keep bugs at bay. Being already then alarmed at what mankind was doing to the environment, I was quite pleased — especially when I discovered that in most cases one can outsmart insects or learn to live with them. By learning their habits they can often be avoided. Mosquitoes, for example, generally stay out of the house if one closes the curtains before putting on the lights at night. A good vacuuming can keep silverfish and fleas at a minimum, and household spiders are more acceptable if you think they bring good luck. Even wasps can be welcome if you know that they eat aphids off your fruit trees, and a wide variety of less noticeable insects are needed by the birds we all want in our gardens. A shallow bowl of water placed outside can keep bees from getting cross on a sweltering summer day, and most insects prefer to stay outside if there are plants to hide in. There can be a harmony in it all, and once one starts to appreciate insects for the fascinating creatures they are, their abundance serves as one more proof of the richness of Mother Nature.

Because of the power exerted by the magic of childhood, Danes remember summers of their respective childhoods as being flawless days of perpetual sunshine. Actually, such summers do occasionally occur, such as the one in 1975. The good weather lasted day after day;

we ate every meal out in the garden, and it was truly a time of wine and roses. We moved up to the family's summer place on the beach of the Kattegat, and we enjoyed weather like that of the Riviera. It was eerie to wake up each morning and see a blazing sun already high in the sky, heat shimmering on the azure waters, making the bronzed figures of early morning bathers appear to move in slow motion. The sea was crystal clear, a sheet of unruffled blue with great stretches of inviting sand shoals exposed in the stillness of the water. We spent hours on the beach and sat late into the balmy evenings, drinking white wine and shelling tiny pink shrimp, while we watched the children skip pebbles on the sea. We thought it was a perfect summer, but then we left the seaside and drove home, past gardens, fields, and forests scorched by the sun and parched by the drought. After weeks of isolating ourselves in the Mediterranean atmosphere of the beach, we were appalled at the damage the heat wave had wrought. I decided then that Denmark just wouldn't be Denmark without a few summer days when the rain falls steadily for hours on end, keeping everything lush and making for a sparkling, clean world when the sun breaks its way through the clouds.

Furthermore, with the proper attitude, a person living in these climes can end up longing for the dark months. On sunny days, I became obsessed with enjoying every waking hour I jumped out of bed, often at the crack of dawn, my head buzzing with a half a dozen conflicting desires: I wanted to spruce up the garden, go canoeing with the kids, hang up great washes of clothes, plan a barbecue for friends who would stay late relishing the light late hours that we have so far north, and I wanted to lie in the sun all day, doing nothing but watch the birds splash about in the birdbath, only getting up to fetch tall glasses of iced tea. All meals were carried out into the garden. Breakfast dragged out an extra hour as we sat on the terrace, speaking in low voices in order not to break a mood so tranquil that one could hear petals fall from the pale pink roses that covered the wall to the churchyard. We moved a table out on the lawn to have dinner under the branches of a pear tree, a golden-green spot where the last rays of the evening sun lingered until its disappearance behind tall birch trees in the churchyard.

It would be bliss if it weren't for the conflicts. While I longed to be brown on days like that, I could practically watch the weeds grow. And if I crawled around in the flower beds pulling up weeds, the only part of me that got brown were my knees, and that went off in the wash. After a couple of weeks of good weather, I was so exhausted that I yearned for a good old rainy day when I could curl up indoors with a book or for an afternoon nap and know that I wasn't missing out on anything.

Sunshine? We have just about all that I can cope with.

7

The Hunting Scene

In a land so rich with traditions, it came as no surprise that hunting was a far cry from the mindless massacre it is in so many parts of the world. Like all living creatures big enough to get attention here in Denmark, game is well cared for. There are many nature lovers, and there are hunters who are often a combination of nature lover, sportsman and gourmet. Fortunately, their common interests serve the same cause: better conditions for the wildlife.

As with most things, this is all tied up with money. Most of the land here is cultivated, and if a farmer or forester is faced with a loss of profit because hares or deer are nibbling away at his tender young crops, he is likely to find an efficient means of exterminating them — Only on his own property, mind you, because like most of us, he probably loves wild animals until he is faced with a choice between Bambi and an acre of future timber. And, because the greater part of land is under cultivation, the result would be very little wildlife left to hunt or enjoy, except for those who want to stalk cats and mice. However, hunters are willing to pay enormous amounts to rent the right to shoot on the farmers' land or in the forests of the large estates. The farmer or forester can be more tolerant of the hare when he realizes that the cabbage eaten is worth peanuts compared to the money he can haul in from the hunting rights. As for the animals themselves, their conditions are improved in order to encourage their presence, and feed is put out for them throughout the winter months.

There is a strict enforcement of hunting seasons in order to encourage the proliferation of game, and the individual hunters are very careful not to over-shoot within their territories, knowing that such a practice would ruin the amount of game to be spotted next year. (This is why I object to the idea of leasing out hunting rights to foreigners; it is the hunter who knows the area well who will respect the conditions for the game.)

I can understand the feelings of those who choose to be vegetarians for ethical reasons; however, with modern farming methods, I would claim that without the presence of meat-eating hunters, Denmark would be a land devoid of wildlife. It is largely hunters who have, for instance, put a great deal of work into reestablishing ecological systems favorable to game.

In times of yore, the royalty enjoyed a kind of hunt called *par force*, which involved riding by horseback through the large forested areas on the heels of a fleet deer, until the poor creature was exhausted. Kings in those days having been in a position to do things in a big way, entire villages were uprooted in order to enlarge the hunt. Consequently, vast tracts of land came under the protection of the crown, ensuring that they remained undeveloped. One pleasant result is a forest on the outskirts of Copenhagen, the name of which can be translated as Deer Garden and which would never have been intact up to our times if there had not been a successive line of monarchs to protect it from land speculation. Thus, thanks to a royal interest in the hunt, we can escape from the confusion and traffic of modern Copenhagen and lose ourselves in this beautiful, unspoiled forest.

For years Finn had a hunt which was tiny compared to a king's, but adequate for him to spend a day trying to bag game and come home covered with mud, scratched by brambles and proud as punch over the game he had shot. Not only did it open a whole new dimension in his life, it furnished many happy hours for the entire family. Late in life, even Paps discovered the joy of going along for the ride. He himself never hunted, but he loved trudging through the forest, seeing the sudden flight of a golden pheasant against a backdrop of flaming leaves, and taking pride in his son's marksmanship.

There were also the unforgettable days close to Christmastime, when the whole family combined Finn's hunting with the search for the many lovely things the forest yields for making our holiday decorations. And there were the distinctly different days in the springtime or summer or autumn, when Finn took us along to learn the many moods, sounds and smells of the forest he knew so well, teaching us to respect the forest as a living unity which needn't be disrupted by one's presence if one is careful.

In the early spring, beginning the 15th of May, the season opens for hunting male deer. Stalking one of these bucks, which are not much larger than a German shepherd dog in bulk, in a forest so lush that one can hardly catch sight of him much less get near to him, is Finn's favorite type of hunt, the *pürsch*. He has sworn that if he ever wounds a deer and doesn't bring it down, he will shelve his rifle; therefore, he has to creep soundlessly to within a range as close as eighty yards of this agile, alert animal in order to even get a chance for a good shot. The deer is aided by a far superior sense of smell and a surefire instinct for when the hunting season is open, plus the fact that if he is very beautiful and in his prime, the hunter who has sole rights to the area might very well be satisfied with the mere sight of him and sit in a trance, choosing to watch him bound away. The season closes again in July, and meanwhile the forest continues to become ever more dense as the undergrowth is transformed from a delicate carpet of white windflowers and pale-yellow cowslips to ferns and grass tall enough to hide all but the tips of the deer's ears.

For the pürsch, Finn rises long before daybreak, in order to be in the forest by approximately four in the morning, when the sun is up. He moves silently through wet grass, every sense attuned to the movements of the forest, tensed to the prospect of a confrontation. More often than not, he returns empty-handed but full of reports of having seen fox cubs playing outside their den or squirrels scolding from the treetops or a clumsy badger trundling home after a night of prowling.

I can sympathize with those who feel distressed about the idea of these lovely animals being shot down, but visit a modern poultry farm or pig stable, and you will change your mind. At least the wild animals have a full life as long as they live. To run free in the forest is far better than being chained in a stable until fat enough for the one excursion in life — a trip to the slaughterhouse. And I can assure you that game meat, all sorts of game meat, is absolutely delicious, and although I don't want to shoot it, I certainly enjoy preparing it for the table.

The skilful hunter takes care not to shoot unless he feels quite sure his prey will die quickly, and he will show respect for the animal by the way he carries it and places it on the "game parade," an artistic display of what has been bagged, to be admired by the hunt party as the hunting horn is sounded.

At first, I felt quite inadequate when my hunter came home ever so pleased with himself for having brought me some dead animal, which

he literally laid at my feet, like a peace offering for having enjoyed an
enormously entertaining weekend with his mates. I could tell by the
light in Finn's eyes that this feathered creature with the loose head was
being envisioned as a succulent chef d'oeuvre on the dinner table.

I used to pore over recipe books and spend lots of money on exotic
ingredients for complicated marinades and sauces. I've since learned
that most of those recipes must have been written by people who were
skeptical as to whether or not the game would taste good. By following
a recipe, one could disguise beyond all means of recognition whatever
bit of game lay buried in the sauce.

If the animal hasn't been hung properly, if it is very badly shot up,
or if you can't stand game meat, I highly recommend camouflaging

tactics such as soaking it in complicated marinades or in milk, but if you like the rich flavor of pheasant or hare and the quality is right, I suggest you keep the preparation simple. Having received the animal with its feathers or fur, one soon learns to determine whether it is old and tough or young and tender and prepare it accordingly.

I suspect that the practice of marinating game arose in climates, where it had gotten a bit tainted before it arrived in the kitchen and from the old days on big estates, where so much game was shot on one day that one had to treat the whole batch of resulting meat as though it matched the least edible specimens. After all, there is nothing more soothing than brewing a mixture of bay leaves, red wine, garlic and thyme to pour over some yucky piece of meat that you really would like to throw out but don't dare because you hate to see a grown man cry.

The best indicator for what to do with game meat once it is cleaned is one's own nose. Smell the meat and choose the herbs accordingly. Of course, I realize that our senses of smell can differ, and I do know that mine differed from that of our dog, Spooky. Proof of that came the time I fixed a badger. At this point I had reached the stage where I smugly thought I could make something edible out of anything Finn brought home. Then, one winter day, he brought home a badger.

First of all, a full-grown, male badger is an enormous creature. This one must have weighed more than thirty pounds. He had the most gorgeous fur and had obviously led a very long and contented life. Badgers build marvelous cities underground in a forest, and I really thought he should have been left there, but, having been shot it seemed a shame that he should go to waste. The only drawback was general consensus that badger meat is far from tasty, and they are only hunted when the forester decides that the population is too big.

Surrounded by a flock of curious neighborhood kids and two pals who happened by the day after the beast was brought home, Finn deftly proceeded to flay him, in order to have the fur tanned. Under the fur was a thick layer of blubber, but when that was removed, there was lean, very appetizing meat, without any alien smells. The friends present were definitely not inspired, however, to share it with us; in fact, friend Demus, who usually has an exceedingly healthy appetite, stuck his pipe firmly in his mouth, announcing through defensively clenched teeth that he didn't want to be invited to dinner for the first six months, figuring that by then the creature would either be eaten or buried.

Not being the sorts who like to admit a mistake, we put the badger, all nicely butchered, in the freezer. Finn thought we could save it for a later feast and me thinking that with a bit of luck we would have a power failure one day, and I could throw it out.

The following month was Easter, and we were broke. The kids had been invited on a posh holiday with friends, and Finn and I thought we could just coast through the holidays with a bucket of paint to give us purpose and the reserves in the wine cellar to give us fortitude.

As fate would have it, we received a long distance call from two dear old friends in Maine, who were planning an impulsive trip to Copenhagen with two of their daughters. We put aside all plans for keeping a low profile and told them to come on over, and I started cooking up a storm. My greatest efforts in the kitchen have been inspired by a lack of cash, and this was serious business. Thanks to Finn's hunt, we had plenty of interesting things in the freezer, but by the end of the week, I began to hit bottom when I plunged my hand inside. The badger problem, though put on ice, so to speak, was again an issue. Should I pawn him off on good friends or on someone I didn't want to see anymore? My dilemma was solved when they decided to extend their stay.

While old Badger was thawing, I made a desperate trip to the library, where I found a book I knew would be useful. It is a recipe book written by a man who is a hunter, and being a good cook, his recipes have not been influenced by a wife who wished to God she could be fixing roast beef instead. He has written recipes for everything one is likely to find in the woods, from the slow-moving snail to the swift snipe.

What he said about badger was, in essence, that if it is a very young animal, it can be roasted and is similar in taste to lamb — So much for that hope! To start with, I knew for a fact that this was a very old animal, and secondly, I don't like mutton. Thinking of all those hungry people, however, I decided to pretend it was young and treat it like lamb. I sprinkled it generously with lemon juice and garlic, barded it with bacon, and put it in a slow oven. I began to feel reassured when the kitchen started to smell deliciously like roast lamb, and I was delighted a few hours later when it sliced nicely, and the juices made a scrumptious sauce.

It was super — Everyone, even the kids, were wild about it. However, poor little Spooky had spent the entire afternoon anticipating this roast, thinking all my efforts were for her. She had looked so disappointed when I whisked the platter into the dining room that I decided to reward her patience by giving her a generous slice when I brought the few remains out to the kitchen. Greedy as all dachshunds are, she jumped up eagerly and grabbed it between her teeth.

Then she did something very peculiar; she stopped dead in her tracks, rolled her eyes up to give me her most apologetic look and dropped the meat on the floor. Looking guilty, as only a dog can look guilty, she proceeded to roll in it, just like she does when she finds an old, dead seagull rotting on the beach. I never have been able to decide whether to take that as a compliment to the badger or an insult to my cooking. I decided not to tell our people-friends about Spooky's behavior, and I fortified my silence by keeping in mind a useful phrase: *à chacun son goût.*

8

A Bird Song Tour

ere in the North, one can tell what month of the year it is by the sounds of the birds. All year long one hears the rakish scolding and inspired warbling of the blackbird, but when the sun comes out on a clear, frosty day in February, and the tiny tit begins its pleasantly monotonous, cheery call, it is like the first line of a cantata, and all the rich orchestration is yet to come, piece by piece, until the intense crescendo of springtime.

Finn, who has always preferred the sounds of the forest to the chattering of mankind, taught me the pleasure of what here in Denmark is called a "bird song tour", an outing taken sometime between the middle of May and midsummer night's eve, which is roughly the day when the birds begin to limit their singing and concentrate on other activities.

We lived within walking distance of the woods, but Finn preferred to plan one of these tours in the forest where he hunted — a two-hour drive. In order to be quietly settled within the heart of the forest by daybreak, this meant getting up no later than one-thirty in the morning on the appointed day and hoping for good weather on the other end of the line. One year, however, the project was greatly simplified when a friend who owned a cottage on the edge of the forest told us that the house was at our disposal during the month of June. This meant that Finn could pursue the pürsch, and we could stay in bed with the window open if it was pouring down rain when we wanted to listen to the birds.

To describe Henning's cottage, I really must describe Henning, for he is a part of my picture of Denmark, though his type was ever so rare. He was a very distinguished looking gentleman, with silvery hair and a face that had a perennial tan, in the nice leathery way you see on a man who has the money and leisure to pursue the outdoor life all year around. His looks and background had provided him with the traits that made it possible for him to go through life with an aura of dignity and gentility, like a successful actor in an appealing role. He looked so much the part of the leader that it really didn't matter that he wasn't especially capable; he was a reassuring presence in our somewhat shabby times.

Notorious for driving a car as if he still lived in the days when Denmark's roads were uncluttered by motored vehicles, he didn't give a fig for one-way streets. Oblivious to the honking of horns from oncoming cars that were going in the right direction, he maintained an admirable sang-froid, while designating to his distracted passenger buildings in Copenhagen where he had attended grand parties or intimate dinners. Once, when driving Mums and Paps home, he mistook a path through the woods for their street, and when his mistake was pointed out to him, his only comment was, "Hmm . . . I thought there seemed to be an extraordinary amount of trees."

Henning's cottage was very romantic. The half-timbered walls sagged with age, as if weighted down by the low-hanging thatched roof. When he bought the place, it had been deserted for some time, and its last occupants had been a Polish family who had lived in it much as farmers who were poor lived a hundred years ago. They kept livestock indoors to augment the warmth of the old woodstove, and they had turned to drink to try to keep up the illusion of a romance that had produced too many offspring to make it easy to keep up illusions any other way. It was, in effect, a ruin.

Henning had had it restored without sacrificing its original charm. The dirt floors were covered with tiles in the kitchen area and wood in the living area, but the rest of the changes were minimal. One entered a kitchen with a pantry, flanked on the one side by sleeping quarters and on the other by a small parlor with a dining area and fireplace in the latter room. The walls were covered with trophies from Henning's long hunting career, and there was a coziness about this room which made it seemed lived in, even after months when the house was shut down.

There were no modern conveniences, except for electricity. The water pump in the garden had been idle for years, largely, I suspect because of the lovely little bird that had a habit of making a nest inside it. We all knew we mustn't disturb her and gladly fetched water from a neighboring farm, giving us an opportunity to reacquaint ourselves with the healthy outlook of appreciating each precious drop.

Honeysuckle climbed one side of the house, and the small meadow all around was filled with wildflowers. One of the boundaries of the property was marked by an ancient elderberry, more like a small tree than a bush, and under the elderberry was an enormous pile of oyster shells, Henning's legacy to the land, for, as he put it, he wanted it known that "Here lived a gentleman." I'm sure it is there to this day, being too large to be easily removed and, perhaps revered, being too impressive to be ignored.

Two sides of the property opened out onto fields which were alternately sowed with grain or sugar beets or rapeseed. The grain was like a green sea in the early summer, the sugar beets were deep green against the rich black loam of Lolland, and, when the rape bloomed it was like liquid sunshine spilled out as a happy inspiration. The other sides of the meadow ebbed out into a beech forest that was dense and mysterious at night and lacey and inviting when sunlight was filtered through its branches, dappling the undergrowth.

During the summer, hares frolicked on the fields in the early morning and late afternoon, boxing like kangaroos, a sight that invariably brought to mind a rather absent-minded friend of ours. Early one summer morning he had come back to the cottage after unsuccessfully stalking deer. Upon finding the privy occupied, he went to the edge of the field, and, while squatting there in God's green nature with his trousers down, he amused himself by looking at the landscape through

the telescopic lens of his rifle. Unnoticed by our friend, the farmer who owned the land had come out on the other side of the field, to enjoy in his more dignified way the sight of the lush grain.

Seeing in the distance a hunter crouched low with a rifle pointed roughly in his direction, the farmer panicked and started waving like mad. His attention caught by all that movement in the distance, our friend zeroed in on the farmer to get a better look at what he thought would be hares. It is only due to the Lollander's stoutness of character that the farmer didn't drop dead of fright, but he was hopping mad. It didn't even pacify him that our pal hurried over to apologize and tried to reassure him by pointing out that there really wasn't cause for alarm, hares being out of season.

All these images came to mind, as I anticipated a few pleasant days in Henning's cottage. A good friend of ours, Alex, from San Francisco, was visiting us, so we decided to bring along a tent to provide extra sleeping space. It would clearly be an advantage to load the car a day in advance. With that in mind, Finn took that day off, too. Unfortunately, the weather was so splendid that he couldn't resist "just one hour of tennis" in the morning.

I know how long one of his hours is when he is playing a game, but that day he really out-did himself. From nine in the morning until four in the afternoon, he played almost non-stop. The "almost" was a lunch break with his partner, and they spent the rest of the afternoon competing both in tennis and in drinking the partner's home-distilled alcohol. Finn won both contests. I will say, however, that despite his condition, he did load the car, and we were off bright and early the next morning for three days of the good life.

Though we left at the crack of dawn, the sun was already high in the sky when we arrived, and the small cottage appeared to be a shimmering mirage beyond the fields. We pitched the tent in the meadow and installed the kids' things inside. Bjørn was at a stage where he was obsessed with the fear of losing things. For anyone who thinks their child is badly in need of psychiatric treatment, I will say a word of comfort. Any problem a kid can conceive of having, our son has had, and he has turned into a very likeable, normal adult. (I won't, however, comment on the mental health of those of us who saw him through his various stages.)

At any rate, this was Bjørn's anxiety-over-things stage, and the only way I could make him relax that day was to advise him to count everything he had brought along. "Then you can write down the number and count everything on the day we pack the car. That way you will know you haven't lost anything."

He was about eight years old that summer, and his freckled face lit up with a smile when he had been given such an easy solution to all his problems. I crawled out of the tent after our little chat and joined the others to drink a cup of coffee and plan our stay. From inside the tent we could hear, "One, two, three, four, five, six . . . , twenty-two, twenty-three, twenty-five," then a pause and, "Phooey! I forgot twenty-four. One, two, three, four, five . . ." While we tried to suppress our laughter, the poor little tyke went on like that until he finally counted himself to sleep.

We decided to do a bit of foraging before lunch and then go fishing for trout for our evening meal. At a nearby farm, we bought fresh-laid eggs from hens that had plenty of greenery to eat as they scratched about in the hot dust. With large, capable hands the farmer's wife picked two baskets of strawberries from a sloped patch soaking up the sun. They were big and scarlet, their sweetness undiluted by any recent rain. We also bought potatoes that had been dug up that morning.

With all that to whet our appetites, we returned to the cottage, where we made an omelet browned golden in butter, sprinkled with parsley picked by the white gravel path that ran around the house. We had cheese and home-baked bread and the glistening strawberries in a large earthenware bowl, and we set the table out in the sunny meadow with a gentle breeze blowing from across the fields.

The trout pond in the forest was a brainstorm of a friend of ours who is a forester. In 1969, when Denmark was ravaged by a hurricane, thousands of trees were uprooted, among them a good many giants with large crowns and shallow roots. Faced with clearing up the forest at a time when timber prices were unnaturally low, Carl had a large pit bulldozed in the middle of the forest where there was a clearing, and he dumped the windfall of logs into the pit. The autumn rains that followed took care of the rest, for wood left soaking in water is preserved from rotting. When prices were back to normal, he could retrieve the wood and stock the resulting pond with trout. He had told us we could fish there that day, and it seemed a most entertaining way to get our dinner.

With his usual irritating efficiency, Finn landed a large trout within minutes and left for the evening hunt. Every bit her father's daughter,

Lani had soon caught her dinner, too. Having a good sport like Alex along turned out to be very handy, he being the one who willingly waded out until his hat floated, removing our hooks from the snags that Bjorn and I kept catching. Finally, we each had a fish, with Alex having done everything short of putting them on the hooks for us. When we got back to the cottage, the kids were put to work cleaning the fish, a part of the bargain which they executed with great zeal, and it wasn't long before the delicious smell of fried trout could greet Finn as he made his way back from the pürsch, tired and happy after hours of being part of the forest.

We agreed to get up very early, in order to be in the forest when all the night creatures had found their hideaway to settle in, and the daylight life began to stir. If one is quiet enough one can even be rewarded with the sight of a deer fawn shyly sidling up to his mother's flanks. It was still dark outside as we hastily threw on sweaters and jeans and went out into the forest. We crept stealthily along the paths, feeling the cold dampness of night dew. The nightingale was singing his finale, his clear trill like magical chimes somewhere in the boughs above us. There was the feeling of excitement akin to the sense of mystery one felt as a child during after-bedtime prowls. Finn silently motioned us together like a troop of straggly soldiers and told us where he would be in the woods, directing us off in another direction. Looking like a partisan, he shouldered his rifle and disappeared into the darkness, while we stood very still, ears cocked.

The sun still hadn't risen, but there was an almost imperceptible change in the nuance of lighting. We heard the dusky wings of an owl coming to roost nearby and were unable to see him in the shadowy trees which were just beginning to take form in the pre-dawn light. The song of the nightingale gradually became overpowered as the myriad of other birds in the forest started to make their sounds. It began sparsely in all directions, small cheeps, followed by more elaborate songs, until the entire multitude was singing — the finches, the tits, the song thrushes and blackbirds, pigeons with their contented cooing, and pheasants with their peculiar call, like something coming out of a hollow piece of wood. Off in the distance we could hear the elusive sound of the cuckoo who calls while in flight. The nearby pond was alive with the trumpeting of geese and the unmelodious calls of mallards and coots. One could hear an oriole and a goldcrest, and the plaintive weep-weep of a buzzard.

The collective sound reached a thrilling dimension and then gradually dispersed as all the members of the orchestra started to go about the serious business of finding food for their off-spring. Suddenly we were aware of the fact that we had been standing still for a long time, and that the bottoms of our trousers' legs were cold and wet against our ankles. We walked back to the cottage, mindless now of the noise we made as we pushed our way through the undergrowth, and, once there, we hurriedly grabbed a cold roll, eating it as we threw off our wet jeans and crept in under feather quilts.

Soon our beds were snug and warm, and, much to Finn's disgust, we were sound asleep and the sun high in the sky when he returned, expecting the smell of hot coffee, and bacon and eggs.

When we did have breakfast, it was out in the sunshine, with the summer sound of a lark singing over the fields. Utter contentment. I'll tell you this, my friends, even if you don't like bird song, an outing like that is worth it, just for the bliss of crawling back into bed for a few snug hours before a well-deserved breakfast.

9

Country Living Is a State of Mind

Finn's hunt kept us in touch with country living, a constant reminder of a dream that we had both always nurtured. However, we also had strong ties to the pleasant suburb where we lived and to the old house so full of memories. At the time, it seemed simpler to stay put and move bits of the country into the city. Most suburban people who want a touch of country buy a wagon wheel or old pump for the front lawn and let nasturtiums grow around it. Finn, however, likes genuine things. He bought live chickens.

The substitutes for country living started innocently enough with a few herbs in the back garden, but that soon expanded to everything from strawberries to tomatoes and chard. Somehow, taking care of all these things came under my domain, although Finn demonstrated a keen interest in the crops when he gave attractive ladies guided tours of the garden. Even so, when he and Lani started talking about raising chickens, I didn't even get alarmed. We lived in a very respectable neighborhood, and the idea was too farfetched to be a worry. I listened to their plans with the same amused indulgence one has for the daydreams of a child with an overactive imagination.

Springtime usually found me trying to find practical solutions for Finn's ever more ambitious garden schemes. As for the chickens, I adamantly stated that if there was time for them to make a chicken pen, there should first be time to help me with the garden work. Of course, they assured me that they fully intended to work very hard this year, and, indeed, it appeared they were serious when I observed them clearing out an unused corner of the garden at the back of the house. However, I knew there was something fishy when I watched furtively from the back windows and saw them making gesticulations which clearly indicated the outlines of a chicken pen.

Having obviously lost the battle, I still hoped to be able to dictate the terms of peace, and I was very firm when I said that there could only be hens — no roosters. Finn readily agreed, but, in retrospect, I recall that he could have had his fingers crossed behind his back. In any case, he knows me well enough to have been confident that I would melt when he came home with the most cunning pair, a cock and hen so clearly in love that one would have had to be heartless to have banished the rooster, even when he started crowing at four the following morning. They were of a French bantam race called *mille fleur*, so we named them Napoléon and Joséphine.

Joséphine was a proper little hen who went about her business in a very self-confident manner, but Napoléon was so infatuated that the feather dusters on his feet barely touched the ground as he pranced around behind her bustle. She had soon laid sixteen eggs and then went all broody. We removed three eggs, in order to make it easier for her to sit on the remaining ones, which she rotated each day in an order known only to herself. She even seemed to have an idea of what to do with her enamored spouse, for she gave him one egg to sit on as he joined her in their nesting box. He looked a bit silly sitting there but was so happy at being able to be at her side, that he seldom left her for a moment. The final result was five fuzzy chicks which Joséphine herded around all day and carefully led into the chicken house at night.

All was idyllic, until Joséphine got it into her head that her chicks should be versed in the ways of the wild and refused to go in at night. She stayed outside, tucking her babes under her wings, safely protecting them from the velvety blackness of starry nights. None of us felt capable of interfering with Joséphine, and she was allowed her eccentricities, until the night the fox got a whiff of French chicken.

We had all gone to bed, thoroughly exhausted, on the evening before a dinner dance we were giving to culminate a visit from my cousin, Alan. It had been a very busy week, and I was too tired to lie awake worrying about all the things that needed to be done in the morning. I fell asleep as soon as my head touched the pillow, but two hours later I awoke with a start. Joséphine was cackling like mad, and my first thought was the neighborhood fox. I jumped out of bed and ran to the window to see him bounding around on the netting covering the chicken enclosure. Our courageous little hen was on the top of the peaked roof of the hen house, just under his feet, where she must have figured the commotion she was making would have the maximum effect.

I would like to repeat, at this point, that we lived in a very quiet neighborhood. The houses along our street were just as silent at three a.m. as the graveyard behind us. Not only was our hen making a hell of a racket, but by now Finn was aroused from his slumber and was quickly assembling and loading his shotgun. I dove under the quilts again, covering my ears and just peeking out with one eye to get an unforgettable glimpse of the great white hunter, dressed in a tartan plaid robe, standing on the window sill, with the barrel of his gun stuck out of the upper window; he was a striking figure with hairy legs and slightly droopy jockeys.

The blast was deafening, and just in case none of the neighbors had heard that, Joséphine recommenced her cackling, more frantically than ever. I expected Finn to go down immediately and comfort his poor hen, but he was getting dressed and asking me to find his hunting horn

so he could blow *Death of the Fox.* "You're kidding," I said. But I could see he wasn't kidding.

Exasperated, I ran downstairs and out back, carefully lifted Joséphine down from her perch and watched her fluff her feathers into place and settle down to gentle clucks as her chicks reappeared from all possible hiding places to scuttle back underneath her motherly wings. As for the fox, he had bit the dust, or, more accurately, the hay on top of the compost pile, and Finn came down to admire him, bugle in hand. Just then we heard a car drive slowly up our street, and I had a strong feeling it would be a patrol car trying to locate the scene of a crime. Finn, who was fully dressed, suggested that I, in my flimsy nightie, should go and tell them that everything was alright, but I was already high-tailing it back to bed, muttering something to the effect that I wished some Hamlet had advised me to get to a nunnery.

I gave no more thought to the fox the following day, as I rushed around making preparations for the party, but I happened to be the one who opened the door when the first guest rang the bell. She stood on the stairs, in an elegant dress, looking horror-stricken and making unintelligible noises while she pointed towards a pile of stones at the top of the driveway. Being ever so pleased with himself, Finn had proudly draped the dead fox over the stones with a candle by its head. Risking my hero's displeasure, I quickly stashed the corpse in the garage and hid the key until the party was over.

Three of the chicks survived the ordeals of youth, and we named them Flower, Fleur and Flora. We later acquired two beautiful Danish hens, with colors like game birds, and named them Frøken Sauer and Frøken Simonsen, followed by two buxom golden shavers, named Marilyn and May. Each hen had her own personality, but being Napoléon's favorite, tiny Joséphine ruled over them all. They lived bravely through an ice winter and enjoyed a lovely springtime and hot summer days when they took dust baths and spread their wings in the sun.

The trouble with chickens is that sooner or later one is faced with either slaughtering them or watching them struggle with old age. At the beginning of a winter, Finn saw it as his duty to slaughter them. I had somehow gotten into the practice of letting them out in the morning and feeding them during the day, but Finn spared me the job of plucking them when their days were done. He always looked a bit teary-eyed afterwards, and we made a practice of putting them in the freezer unlabelled so we could enjoy their extra delectable home-grown quality without being overwhelmed by feelings. However, we had to give Napoléon and Joséphine to friends, not being able to devour them.

We assiduously avoided naming our next batch of chickens, except for the magnificent cock which we called Luigi, knowing that he would probably irritate me to the point that I would be able to wring his neck personally and pluck him with pleasure. The batch of Shavers we bought this time had never been outdoors when they were delivered to us one November day. They were in a state of shock the first two days, looking startled every time a leaf fell or a sparrow chirped. They were extremely docile and uncomplaining, but that first week must have been comparable to being evicted from a heated apartment to the hardships of Siberia. They huddled together, keeping their magnificent plumage immaculate and conversing in small clucks. Good, I thought. These will be quiet and devoid of personality. We even had to pick them up at nighttime and put them safely in their house.

Soon, however, Luigi cautiously began practicing his crow when locked up at night, and, once he felt confident that it was a call worthy of someone with his splendor, he started giving us the full blast of it all day long. I could see that this was to herald in a period of increased sociability with all the neighbors while we tried to make sure they were pacified. Although our modern world is filled with the nerve-shattering sounds of power mowers, electric saws, and hedge clippers, stereo sets and even motorized gravediggers, the crow of the rooster is not on the acceptable list, and Luigi had the volume that little Napoléon had lacked. Fortunately, we had very nice neighbors who all seemed to be sound sleepers. Furthermore, the neighborhood being a very old one, there were no zoning laws such as would have been in place in a modern area, preventing the presence of livestock.

Not only did Luigi learn to crow, the primitive living conditions inspired him to other patterns of rooster behavior, clearly indicated by the amount of mud all over the hens' backs on rainy days. The once-so-inhibited hens soon were laying enough eggs to pay for the keep of themselves and their over-sexed friend, and they all learned the joys of scratching in the dirt, nesting in the sun, and communicating their discoveries in an increasingly varied chicken babble. As Finn and Lani had obviously foreseen, I became a devoted chicken owner. Somehow, I found that I was stuck with unwanted work, but it really didn't matter.

I realized how attached to them I was the day they ran out of chicken feed, and I found myself frying buttermilk pancakes for their breakfast. Luigi looked alarmed at this innovation, and the hens walked around and around their feed trough, discussing in small clucks the possibility of the mess being edible. Once they had tasted it, their clucks turned to happy chortles which they usually saved for days when we spread fresh hay out in their pen, and Luigi flapped his wings loudly and gave out with a masterful crow, taking the credit for their satisfaction.

Having chickens taught us a great deal about our feathered friends, but it also taught me a lot about myself. I'm an absolute twit. Not only did I give in to the idea of having hens, I fell for the looks of roosters, and that even though I knew I would be the one they would keep awake. Just as there is a balance of power among nations, there is one among couples. Right from the day I moved to this country instead of making Finn move to mine, I had stepped into the role of the weaker part. It isn't even that I'm weak, he is simply too crafty.

He has me over a barrel in two ways: One is that he gets hay fever and starts to sneeze when there is something annoying him. This never fails to evoke my sympathy, and it was years before I discovered that these outbursts were more apt to occur when there was some

annoyance which he could count on me to remove. The second way I've lost the advantage is that I wake up at the drop of a pin while Finn sleeps through nearly everything.

Luigi's nocturnal practicing of crowing definitely got out of control. While it was very disturbing when he was shut up in the chicken house, it was deafening when he was out. He started crowing around three a.m. one winter morning and continued with approximately fifteen minute intervals throughout the night. When I complained in the morning, Finn took a vicarious masculine pleasure in having such an active rooster. I struggled through the day, absentmindedly tending the house and meals while I speculated over the possibility of inventing a muffler for roosters.

By the time we went to bed that night, I thought I would immediately doze off, but I had been so tired during the day that I hadn't eaten enough. My stomach refused to let the rest of me go to sleep before I had had a snack. As I got out of bed, Finn was roused and he groggily asked me what I was doing. "I can't sleep. I'm going down to get something to eat."

After having pacified my hunger, I crept back into bed, grateful for a nice warm partner to cuddle up next to as I felt myself blissfully dropping off. An hour later, I heard a tapping noise which I took to be one of the kids trying to awaken me by lightly tapping on the door, but as I lay there listening for further sound above Finn's snores, thinking I might have dreamed the first sounds, I heard the unmistakable noises of hens, busily pecking at grain in their feed bowls and clucking contentedly. A loud squawk made me leap out of bed and look out the window.

The snow on the ground made a bright backdrop for the scene I couldn't believe that I was seeing. The hens were milling around, and Luigi was riding herd on them, and it was one a.m. "Finn!" I said. "You told me you had shut the hens in. Do something! They are all out of their house."

Finn woke up with a grunt and said in a far too reasonable tone, "What do you want me to do?"

With the rising hysteria it takes several sleepless nights to cultivate, I tried to avoid waking the kids by screaming in a stage whisper, "Well, for a starter, you could go down and lock up the bloomin' birds. With Luigi out I won't be able to sleep at all!"

Without even lifting his head from the pillow and still sounding very reasonable, Finn said, "But darling, you already told me you can't sleep," and he resumed snoring.

While counting to ten, I stomped down the stairs, put on winter boots and an overcoat, found the flashlight, and stormed out of the house, heading for the back yard with blood in my eye.

Evidently Luigi had an instinct for survival, for by the time I had reached the pen he had shooed all his hens into the house and was looking at me with a startled expression under his floppy comb. He was so intimidated that he didn't crow until nearly six the next morning.

Finn came to the breakfast table wreathed in smiles, gave me his usual nice-smelling aftershave kiss, and had the nerve to ask, "Did you sleep well, darling?" And this is where the balance of power comes in. If I had started to nag, he would have started sneezing, and I knew I'd be a goner.

In all fairness, I should say that at heart he is the most chivalrous of husbands, and if I had been a heavy-sleeper, he probably would have become a light one to take care of me. Take the night he woke up as I was climbing back into bed.

"Where have you been?" he asked. I told him that I had just checked the downstairs rooms and the cellar, because I had heard a noise in the house. At the thought of me throwing my hundred pound frame into a battle with a burglar, Finn sat bolt upright in bed and said sternly, "Promise me — you must promise me that you won't ever get up and check the house for prowlers. If you hear a noise, wake me up!"

"Alright, darling," I said contentedly, as I snuggled down next to this masterful heap of muscles.

Ten minutes later, I again heard this peculiar sound and promptly awakened Finn. He was a bit cross, but listened as conscientiously as one can while trying to remain asleep, and after I nudged him back to consciousness, he muttered, "Oh, that's nothing," and fell back into a deep sleep. (By the way, I never did find out what the noise was, and I suspect it was a ghost sending messages in Morse code. Not knowing Morse code, I will never find out the truth. I toyed with the idea of trying to count the knockings, but that put me to sleep.)

The next rooster we acquired was Caruso. He was simply magnificent, both in plumage and size. The trouble with Caruso was that he so ferociously protected his hens that I finally ended up flatly refusing to enter the pen. In the beginning, I discovered that if I growled like a dog I could keep him at bay long enough to put feed out for the chickens, but that ruse became rather alarming to anyone who happened to catch sight of me from within the churchyard. Besides, he soon became immune to that ploy and even flew at me if I had a club in my hand. He was delicious as coq au vin.

One incentive to our farm life within city limits was an interest we had in ecological gardening. All that lovely chicken manure was a wonderful asset in enriching the soil in order to grow a good many of our own vegetables. Once having made the decision not to use chemicals for the soil or pesticides on the creatures labeled pests, one finds that insects are not only helpful in maintaining the balance, but those insects that we consider destructive are useful, too. Of course, they provide food for the birds and toads whose help we need in biodynamic gardening, but they also provide clues as to what things are out of balance. An overabundance of snails indicates a need for more mulching to "sweeten" the soil, and an attack of aphids often comes when a plant needs water, something which can also be helped with richly mulched soil. All in all, insect watching becomes an intriguing activity when one allows time for it, and with the improvements that naturally occur when the soil is treated properly more varieties make their appearance.

I've only tried to play God once with an insect. I discovered him on my prize lily which had just come up, a tender green plant which grows to bear a cluster of fragrant white flowers. He was fire-engine red and very shiny, a beautiful little creature crawling around on the spiky leaves. I liked him until I noticed that he wasn't merely climbing to the top of the stalk in order to get a better view. He was munching away at my beloved plant. I decided he could just as well be eating something more plentiful, and I carried him in my closed palm to the other side of the garden where I put him in a bed of pansies.

The next morning, the tranquil mood of my early morning inspection of the garden was again shattered when I found him back on the same, rapidly diminishing lily plant. This required drastic action. It's always nicer to let others do your wrongdoing, so I marched down the street and threw him in the garden of a friend who uses pesticides, leaving him to his fate, but not actually destroying him since he was so pretty.

The next morning I found him back on what little was left of our lily, and this time he had a girl friend with him. They were celebrating their union by polishing off the remains of the plant. With a fleeting

respect for all of the patient Hindus in the world, I squashed them
both. The lily somehow managed to survive and multiplied. The scent
of its blossoms filled the evening air, but no more red bugs were
drawn to it. I try not to think too much about the possibility that I had
destroyed the last living specimens of the red lily ripper.

With chickens in the back, the foxes continued to make forays into
our garden, but we soon acquired a cat that would scare the daylights
out of them if they came around while he was out. Having been a tiny,
wild kitten when we got him, he grew up in the shelter of Spooky's
basket and feared nothing. Sam was, like all kittens, wonderfully
amusing to watch as he grew and became more acrobatic. One tends
to forget that all the skills a cat develops aren't for our amusement,
but part of a training program in the art of catching birds, or, in Sam's
case, birds, mice, squirrels or anything that moved.

He turned into the most beautiful, affectionate, terrible cat you
can imagine. He was soft grey with a snowy white breast and paws,
and white markings on his face which served to give him a wide-eyed
look of innocence. If I believed in reincarnation, however, I shudder
to think what might have been lurking under his graceful exterior. I
thought at first that if he were a well-fed cat he would be too placid
to be interested in birds and too fat to catch them, but he merely got
very large and kept up a training program that turned it all to muscle. I
hung a bell the size of a plum on his collar, and to make it even more
difficult for him to plan a surprise attack, I added two smaller bells.
All these banged together to accompany his movements, much like an
oriental orchestra.

It cramped his style, but definitely didn't put him out of business,
and when it suited him, he could get the collar off on a branch of a
tree. He was capable of catching a bird on the wing with just one paw
as he leaped from a table top. Squirrels he devoured, leaving only the
tip of the tail. In the beginning, he proudly laid his prey at my feet,
expecting praise, but I soon learned to let him out during the nighttime
when I wouldn't have to witness his prowess. For his part, he gave up
on trying to understand humans who would praise him for killing mice
and rats when birds were infinitely more difficult to catch.

Finn, like many Danes, absolutely hates cats and had warned me
that Sam would be bad news for the birds. He was no comfort at all
when I asked him whether we could assume that all the birds who
survived the summer had learned to be cautious when they heard

Sam's bells. "I think it would be more reasonable to assume that the birds that are no longer with us are the birds who know what those bells mean," was his laconic reply.

Despite his distressing habits, I adored Sam. He was truly a splendid animal, fascinating to watch. Even Finn admired him. An insatiable curiosity drove him to explore things which our dog shied away from instinctively, like the gushing sound of water disappearing down a drain. The dog was lovely, but ever so soppy — affectionate towards everyone, particularly ladies with nice perfume. Sam was all mine, and he followed me everywhere. If I was weeding in the flower bed, he was always within reach, hiding in a bush waiting for a chance to pounce on my hand, considerately retracting his claws as he did so. If someone opened the garden gate, he growled a warning, and crouched low, ready for the kill.

Soundlessly, he could leap up on our bed, and I would sometimes wake up to find him at my side, lying on his back, his paws tucked over the edge of the covers, loudly purring. The dog doted on him, and Sam loved to tease her, stretched out under the legs of a stool, ready to bat Spooky on the nose when she approached, or jumping her for a wild tumble that ended when the cat got bored and licked his fur smooth while Spooky stood watching, happily wagging her tail. A cat is such a sensual creature, so fastidious, and so graceful that one can forgive them for a lot. However, I have to laugh when people claim that their cat doesn't take birds. Perhaps that is true if he is the result of several generations of cats that have been kept indoors, but a wild animal is just under the surface of most cats.

We never did get a cow to have in the garage, though that was a prospect that worried me considerably. I'm sure that if we had, I would have discovered that we could have learned a lot from that sort of creature just as we did from all the others. Seeing a flock of doves perched high on the bobbing branches of a giant birch tree, clearly enjoying the fun of the gentle movement and the glow of the afternoon sun, or watching the cat move with elegance across a frosted lawn, contentedly warm and proud in a fur he enjoyed without a single thought to this year's fur fashion, reminded me of the real meaning to life. To be warm and well-fed right at this moment and be able to take pleasure in the variety show offered by the wind and weather is far more fun than anything we humans have been able to devise.

10

Kids

C hickens, cats, dogs and insects would not have been enough, however, to make me put down roots in Denmark. For that, I have to thank our children. The happiness one can receive from a child can make all other factors pale, and the sense of purpose they give one all during the years when they need the security net of a family is enough to make everything else seem unimportant.

However, one of the main reasons I can give for not moving to a foreign country is that once one's children have reached the age of two, they begin to have a definite edge over you by having learned the language from scratch. Small babies are delightful, and for the first year anyone who is good at changing a diaper will enjoy the feeling of being the most important person in that small creature's world. But then the little critter starts to talk.

Being the sort of parents who still believed in parental authority, we could see the disadvantage of me trying to sound authoritative in a language like Danish. First of all, my mispronunciations were a constant source of amusement to all and sundry. Secondly, Danes use a tone when speaking to small children similar to the one used for puppy dogs, and I had more experience with tending children than housebreaking dogs. Therefore, we decided to speak English with our children, a practice which resulted in them growing up thinking that Danish was the official language for the grownup world and English was baby talk.

When they began to come into contact with other children, they suffered from a disadvantage. They hadn't learned to swear in Danish, and they didn't want their friends to know that they spoke baby talk at home. Not only that, but we had taught them to be well-behaved during a period when the prevailing trend in Denmark was free upbringing. When they entered school, we were turning them loose in a jungle, and they weren't equipped with the salty sort of language that can be so useful in the situations that were bound to arise.

Our kids never complained about all this, however, and their friends proved to be quite tolerant of my shortcomings. This might have been due to the thousands of cookies, cakes and muffins I baked over the years. More interesting were the conflicts that arose due to our peculiar ideas about discipline, and those conflicts were always smoothed over by the fact that most children are irresistible.

There was, for example, Simon, a tiny boy whose father was a native of Greenland. Simon had an irresistible Bugs Bunny smile and silky dark brown bangs that nearly covered his coal black eyes, giving one the feeling of being spied upon by a mobile bush. When he and Bjørn were four he was half Bjørn's size, but easily mastered the situation by having command over a vocabulary that would instill respect in a dock worker. With an angelic expression on his face, he sent four letter words winging over the neighborhood, and he led a lawless life that was the envy of all other small boys. Simon used to spend hours at our house trying to liberate Bjørn, and we spent just as much time afterwards trying to put Bjørn back into a form acceptable to his grandparents. I saw Simon as a healthy contrast to our methods, Bjørn saw him as a mini-hero, and Finn saw him as a threat to the harmony of our home, especially after the time Finn had to repair our washing machine.

Simon had leaned his head back as far as he could in order to look at me from beneath his fringe of hair and, in his most appealing manner, confided in me that he had put a hazelnut in our washing machine. I chuckled and patted him on the head, thinking he was just teasing, and gave the matter no more thought.

Soon the washing machine was over-flowing every other time I used it. This was very inconvenient, because in those days we lived upstairs, and it was installed in a cabinet in our kitchen. Getting it out to repair it meant removing a built-in table and a radiator and filling the kitchen with nuts and bolts and odd bits and pieces. Not repairing it meant that Faster Eli would have to use an umbrella to work in her kitchen. I had forgotten all about Simon's hazelnut, and Finn was in no mood for helpful suggestions anyway, so I left him to struggle with fixing it and hoped it would be in place before some weekend guests arrived.

I think it was about midnight when he finally had reassembled the

machine, not having found anything mechanically wrong with it. We started it up, and within minutes the kitchen was flooded. He had to take it all apart again, and this time he found a small hazelnut in one of the intake hoses. I was very grateful that it was by now three a.m., because in order to protect Bjørn, I was forced to squeal on Simon.

Little Per was another neighborhood feature. With his blonde hair, big blue eyes and rosy cheeks, he was what one would imagine a Gerber baby to look like at the age of four. He barreled around the block on a little red tricycle, preferably in the middle of the street where he could pretend it was a car. His worst habit, as far as Finn was concerned, wasn't that he was risking his life but that he rang our doorbell during the dinner hour. Finn is the most unorthodox person I know, but he expects good manners from the rest of the world, including little Per.

We sat having dinner one fine spring evening, that time of year when the days are long and the kids sit on pins and needles waiting to go outside and play. It's a bewitching season when children rediscover the things they had forgotten during the winter months: Hopscotch and softball, riding bikes and skipping rope. They compete to be the first one to wear short trousers and take off woolen tights. They forget the time and hope that their parents will forget it, too, as they relish a newfound freedom. That was all the good news. The bad news was that Per had started ringing on our doorbell every evening just as we sat down to dinner, disturbing us and making it even harder for Lani and Bjørn to sit still. We tried ignoring him, but when he persisted, I had to open the door.

"Can Bjørn come out and play?"

"No, Per. We're eating dinner. And, by the way, please don't ring the doorbell again. Finn doesn't like his dinner disturbed, and Bjørn will come out as soon as we're through."

I gave him a friendly smile as I shut the door, thinking what a pretty picture he made through the mullioned windows of the double front doors.

Five minutes later we heard a crash and the tinkling of broken glass. When I ran to the door, I saw Per high-tailing it down the driveway. I knew he would be back, because he had lugged his cherished tricycle up to the top step in order to bang on the ill-starred window of the doorway, and he had to leave it behind when he made his getaway.

We watched for him, and I reminded Finn that little Per was only four and couldn't help that he had no upbringing. Finn was livid about the doorbell ringing and the broken window pane, but all anger vanished when we saw Per make his return, peeking around the garden gate and scurrying up the drive. With great concentration, he climbed up to stand on the seat of his precariously perched tricycle and piddled through our mail slot.

Trying not to laugh, Finn flung open the door. Looming above the startled little boy, he boomed out in his deep voice, "Young man, you mustn't break our windows and I forbid you to pee in our mail slot."

I expected little Per to burst into tears, but he looked up at Finn with his angelic face and said, "Can Bjørn come out and play now?"

Although we were going against the tide in raising our children by antiquated norms, Finn never wavered. It was more difficult for me, having been raised in an environment so entirely different from the one our children were being subjected to. Where I came from, obnoxious children could always be sent outdoors without fear of them freezing, and my father's ideas of disciplinary action were too bizarre to have left me with a feeling of having conformed to any system.

Ours had been a household where the only memorable ruling was about not squeezing the toothpaste tube in the middle, and I was only corrected for sassing or for balking at trying some peculiar food. Usually the punishment consisted of being "ostracized" (any disciplinary action which could improve our vocabulary was considered most suitable) or being put to the task of writing some inane sentence a hundred times. The former punishment always resulted in me doing everything in my power to rejoin the fold, and the latter merely developed my theatrical sense, as I sat writing far into the night, knowing how sorry my father would be when I went blind.

Because human offspring are dependants for so many years, I think one should always try to mould them into small persons who are appealing enough to be cared for if they should be orphaned, and here in Denmark, that means that they also have to be bearable for hours on end spent indoors. From the time of Henry James until the end of the fifties, American children were conspicuous for their bad behavior when they were compared with their European counterparts. However, by the time Lani and Bjørn came on the scene, a reaction to the strict rules of the old world had resulted in a trend for free-upbringing here in Denmark, and American toddlers were perfect angels by comparison.

Parents began to cower under the reign of terror produced by their children, but they showed admirable tenacity in trying to continue to allow children freedom, no one wanting to admit that he was ready to wring the neck of his own kid. The ticket was to turn them over to institutions equipped with plastic furniture, unbreakable toys and professional care by people who developed a tolerance for noise, knowing that they only had to stand it for eight hours and were being paid to do so.

I could definitely see the wisdom in teaching our children more regimented living, in order to equip them with the backbone to be able to cope with their father, but I did look wistfully back on the hours my brother and I spent running freely in the jungles of Hawaii, and I stood firm with one compensation for keeping the kids in line most of the time. I allowed them to jump on our bed when they were feeling especially exuberant. It seemed a pale substitute for swinging from vines and climbing trees, but it did look like fun when they jumped up and down to beat the band, rosy cheeked, tousled and shrieking with pleasure.

03　　03

Soon enough the kids started school, and their circle of friends widened from those who had grown up used to the idea that Lani's and Bjørn's mother talked funny, to a whole new crowd of youngsters. I encouraged ours to have parties for the entire class, thinking I could buy their tolerance with American hospitality. (In looking back over the years, I can see it would have been far less time-consuming to have taken Danish lessons.)

Lani's girl friends came home with her and played quietly for hours with the sort of things girls like, and I thought my plan would be duck soup. Then Bjørn started school and invited all the boys home.

I heard them coming when they were more than a block away, and before I could greet them, they had pushed me aside in their headlong rush up the stairs. The food I had thought would keep them occupied for at least a half an hour was consumed within five minutes, except for the more sticky bits which they clutched in their hands as they explored the house.

I had made a treasure hunt for them with elaborate clues, thinking it would take them at least an hour to sort out the mystery and dig up the treasure which was buried by a birch tree in the back yard. Twenty minutes flat, however, and they had dug up the treasure chest which really did look like a pirate's chest. It was filled with Danish five øre coins that were roughly equivalent to the American penny, and I had polished them to a deceptively opulent gleam. Naively assuming that seven-year-olds would be unaware of inflation, I had thought they would be thrilled when they saw all those shiny copper coins.

They opened the chest and, sure enough, they began to exclaim, "Gee, look at that!"

"Wow, look at all those shiny coins!"

Until the gravelly voice of a future bank director shattered the mood by saying, "Aw shucks — they're only five øre coins!" With that, they all lost interest immediately and stormed back into the house to find something else to do, except for two boys who remained outside, breaking down tall stalks of goldenrod in the back yard.

I was planning to pull these plants up anyway to clear space for a herb garden, and it struck me as a brilliant idea to leave them to it, thereby keeping them occupied with something that seemed appealingly destructive while actually being a help to me. I herded the rest of the boys together and suggested that they made a hut covered with goldenrod. Within seconds they were energetically making a shambles of that flower bed.

I went back inside to keep an eye on them from the kitchen window while I made some more refreshments, quite pleased with myself for having hit upon such a good idea. Minutes later, one boy had discovered that by stripping the green bark off the long stalk, it became an excellent whip, and he began lashing the others vigorously. During the heat of the battle that followed, I managed to make a quick call to Finn's office and plead with him to come home and help me.

Somehow I got through the next half hour, and when Finn arrived home, he put on his most awesome officer's tone and, with sharp commands, soon had them lined up like a small troop of foot soldiers. He divided them up into two platoons, and barking brisk orders, he sent them scurrying around in a fierce competition to tidy up the garden. Each time a small soldier reported back to Finn with a candy wrapper or goldenrod "whip," the little guy had to make a snappy salute and an about face to run off after the next piece of litter. The most unruly of the boys were lapping up this first taste of discipline, and they all dragged their heels when their parents came to take them home. We had established a bad reputation as militarists, but the kids had loved it.

Lani's parties were lovely, tame affairs, little girls being more subtle in their animosities. The girls were especially charming when invited to a real tea party and told to dress up like fine ladies. (The only jarring point on that occasion was that one little girl showed up wearing her mother's wig, and I spent most of the day wondering how her mother was managing.) So, when Bjørn was eleven, I thought that by inviting both the girls and boys to a party we would get a much more reserved group, and to further intimidate them, I planned a grown-up style sit-down dinner.

"Just wait," I assured Finn, "they'll act like adults when they see this setting." (After the party, I tried hard to refrain from guessing which adults might have provided them with their behavior patterns.) In the rumpus room in the cellar I set up a long table with real linen and pretty dishes, rather than paper plates and napkins. Even kids love quality, and everything started off very well. It was a costume party, and they all looked so sweet in an imaginative variety of outfits.

Lani helped Finn and me as we ran up and down the cellar stairs, bringing in steaming platters of spaghetti Bolognese and what seemed like an endless amount of fresh bottles of soda pop. A couple of the boys got up and made speeches, and they were all saying that they liked the food. One very dignified little girl had quietly, but firmly, refused to taste the spaghetti and meat sauce or the salad, and she now politely informed me that she wouldn't mind tasting the dessert. It was at that point that one of the boys stood up on his chair and, holding a bottle of soda pop in one hand, shook it vigorously so that it could be sprayed all over the girls, who giggled and shrieked and yelled at him to stop.

Finn put the fear of God in them so that we could serve the layer cake, but everyone had eaten so much by then that they left half the cake on their plates, only to ask for more of it hours later. Before any of them got the bright idea of throwing cake, we herded them out, with the exception of the dignified little girl who was on a dessert diet.

At that age it is impossible to organize the boys and girls in one sort of activity, unless you have the managerial talents possessed by Finn, and, by now he had made a grumbling retreat into the television room, with a bottle of wine to soothe his nerves. One boy joined Finn, eyed his wine, and challenged him to a game of chess. Some of the kids disappeared out the front door before I could stop them, and the rest stormed upstairs to dance "cheek-to-cheek" in Bjørn's room.

There soon was a big commotion taking place up where the dancing belonged, and I went up to see whether I could be of help. The din was deafening, and I had to turn down the music in order to try to listen to what they were telling me. It turned out to be a problem about not being able to squeeze more volume out of the tape recorder, and each boy was offering his expertise to sort it out. Soon the dancing was in full swing, and I heard Hans remark to Maria, who wore such a skimpy costume that she was to come down with pneumonia the following day, "Yuck, you smell like perfume." Sitting on the sidelines watching the cheek-dancers was one dejected soul who confided in me that she would like to dance, but they had all told her that her cheek was too high.

The group who had dashed out the front door came back, furnishing me with a breathless account of what was taking place through our neighbors' windows. I began to watch the clock and look forward to the hour their parents were to fetch the whole lot.

Søren, the class terror, whom I would have voted the boy most likely to succeed, was in the cellar hammering loudly on the door to the toilet. Finn rushed down to help him out of what he judged to be a desperate situation and explained to him that there were other toilets in the house. Girlish giggles from within revealed that the occupants were Pia and Eva, two little beauties who had spent hours painting on a glow like the one they had underneath all the paint. Søren went back to his hammering, and, in exasperation, Finn said, "Young man, why don't you use one of the other toilets?"

Søren merely looked at Finn like he was a dimwit and patiently explained that "This is more fun." That was when I discovered a long line into a room where the kids were telephoning home to ask if they could stay another hour or two.

Somehow we got through the evening, and Bjørn was the hero of the day, because they had all had such a good time. This made up a bit for the embarrassment Bjørn felt over having parents who kept chickens in the back yard, but he had also discovered that it was more fun to join the demolition squad at other people's homes than to see them run wild in his room.

It wasn't very long, however, before Lani's and Bjørn's friends developed into delightful young people, and I look back with fondness when I recall the many pleasant hours we spent with them. We always had time for them, but best of all, they always had time for Finn and me.

છ 03

It was an interesting experience to see our children growing up in a Danish framework. I was unable to help them much by sharing my school experiences — those having been so very different, but they managed very well on their own. There are good things and bad things about both the American and the Danish education system, but what I especially liked about the Danish one, when it was at its best, was the comradeship that could develop in a good class.

From the first grade through the ninth, a group of pupils is kept together. This is, of course, a disaster if the class has an unfortunate constellation or an inadequate class teacher. But when it functions well, these young people, with all their different personalities, grow up together, learning to be tolerant of each other and supportive of those who need it. When they become teenagers, they usually remain a group, quite unlike the dating system that was so important a part of a young American's life when I was young, and there seems to be more room for the "oddball" who often serves to make life more interesting.

The nice thing about raising children is that if you love them enough, most of them turn out to be surprisingly well-adjusted, responsible people. Little Simon is a charming young man, well over six feet tall, and many of the children who were far less charming tried out their very worst stages on their parents and emerged into the outside world as delightful young adults, miraculously transformed, either due to peer pressure or genetic factors. It makes one think there is hope for anyone, as long as somewhere along the line they get the idea that someone really likes them for what they are.

11

Housekeeping

The house we lived in was bought by Finn's grandfather in 1902 and was four years old at that time. A prosperous middle class was expanding to the north of Copenhagen, into what they termed "villas," and those built along our street were parceled out from farmlands owned by the church. Therefore, the original deed stipulates that a certain number of barrels of grain was to be paid to the vicar each year, to compensate for that loss of income.

When Finn's father and Eli were children, the street was a tree-lined feature separating the churchyard from field and a forest. During World War I, soldiers camped on those fields, and their officers were quartered in the attic, an accommodation required by law, but, undoubtedly something which quite suited Julius with his keen sense of duty. He himself was exempt from being called back into active service, because as suited a man of his standing, his girth was too great for any trousers or belt in the army supplies.

Julius's waistline was a yearly record of the family's prosperity. He and his wife, Emma, loved to entertain, and a dinner party in those days consisted of so many courses that merely sampling a small taste of each one would be a formidable undertaking for us lesser mortals. To make such a spread, a large inventory was required: Linen, china, silver for each course, and an array of glasses. Chairs and sofas were designed to bear a ponderous weight and made from materials that wouldn't deteriorate for many years. However, undisturbed by the constantly changing fashions such as we have today, a man in those days could acquire, during a long lifetime, a handsome style of living and feel confident that it would not only be a credit to him, but a good start for future generations within his family.

Taste can always be discussed, but there is no denying the quality of the household goods which were bought in Julius's time. Not only were furnishings solid, they were respected for their quality and cared for to insure their lasting. I can't help but compare the sense of achievement a man like Julius must have felt with the sense of frustration many a successful person must feel today when there is always something new that simply must be acquired.

The house was quality, too, a solid brick structure with windows, doors, and paneling made from properly aged wood. It only needed a loving hand, after many years of neglect, but an old house is like a slowly sinking ship. As soon as one finishes plugging up one leak, another part needs bailing out. However, even a ruin, when old enough, has a certain charm, and in a climate as hostile as the Danish one can be, many old houses emit a comforting atmosphere that is too expensive to reproduce in a newer, more efficient dwelling. That is why so many people live in old villas and face the never-ending task of restoring windows, replacing plumbing, and wondering how long the roof will last.

The house itself seemed part of a conspiracy to keep us from abandoning it. Just when we might have felt like throwing in the towel, sunlight entered a window at an oblique angle, lighting up oak paneling that couldn't be found today. The satiny feeling of the mahogany on the banister filled one with owner's pride, and the parquet floors were of a quality unsurpassed by anything new. The more one works to restore the original beauty, the more veneration one feels for the old wreck, and there is no leaving her.

There are those who solve the problems of restoring an old house by working very hard to earn enough money to pay someone else to do the work. Because we had decided that my place was in the home, that option was out; consequently, our experience with Danish skilled workers has been limited, but memorable. They are worth knowing — a proud lot and very much a part of what I consider best in Denmark.

At first I scoffed at the long apprenticeships, having known plenty of capable workers in America who became painters or carpenters simply by "getting on with it." But I learned to respect the amount of knowledge a Danish skilled worker will have about all the elements necessary to insure true quality, and, even more important, the amount of personal pride he will have acquired for having done his apprenticeship and passed the apprentice test.

Finn's great-grandfather Bernhard was a cabinetmaker, and in cleaning up the cellar, we discovered a portfolio of freehand drawings he had done, as part of his training when just a boy. They were geometrically perfect and beautiful enough to merit being framed. He himself had made the oak paneling in the dining room, as a finishing touch to compliment the buffets, side tables, chairs, tables and cabinets he made for his daughter Emma.

With reverence for all such details, we launched into the never-ending task of trying to re-create the proper setting, and one of the most tiring jobs was restoring the mullioned windows and keeping the paint in good repair on the maze of sprockets. This seemed all but hopeless on the windows that faced southeast, thereby getting the full effect of the strong Nordic sun which mercilessly burned off the paint and putty, bringing me to the reason why I have so much respect for the true skilled worker; I compare him to Frederick. He taught me the lesson never to hire a skilled worker to do something other than his own skill has taught him. Whether or not he is capable of doing the job, he will possess the other qualities of the Danish working class: He'll be opinionated, cheeky, independent as all get-out, and too charming to dislike.

In the early years of our marriage, Finn didn't really trust me with that sort of painting, and with his work and all our other activities, I felt we could use some help with the windows in the upstairs sitting room. A real painter was far too expensive, but friends on our street warmly recommended Frederick, a retired bricklayer who was, by his own account, capable of doing anything. He had been doing some work for them, and he was very likeable, overflowing with self-confidence and, best of all, he was cheap. Finn was a bit skeptical about the whole deal, but he had so many other things to do that spring that he was grateful for the fact that I wouldn't be able to nag him about those windows.

Frederick assured us that no one could paint windows like he could, and my American background gave me no reason to doubt that possibility. It was arranged that he would come the following week. He was willing to work for rock bottom wages, but he wanted us to throw in a lunch and the amount of beer that he needed to keep going.

The matter of painting was quickly settled, but he went more into detail as regards the lunch. In entrusting me with this important meal, he made it clear that I would be competing with none other than the "little missus," and he expressed a bit of doubt as to whether or not my lunches could meet her standards. I was so eager to have the paint job done, that it didn't even occur to me that I was being manipulated.

Frederick showed up bright and early on the appointed day, and I led the way upstairs, a stack of newspapers under my arm. I started to spread the papers out to protect the carpet, but Frederick assured me that that wouldn't be necessary, and he quickly converted the room to a workshop by putting down all the buckets and paraphernalia he was carrying. After several trips up and down the stairs, he cast a glance about the room, which was furnished in Danish antique farm furniture, and slung his tool chest up on a seventeenth-century oak chest which he clearly thought was a weird piece of junk to have in a respectable home. (Another thing about Danish skilled workers is that they can be terrific snobs.)

I hadn't had time to take down the curtains and started to climb the ladder to do so. Shouldering me aside, he made it clear that all details were best left to him. He pulled the curtains down in a heap, and I started to pick them up, saying I'd better wash them.

"These?" he said, "they're too shot to bother." And to demonstrate his point, he pulled at one of them, ripping the poor old thing half way down the middle. He was momentarily taken back, but then he shrugged and said, "My little missus always insists on new curtains when the windows get fresh paint." I was young and inexperienced, more embarrassed for having curtains unworthy of Frederick's approval than annoyed with him for being such a pain. It was clear by then who was running the show. That was when he said he could use a beer.

With the first beer of the day in his hand, he listened condescendingly to me as I told him that I wanted the windows painted with pure white paint. This, however, he was unwilling to do, informing me that here in Denmark my ideas about window paint were entirely erroneous. The white had to be tinted, and it would be best if I also left that sort of thing to him. Feeling completely powerless, and seeing that the room was already reduced more or less to shambles, I decided to use that day to whitewash the bathroom ceiling. There's nothing like a messy chore to keep one's mind off another mess. Left alone, Frederick dug into his job with the enthusiasm a kid shows the first time he tries finger-painting in kindergarten.

Meanwhile, I organized my work. When whitewashing, it is very important to remove the layer of earlier whitewash, and I had found a rather bizarre, but most efficient means of doing that. I removed everything from the bathroom, put on my messiest clothes and an old raincoat, climbed up on a ladder with the "telephone shower" in hand and turned torrents of water loose on the ceiling.

Quite content with the result and unmindful of my appearance, being used to doing mucky work, I decided it was time to offer Frederick a cup of coffee. Although people who fix up old houses often walk around looking like casualty cases from sabotage at a paint factory, the look on Frederick's face made it apparent that he didn't approve. He was horrified when he heard what I was doing. Mrs. Frederick, who got new curtains all the time and probably went to the hairdresser's once a week for the money she saved on Frederick's lunch, obviously wasn't in the habit of doing whitewash jobs. He assured me that all such chores would be done by him as soon as the windows were painted, and when I implied that we had only budgeted for the one job, he looked at me with a hurt expression and disdainfully informed me that he wasn't working for the money, and he wouldn't hesitate to extend credit to such a nice lady.

Finn came home for lunch, and we were joined by a friend of ours. Seeing as we had company, Frederick was content to have his lunch served in the room where he was working, and he seemed to approve of the food and the beer and snaps to wash it down. Just to be helpful, he suggested to me that I leave the carrier case with beer upstairs, so he wouldn't have to bother me. He soon returned to his work with renewed energy and could be heard juggling windows, dropping putty knives and stumbling over buckets. Neither of us wanted to see what he was doing, and we concentrated all our attention on our guest. By the time she left, Frederick had finished his fifth beer and was on his way out, promising to come just as early the following morning.

We went upstairs to view his progress and stood aghast in the doorway. The room looked like a recently abandoned seagull colony, except the white droppings were putty and paint. He had, at one point, evidently put a foot in a paint bucket, and white footprints could be seen doing a fade-out across the green carpet. As for the windows, there was so much putty and paint on them that it interfered with our view. Almost in tears, I promised Finn I would never again ask for someone to help us with painting if he would just get rid of Frederick for me.

Finn worked far into the night cleaning up the mess and spent the next few weeks of spare time scraping off what Frederick had smeared on in order to paint the windows properly. However, Finn proved to be just as inadequate as I was when it came to actually getting rid of Frederick.

When he showed up in the morning, Finn gave him some song and dance about it being urgent that he help me in the garden and leave the windows for now. We had, at least, gotten him out of the house, but he was soon wreaking havoc in the garden. With characteristic energy, he started digging where we had asked him to, but after heated disagreements with him as to which plants were perennials and which were weeds, I could tell that our visions of what a garden should be were too different to be reconciled. When I had reached my wit's end, I did something truly contemptible. I recommended him to one of our neighbors, thinking she was capable enough to be able to sort him out.

Suddenly it dawned on me the reason for Frederick's success in finding one job after another in the neighborhood, but it wasn't until years later that we sheepishly admitted to each other that he had been tossed about like a hot potato. He did miss our house, however, and on more than one occasion he stopped by to tell me that we gave him the best lunch.

ल ख

The next time we had to have help was to make a bathroom, and we were very impressed with Benny, the bricklayer who did the tiling. "That's the sort of man to have working for us," Finn said. "He's so talented one could call him an artist." So, when the first energy crisis hit, and we started to turn off the heaters, we called upon Benny to build a fireplace in the upstairs sitting room. When one adds such a feature to an old house, it is important to get someone who can make it in the correct style to match that of the house, and we knew Benny was our man.

We were about to discover the power a real skilled worker exerts over the rest of us. First of all, a person who can do something much better than anyone else can is far too much in demand to be available right when you want him, and secondly, a prima-skilled worker is like a prima donna, likely to walk out at the drop of a hat if his employers don't live up to his standards. We have had many good hours with Benny, but we were never in doubt as to who was actually the boss. He agreed to do the fireplace which pleased us very much, for the truth is that he could get plenty of easy work tiling swimming halls and public buildings, and the pay is the same. He dropped by to make a bid, and we tried to agree on a date for him to begin. Feeling very good-natured about being flexible on my part, I laughingly said that anytime was fine with me, except the week before Christmas. This was late October.

A week before Christmas, Benny showed up. Meanwhile, we had become more and more desperate to get alternative sources of heat as the Arabs increased their threats to turn off the oil. We felt like hugging Benny, our savior, when he waded in one afternoon, big blue eyes, wispy blonde curls framing an angelic face, bits of sand and mortar dribbling from the bricklayers' white overalls that covered his two-hundred pound frame. He trundled upstairs with buckets and bags and big heavy tools, carefully removing his wooden clogs at the entrance each time he made a trip. I had called Finn, and he hurried home to help out and to offer Benny a drink. By then, Benny had beads of sweat on his upper lip and a few beers were just the ticket to re-establish his moisture balance, something Danes take more seriously than do people who live in the desert. He sank gratefully into a chair to rest after all his exertions and entertained us with stories about his life, while the sun sank in the west.

Just as we were wondering whether he would ever start work, he got up and walked over to the corner we had picked out as the site for the fireplace, and, with a grand flourish, he used a carpenter's pencil to mark horizontal lines on the wall. Then he made a mark on the ceiling where the hole for the chimney would be. With a hammer and chisel, he chipped away the lines on the wall, dispersing great clouds of chalky dust which floated throughout the upper floor and sank quietly, coating everything from the attic to the cellar. He then made a hole in the ceiling and out through the roof, exposing the early darkness of a winter sky and a few bright stars.

There was to be a corner fireplace, suspended within the angle of the two walls, and there where he had chiseled the lines on the wall he formed a structure which was to brace the weight of it and explained that having done that, he had to wait for it to dry. "Well," he said, beaming with satisfaction over having started so well, "there's nothing more I can do today." As an afterthought, he placed a bucket under the hole in the ceiling and said, "See you in the morning."

There wasn't any point in objecting to being abandoned like that. Benny was a prince, but we knew that under that placid-looking exterior lurked a fierce enemy if he felt bullied by a customer. He would work for you for nothing, but he would walk out on a lucrative customer who started to get bossy. We also knew that in his own apparently erratic way we could trust him to get the job done far better and more quickly in the long run than anyone else. The only problem was to try to keep this in mind when the north wind was herding the last cubic inch of warm air out of our home and up through the roof. Those were the days when we only had the upstairs of the house. Faster Eli could stay nice and snug downstairs, but we had to pack the kids off to friends, a sub-zero flat not being the coziest place to be during the Christmas season.

Needless to say, Benny didn't show up the following day or the day after that. Finn stayed at home, not wanting to leave me alone in such misery, and he used the time to put up a wood stove in the hallway, hard work which kept him warm. I ensconced myself in the guest room, where I could close a door and turn on a heater. There I made Christmas decorations and ate raw cabbage, believing that could ward off a cold I felt coming on.

Benny showed up at long last around noon on the 23rd. We were so desperate by then that instead of yelling at him, we felt like hugging him. Feeling so welcome, he became very garrulous, and while we anxiously watched the clock, he constantly paused in his work to watch us and make sure we weren't missing anything in the wealth of stories he entertained us with. Finn kept him supplied with materials to speed up the job. Benny's movements were slow and graceful, like an underwater ballet, but there was never a wasted motion, and, with a sure hand, he put the final brick in place and smoothed the last dab of plaster. Where there had been chaos, there now was a beautiful fireplace. There was a moment of suspense as Benny placed a crumbled newspaper on the hearth and lit it to test the draught. At the sight of smoke swiftly rising up the chimney, Finn brought out a beer to celebrate Benny's success.

Finn's knowledge of tradition proved to be fortunate, for as we sat in front of the fireplace, drinking beer and contentedly watching the small pile of ashes, Benny told us about a job he had where the house owner had forgotten to give a round of beer when the fireplace was tested. He was a very wealthy man who had pulled no stops when building a luxurious home in a posh neighborhood, and Benny and his mates had worked hard to complete the fireplace. They had all developed a great thirst for the beer they expected and were quite pleased with themselves when the very tall brick chimney proved to have a fine draught. Unfortunately, the old cheapskate who owned the house only nodded his satisfaction and forgot the beer. The bricklayers took their revenge by buying some beer themselves and bricking in the empty bottles all around the top of the chimney, the necks of the bottles pointing inwards to produce a whistling sound when air passed through the structure. Benny claimed that architects and engineers were repeatedly called out to check the owner's complaints about that infernal whistling, but either they were unable to discover the source or were too amused to tell what it was.

When Benny left, Finn and I worked like beavers to clean up the mess, put everything in place, put out the decorations, and heat up the place. We were able to fetch the kids home to a tidy Christmas day and invited all the friends in who had pessimistically invited us to spend Christmas with them. The fireplace proved to be a very useful improvement, and with Benny's help we were able to build an even finer one on the ground floor when we one day took over the rest of the house. By then, however, I had learned to be stoic about losing all control over the course of events whenever he was around.

12

Easter

Usually these outbursts for improving the house didn't come at Christmastime, however, but at Easter. Easter is the time when the snow has melted, and the house and garden are revealed in a shocking state of neglect. The blinding northern light, coming in one's windows without a softening effect from leaves on the trees, exposes every flaw in rooms that have been closed up during a winter when smoke from the fireplaces has coated the walls and woodwork, and spiders have quietly spun webs in winter-dark corners and allowed them to become coated with dust. Everything seems to need paint and new coverings, or at least a good cleaning. With the same nesting instinct each year, most housewives corner their husbands in ambitious plans for spring projects to spruce up the roost. The husbands, on the other hand, might very well be stirred by nesting instincts of quite a different nature and long for carefree times of yesteryear.

One thing for sure, Easter couldn't be ignored. Everything was closed down for three days, and there is a tradition for something significant taking place. Where there was a conflict of interests in our household, we tended to compromise. I made plans, Finn acted like he was agreeing, and then proceeded to do whatever suited him.

Before he had really put this into a system, though, I did get some darned good work out of him. Take for example the Easter that began so well with Finn starting to fix up our attic. Since the days in World War I when soldiers were quartered up there, it had been used only to dry clothes, and one reached the clotheslines by following a path that had narrowed steadily as various members of successive generations added their contributions to the junk that was stored up there. We wanted to make this space into proper guest rooms, and after the gigantic task of emptying the piles of fascinating debris (most of which ended back in use), Finn set about insulating the sloping walls and putting

Oregon pine boarding between the old oak beams that supported the roof. The task was demanding, for each board had to be fitted, no two measurements in such an old house being exactly alike. I was ever so impressed with his work. He also had to put down flooring, the old floors not having been intended to beautify the room.

It being cold up there, he could count on being in relative peace from me, but one day the sun was shining, and I had listened to his hammering so long that I decided to join him in the novel surroundings, bringing a tray with hot coffee and fresh-baked apple strudel. I hummed to myself with contentment over all we (meaning Finn) were accomplishing and went upstairs on tip-toes, wanting to surprise my hard-working husband. When I reached the top of the stairs I didn't see him at first, but then I spotted a mattress that nearly covered the part of flamed beech parquet flooring he had already put down, and Finn was stretched out on it, smoking a pipe and blowing smoke rings up to the ceiling as he sporadically struck the floor with the hammer.

After that little episode, I thought it wiser to motivate him to do jobs that I could see, and during that time of year there are always things to drive off to the dump. Among an abundance of useless junk, we had a roller which had formerly been used to make the lawn smooth. It was far too heavy for me to be able to roll it at all, and Finn copped out by claiming that it did more harm than good in tending a lawn. He added it to the contents of the trunk of the car and off he drove.

The community dump yard was a nice, tidy affair where one could sort various types of trash into the designated containers. On the scene daily was a somewhat exclusive little group of bums without any official status. They have since been banned from the place, but we think they were quite useful. At least they made money off the perfectly good things people throw away nowadays, thereby aiding the environment and helping support the breweries. Whenever Finn had something he thought they might like to get, he pointed it out to them, and they, in turn, were on the lookout if there was something he wanted to find. That spring day, there were three of them, beer bottles in hand, sitting in the bright sunshine on a tacky old sofa, surrounded by treasures they had gleaned from the day's trash.

Trying to look casual, they all sauntered over to the car when Finn drove in, but they had spotted the roller, and although it is weighted down with cement, the scrap iron on the outside was worth taking.

Finn grinned and said they were welcome to it, but the three of them together couldn't lift it out of the trunk. Never being able to resist a chance to show off, Finn asked them to move aside and lifted it out, carrying it over to a container and chucking it inside. The dump yard trio now found it even more impossible to lift, and Finn was so pleased with himself that he obligingly hauled it out of the container and carried it single-handedly over to their treasure trove. He had, of course, established a lifelong reputation among a very critical following, an opportunity that doesn't present itself too often in our civilized times, but what they didn't know was that by the time he got home, he could hardly get out of the car. His back was out of whack for the rest of the week.

He tried to act like nothing was wrong, but I knew as he walked up the driveway that he wasn't all stooped over like that just to get a better look at the flowers. I could see that this wasn't going to be the sort of work holiday I had planned on, but there was one compensation — Though I would have to do without Finn's help, a bad back guaranteed that he would be leading a rather quiet life for a few days. I figured that once I settled Finn in a good straight-backed chair and installed a game of backgammon in front of him, with the kids taking turns letting him beat them, I could do some painting upstairs. Finn first insisted on taking a look around the garden to see if any tools had been left out, while I went into the house to make a pot of tea to perk him up.

We soon had a fire crackling away in the fireplace to take the chill off the room. The fitful April sun darted behind dark clouds, making the fire look bright among the green fabrics of the room, or came out dazzling, lighting a bowl of daffodils. At least Finn could feel miserable in a cheery scene. Not being used to seeing their father incapacitated, the kids were treating him like a cross between an invalid and a chained bear. I disappeared to get on with the painting.

As usual, some of our windows needed a big going-over, and I had just scraped the old paint, cleaned the woodwork, and was about to dip a fresh paintbrush into an inviting bucket of white oil paint, when the doorbell rang. Some friends from down the street were standing on the steps, looking like a couple of kids who had been invited to a birthday party.

"Hey, come on in," I said. "This is a great surprise. You won't believe this, but Finn is confined to a chair and will love having some company." They joined Finn as I hustled about to get fresh tea, more cups and slice some cake, mentally noting that it was early enough in the day not to have to worry about them staying for dinner.

I had no sooner served tea to the first couple when the doorbell rang again, and, of all coincidences, another neighborhood couple was standing on the stoop. I sent them up with the others, thinking how amazing it was that Danes who were usually so reserved about dropping by unexpectedly should be doing so today. I cleared away the tea things and started serving drinks, when the bell rang again. It was one more couple, this time with kids who were at the sticky-finger stage. My pleasure over Finn's good fortune at having company in his hour of need was beginning to fade, as I ran back and forth, refilling glasses. One of the little kids was trying to feed a daffodil to the dog, and Lani and Bjørn were starting to get hungry, but I was trying to stall them, being in no mood to make dinner for eight extras.

I took a minute to sneak back to my paint job but decided it wasn't even worth considering, and, reluctantly, I put the lid tightly back on the can and the brush in water. Since I believe so strongly in making the most of the moment, no matter how ridiculous that might seem at the time, I took a deep breath and joined this increasingly rowdy crowd. One thing was clear: they had by now had so much to drink that a meal was unavoidable.

It was very late when I followed the last of them to the door, and as one chap was leaving, he chuckled and said, "Don't forget to take down the watering can. It's after sunset, and there might be the same rules for watering cans as for flags!" I stared at him as if he were total bonkers and asked, "What watering can?!"

"Oh, the one old Finn-boy hoisted up the flagpole to let us know there were drinks on the house. He passed the word about the signal last week and told us to watch out for it. Leave it to good old Finn!"

My curiosity aroused, I went back into the house, picked up a flashlight and made my way out to the tall flagpole in the front garden. The beams of the light could just reach the green watering can, dangling innocently in the breeze. I quickly took it down. If I couldn't paint, at least I wanted to sleep late the next morning, and no telling who might spot the signal next.

CB   CA

I finally got much wiser. I decided that from now on Easter should be reserved for play, no matter what I otherwise felt like. For many years, this meant spending Easter Sunday in the country with Finn's parents, and like with everything we did with them, the day was shaped by tradition. The sameness of the routine made the odd factor which occurred due to weather or special added guests far more memorable. To describe one Easter Sunday is to describe them all, variations on a theme, and one that comes to mind was in 1973.

The beach was often inviting at Eastertime, its icy waters a deceptively warm turquoise hue. Winter storms had brought in broad stretches of sand to cover the rocky shore, and the children happily poked around on the water's edge, rediscovering the enchanting world of warmer days. Lani found a rock with tiny mussels clinging to it and pried them loose to bring them up to the cottage in cold, red hands. We boiled them to eat on a small piece of toast, a delicacy that still makes my mouth water.

The light at that time of year is so powerful that one feels the presence of spring, regardless of the temperature. We bundle up and sit like reptiles, soaking up the sunlight in nooks and crannies where the air is still. The sun in the small cottage was so bright that the flames in the fireplace seemed pale, but the room was nice and warm. When we had arrived, Mums and Paps were already busy. Paps, a strapping man who looked much younger than his age, rubbed his hands together and wiggled his moustache in anticipation of the feast to come. The Easter runner was on the table, meticulously embroidered with tiny chicks and spring flowers. And, as always, the beer and snaps glasses painted with red hearts stood waiting to be filled.

There were only the six of us that day, but no corners had been cut. Finn and I were often more practical when we were at the summer place, but Mums never lowered standards, and the feast was the same even after she had grown old and bringing all the ingredients together up there was a real chore. There were various types of herring, also freshly smoked ones from the nearby fishing village, a great variety of cold cuts, homemade chicken in aspic, boiled eggs with deep yellow yolks, resting on a dark-green background of cress, and everything made appetizing with fresh slices of cucumber, tomato and red onions. The food was arranged to be as pleasing to the eye as it was to the palate, the beer was golden and the snaps was chilled to the point that the small glasses were covered with dew as soon as they were filled.

No sooner had we tasted our first bite of Mums' delicious herring before she raised her glass and, in melodic Norwegian, proposed that "we let the fish swim!" The children were drinking the dark, non-alcoholic beer which they loved at Easter time, and they were in just as festive a mood as we were.

When they were small, they usually got restless by the time we reached the cheese course, and they ran off to play on the beach and tumble down grassy slopes of the nearby hills, bursting in occasionally with ruddy cheeks and bright eyes to show us some treasure dug up from a hole in the meadow or fished out of a tide pool. Now they sat with us, eyes still shiny, cheeks still rosy, but this time from the warmth of the room and all the laughter that used to ring around the table whenever we were together and reminisced about other Easters and other days in the cozy little cottage by the sea.

13

Havstuen — the Sea Room

I must have asked a million questions about Denmark as Finn and I spent the many days on the freighter sailing over here. He was so afraid of my being disappointed that, if anything, he tried to paint the picture a bit bleak. I was delighted when I was greeted by such a warm and charming family and taken to their very inviting home on the edge of the woods north of Copenhagen. The one place Finn couldn't really hide his feelings for was the summer place, and it was the most difficult to describe, for the beauty of it is in all the happy hours spent there.

It is a humble cottage perched on the most northern point of Zealand. The small meadow that runs down to the water's edge was once three times as deep, but it has been eaten away by the sea during its many rages. The house is called *Havstuen*, which means "sea room," and the sea is the first thing that comes to mind when the summer place is mentioned. Every day spent there has been colored by the sea in its many guises. The Kattegat, a large, living body of water, touching Sweden on the right and reaching out to the open seas on the left, dominates the landscape and makes everything else seem small by comparison.

As soon as Lani and Bjørn were old enough to wander about a bit on their own, I'd see them sitting on the steps down to the beach, dreamily watching the ever-changing Kattegat. When it is stormy, fierce waves lash at the steps, throwing salty foam on the wild rose that is struggling to get a foothold there; on such days, the distance of ships at sea appears shorter, the water between them and land being filled with whitecaps. The color changes from green to slate, and the seagulls frolic in the strong wind. Other days the water is smooth as glass, and the beach is a broad strip of pale sand and stranded rocks. It can be clear and inviting under a sunny sky, or strange moods can descend upon it, giving the water the look of something molded out of silver, with the sun suspended over the horizon, a heavy, red globe throwing a path of hammered gold towards seagulls, weirdly silent, lifting in flock and settling on the dark rocks protruding out of the still waters. No matter what the mood, the sea always has the comforting effect of making one aware of how very insignificant we are compared to its greatness. It's a whiff of eternity.

The tradition of sailing is an old one in Denmark, and the variety of sailing vessels that pass by on a summer day are entertainment in themselves. If the day is fair, we like to sit in the hot sand at the end of the meadow which is filled with wildflowers that are blue and yellow flecks in a golden background, watching small crafts, well-built yawls, handsome ketches, and lovely old schooners with every variety of size and rigging, sailing by us.

The plants that grow by the beach struggle with the wind the year round, and although the pines that grow on the hillside behind us are large and lush, those close to the sea are bent and twisted by the strong winds and salt air. The hardiest plant is the wild rose, supposedly brought to Denmark by French missionaries who prized them for the rich harvest they yield of large rose hips. On one side of the small meadow is a deep green cluster of wild roses, full of large magenta blossoms in the early summer and huge, bright orange hips in the late summer. On the other side is a patch of heather, alive with lovely, soft bumblebees when in bloom. The lilacs and grayish greens of the heather are breached upon by a bright green patch of crow berries which the seagulls and crows strut about in while eating the small black berries In the springtime the heather turns the color of burnt sienna, like bold brushstrokes to accent the pale aquamarine of the sea.

Inside the cottage are very small rooms, the main one of which is given its personality by Norwegian antiques. In the corner with small-paned windows out to the sea, is a table made out of ash and scrubbed white in Norwegian fashion. There we have our meals when the weather isn't fine, and there we sit on rainy days, doing handicrafts or playing games while the rain runs down the windows in rivulets and the sea throws its spray up over the cliff. Hanging above the windows are colorful ceramic plates with Norwegian homilies, reminding us to love our neighbors but keep the fence repaired, to fish for a wife with a silver hook, and to keep in mind that food is only half the meal, along with other equally wise proverbs.

In another corner, there is an iron fireplace from Norway, indispensable on rainy summer days or during any of our visits during the rest of the year. All around the fireplace are copper forms which used to be used for various types of Danish pastries. On the wall, under the low, knotty-pine ceiling, is a carved cuckoo clock, with a little bird that is too old and tired to come all the way out when he sounds the hour. On the brick floor under the fireplace is a huge copper kettle that kept the family supplied with constant hot water a hundred years ago, but now is more often filled with wildflowers — bachelor buttons, yellow and white daisies, Victorian lace and ripe grass, picked on our evening walks. There is an antique Norwegian rocking chair, from the valley of Hadanger, and there is a small desk, made for Mums when she was a girl starting school. The adjacent glassed-in veranda with rattan furniture is more modern, but it is the room with the antiques that gives character to Havstuen.

As a young bride, I used to resent the inevitable weekend in the country, spent with such a close-knit family. There was little time to relax and enjoy the weather, for we started the day with a large breakfast at a well-set table, served coffee with cakes at ten, and a full spread for lunch at twelve, to be followed by afternoon tea with sandwiches and cake at three or four, dinner at six, coffee on the verandah, and more often than not, tea and sandwiches before bedtime. After at least two of these repasts, the table was scrubbed satiny smooth with hot soapy water, and the rest of the time was well filled by all the other household chores. During my leisure time, I washed diapers and tried to ignore Mums' remarks about how much nicer they would be if I would take the trouble to iron them.

Later, I was able to enjoy the positive side of these family holidays. By resigning oneself to the fact that a holiday for the family is a work day for the home-going housewife, one can be very relaxed about the amount of work that has to be done. I could simply assign myself a free day during the week. It was all worth it in terms of the happy memories the children have from those days, and to be truthful, I, too, remember the meals better than I do the washing up.

By learning the habits of a Danish family and tempering them with a more relaxed routine, I soon came to love the many days spent in this primitive retreat. Weeks spent there on our own were enchantingly uncomplicated. When the weather was fine, we practically lived outside, and the four of us let the one who was hungriest worry about breakfast and lunch. That invariably being Finn, I stretched out in the warm sand and pretended I was asleep until he called us together for some tantalizing snack. We liked to sit down at the water's edge at dinnertime, watching boats sail by the burning red sphere of a slowly setting sun. We used to hail down friends who would come up the bank to join us over the last of our dinner wine and sit talking softly so that we could still enjoy the evening song of the birds and the sound of water lapping against the shore. The kids threw rocks at a boulder jutting out of the sea, and the dog raced back and forth, frantically hoping to catch one, her tail a happy propeller. Darkness doesn't fall until after ten on a summer evening, and if nothing deterred us, we could easily turn in soon afterwards, pleasantly drugged by the heavy sea air.

When we were in the country, we didn't just shop for food, we foraged for supplies. Rather than cluttering my mind with a long list of items one could get off the shelves of a supermarket, we made a trip to the nearby fishing village to buy what we needed for a seafood feast or to a farm to buy chickens and eggs and fresh vegetables. If Finn didn't catch any fish, we bought them from old salts when they sailed into the harbor, and to eat a fine, fresh plaice, one only needs chopped parsley and melted butter to dress it up. We liked to buy tiny shrimp to boil, and the children didn't have to be very old before even they liked the fun of sitting around a large bowlful of shrimp, peeling them and piling them high on a slice of home-baked bread to be garnished with lemon and dill and relished with a glass of white wine, a summer pleasure accented by the feeling of a fresh cotton shirt on a sunburned back.

Not surprisingly, those friends who are accustomed to the best food in the finest restaurants are the ones most likely to appreciate good quality foods served so simply, and some of our very best friendships started with sharing such pleasures in the summer place. Gil and Joanne, from England, were just such friends.

The first time I met Gil was the day before we were to have a party and were expecting out-of-town guests. I had a million things to do, and a nice little man was busily reupholstering a sofa in our study, with promises of being finished that evening. When Finn came home from work and told me that he had invited some Englishmen for night food, I didn't overreact. After all, with the American notion that the English are rather stuffy, I figured they wouldn't stay very late.

At around eight in the evening, the three of them blew in like a hurricane, carrying a potted plant arrangement that looked like something you would send to someone who had just won the Irish Sweepstakes. Gil was their leader, and he was handsome in an unmistakably British way, a head taller than everyone else around, with prematurely graying dark hair and wickedly blue eyes, full of mischief and good fun. On that first evening, we had so many laughs that I think we were all surprised when we noticed that they were still there at three o'clock in the morning. We struck up lasting friendships with two of them and cemented our friendship with Gil with an invitation for him to come back with his wife and children and make use of the family summer place. This last, however, was definitely Finn's idea. He has a wonderfully simplistic attitude towards other peoples' preferences. He figures that whatever he likes, they will like. I could picture Gil thinking it would be a lark, he being as hare-brained and fun-loving as my husband, but from the picture I had formed of his wife, I doubted strongly that she would appreciate such primitive facilities.

They arrived in September, with their three youngsters, and one look at Joanne only strengthened my doubts. She was a glamorous, long-legged, buxom blonde, dressed to the nines, and with beautifully manicured, flawlessly lacquered, long fingernails that looked like they had never been exposed to work. She didn't quite seem the type who would be found roughing it in a tiny cottage with a privy. But as soon as she spoke and one noticed the nice smile wrinkles around her lovely, grey-green eyes, you could tell that she was too warm and genuine to be anything but a good sport. (I was also to discover over the years that she is one of those people who can manage both having long nails and being capable in everything from cooking to gardening, sewing, and decorating.)

Like most English kids, theirs knew how to tow the line when the real authority was around and were independent as all hell once they were unnoticed. Joanne had only to give a withering look to either of the two boys, and they looked like cherubs, but me they had sized up in a minute and put in the category of caretakers and au pairs, there to do the job and otherwise to be ignored. The little girl, Evy, was something out of an English picture book, delicate skin, dark hair in ringlets, and lovely frocks. Her two brothers had involved her in a conspiracy to keep their parents unaware of the spicy language they were teaching her to use, but a four-year-old can't always keep a secret, and she occasionally let slip an expression so incongruous that one looked around for a ventriloquist.

They started their holiday at our home near the city, and there we more or less fell into a routine. We stayed up half the night having a whale of a good time with Gil and Joanne, and when they retired, I always told them to sleep late, this standing out in my mind as the greatest luxury one could wish for when away from home. At the crack of dawn, I would hear the pitter-patter of little feet as their three children descended the stairs to start the day. Evy always began with a regal demand for some breakfast cereal we didn't have, and the boys absentmindedly ate whatever I gave them, their minds already teeming with plans for the day. Finn left for the office, and our kids, who were five and seven at that time, stood wide-eyed, taking a vicarious pleasure in seeing Steven and Jeremy, who were slightly older, do all the things they didn't dare do.

By late morning, I was worn to a frazzle and looked it. That was when Joanne and Gil came downstairs, looking super, refreshed and elegant in the latest fashion. About then, Finn would come home for lunch, give me a peck on the cheek, take one long look at Joanne, and sweep her off to see something or someone, pointing out to me as they left that this would give me a breathing spell so I could get organized for dinner. It is real proof of how loveable Joanne is that I didn't even begin to dislike her. Of course, by the time the whole herd of kids was again tucked in their beds at night, I felt such freedom that I forgot all about being tired and stayed up just as late as I had the night before.

After a few days like that, we drove in two cars up to the summer place, accompanying them in order to help them settle in and make sure all was satisfactory. However, it turned out that not only was Joanne a good sport about staying in the summer place, she talked us into joining them, making the cottage even more tiny. It being September, the season for lolling in the sun was on the wane, and we were well into the season for eating. Stephen, Jeremy, and Evy reacted to these smaller quarters by constantly being aware of the vibrations of authority and resigned themselves to being perfect little angels, spending hours on their own, gathering poisonous caterpillars and trying to catch fish.

We thought it would be fun for the kids to see the nearby farm where Finn and Gil could buy some chickens, and Joanne and I were only too grateful for the peace and quiet that ensued to notice that the men had taken a bottle of aquavit with them. We did get suspicious, however, when they had been gone more than an hour.

They came home, hooting with laughter all the way down the hill; they had forgotten to take glasses, but they had been taking turns drinking from the bottle cap, and it must have taken quite a number of capfuls to have put them in such a state. We were, of course, painfully sober and failed to see the humor in all they had to tell us about their adventures, but Finn hoped he could get in Joanne's good graces by showing her what good luck they had in finding something for dinner. He lugged a big gunny sack over to her and stood all pleased with himself, waiting for her to look inside. When she did, she let out a shriek and jumped back, finding it filled with decapitated chickens. She assured him that she wasn't ungrateful, but she was accustomed to chickens nicely cleaned and wrapped. The last thing Finn wanted to do was to make Joanne unhappy. He hurried to put the gunny sack out on the meadow and rushed back into the house to turn on the radio and start whirling her around the room.

Gil, who could drink enough to float the Queen Mary and still look classy, made the famous bottle cap toast, "First today!" and threw it down the hatch, while poor Joanne, who was getting a bit dizzy from being twirled around in an area the size of a postage stamp, glanced out the window, and, to her horror, saw Evy in her ruffled white frock, crawling out of the gunny sack, smeared with all the things chickens have on them when they have lost their heads and been stuffed into a bag. Evy was clearly having the time of her life, but that finished Joanne. She beat a retreat to her room, saying she was feeling a bit tired. Gil and Finn felt so contrite that they plucked the chickens, while the kids clamored to get a good view of the various parts being drawn out of the birds as I cleaned them. The barbecued chicken was delicious, but after that, we stuck to seafood. My guess, however, is that it's the chickens they remember best — one way or another.

Otherwise, staying at the summer place provided Finn with an opportunity to relive the pleasures he had when he was a boy and spent the duration of the school summer holiday in the country. Old photographs and letters written to Finn's father, who had to stay in town to go to work during part of that time, reveal how many changes had taken place in the decade following the war. With gasoline rationed, the family had to take the train and a horse cart to the summer place in those days, or they bicycled up — a grueling trip that took the greater part of a day.

During the latter years of the Occupation, the grounds next door to Havstuen were used by the Nazis to intern Polish prisoners, giving an element of danger to the family's habit of listening to BBC behind dark curtains. They soon discovered that the German guards liked to sneak close to the cottage, in hopes themselves of picking up a bit of news from the outside world. In a sudden fit of anger, Finn's mother once accosted an armed German soldier who was standing guard on the beach. Speaking flawless German, she gave him one devil of a scolding for being there. He was a large man with hands like a farmer, and he took her quite off guard when he began to cry. He looked out to sea with tears rolling soundlessly down his cheeks and told her that he wanted so badly to go home to his family.

During his teenage years, Finn had many happy hours maneuvering a kayak, and he could still get all starry-eyed dreaming of getting some small vessel to paddle around in. One day, following a storm, he found a pathetic-looking gray dinghy washed ashore, and although we reported it, it became obvious that no one was going to claim it. It wasn't exactly beautiful, but it served us well. We liked to load it down with a picnic lunch, our little dog, the kids, and a couple of friends and let Finn row us down the shore to another beach, just for the change of scenery. It was always good for a laugh when he rowed up alongside of posh sailing boats and we watched the look of amazement on the faces of the crew as he stood up, holding the oars, and asked in English, "Is this the coast of Denmark?"

The little rowboat made it possible for Finn to put out nets and supply us with fish while we were vacationing, a pastime which was great fun for Bjørn and Lani, who liked to go along when the nets were put in place in the evening and taken in early in the morning. On one particularly pleasant summer day, there were three in the boat: Finn rowing, with his usual degree of concentration, our American friend Alex, with his nose buried in a book and his old hat a tempting target for seagulls, and Bjørn trailing a small hand along the side of the boat, as he watched the fascinating underwater forest of seaweed beneath them. Bjørn was ten and had been told he could row the boat alone if he could swim a hundred meters over this area, but the long tendrils of seaweed seemed to be reaching out to catch him, and with a small boy's fantasy, he pictured even stranger things lurking under the large rocks. "But I can swim a hundred meters, Dad. I got my school badge to prove it."

Knowing Bjorn's aversion to swimming over the area where the boat had to be rowed, however, Finn stuck to his guns, insisting that it was only a valid test if taken there where a boat might capsize.

The peacefulness of this scene was interrupted when Finn's old friend, Demus, emerged suddenly in the water alongside the boat. Like a great walrus he pulled himself aboard, bringing a good deal of seawater with him. He was ever so pleased with himself for having taken them by surprise, but Finn likes surprises best when he instigates them and unkindly remarked that Demus's wet presence was unwanted.

"All right," said Demus, "if that's the way you're going to be, I'll leave!" Whereupon he stood up and made a very nice dive off the side, capsizing the boat as he did so. Hearing the resulting commotion, I looked out to sea and thought it was odd that Alex, still wearing his hat, seemed to be reading a book while swimming in the water. But then I realized they were all in the water, a wonderfully comical sight on an otherwise quiet day.

With a great deal of effort, Finn managed to right the boat while Alex made it to shore without his book getting wet. It was so much like the sort of prank that Finn would have played on Demus that ordinarily it would have quickly been forgotten; however, in the course of events, one oarlock had been lost. Finn was madder than hops about losing it and became obsessed with finding it. The sea was very clear that day, and for the greater part of an hour, he and Bjørn circled around a small area, peering down in the depths, hoping to spot the missing oarlock.

Miraculously, they found it, but Finn then discovered that he was unable to dive deep enough to retrieve it. Telling Bjørn to sit still while he swam in to get a long-handled rake, he cast anchor and hurriedly swam ashore, happy as a clam at having such good luck. Within minutes, he was running back down to the beach, rake in hand, and he turned livid when he saw Bjørn rowing in, the site of the oarlock lost forever. The language he used was decidedly unsuited to the ears of a small child, but Bjørn was armed with a righteous feeling for having done what he considered correct. He stood there red-haired and freckle-faced and unflinchingly explained to Finn that he had to come ashore to take a leak. Knowing the penchant small boys have for peeing everywhere their fancy takes them, Finn was baffled; why not in

the sea? Trying to get the heat off Bjørn, I claimed it was his parents'
fault. It was they who told the kids that if they relieved themselves in
the sea or a swimming pool, the water turned red. But having been a
small boy himself at one time, Finn saw right through that story and
knew that it was more likely a case of Bjørn having been unable to
resist the temptation to prove that he could row the boat, even without
an oarlock.

Most of Finn's worst summer-house-pranks were shared with
Demus, whose grandmother's large, thatched-roofed summerhouse
was just down the beach, and I soon learned to accept that when the
two of them got together it often ended in a competition in playing
rotten tricks on each other, a pastime which seemed to give them no
end of pleasure. On one occasion, however, Finn definitely wasn't at
fault.

Demus was in the country with his family and his sister's family.
After a day of riding herd over all their collective children and a variety
of dogs of assorted sizes, the adults had treated themselves to a steak
dinner with a good bottle of wine. As often happens, a meaningful
dialogue between the women occasioned the opening of another bottle
of wine and a good deal of agreement as to how really impossible men
are. While the candles melted and ran down the checkered tablecloth,
and small night insects gathered to perish in the flickering flames, the
men were forgotten.

Demus and his brother-in-law, Morten, didn't mind the women's
complaints, but they did object to not getting their after-dinner coffee.
Then they had an ingenious idea. Without a word to their wives, they
went quietly out of the house, walking along the beach to our place
to talk Finn into joining them for a quiet cup of coffee, a big whiskey
and a hot game of liar's dice on board Morten's sailboat which was
anchored in the nearby harbor. I had a good book to read, and it suited
me fine to have Finn out of the house so I could enjoy it with a clear
conscience, book reading not being the most sociable activity.

The men were gone for ages, and when they did come back, they
were in great spirits, thinking they had done something really cheeky.
It was agreed that we wouldn't breathe a word as to where they had
been, and they went off chuckling, the light of their flashlight bobbing
up and down along the path down to the beach. Ten minutes later the
phone rang, and one of the wives was calling to ask me whether Finn
had been out with Demus and Morten. I crossed my fingers and lied,

"No, he's been spending a quiet evening with me." Then there was a terrific commotion at the other end of the line as several people tried to talk at once. I turned the phone over to Finn who dutifully repeated what I had just said.

Without knowing it, we had betrayed poor old Demus after all. The ladies had been so absorbed in their conversation that they hadn't even missed their spouses. When Demus and Morten walked in the house, each with the look of the cat that had swallowed the mouse, their wives barely bothered to look up. The third bottle of wine was nearly drained, and they still hadn't run out of complaints. "Didn't you miss us?" ventured Morten.

"Miss you!" hooted Susanne, "Why in the world should we miss you?" After such a putdown, the men felt justified in smugly telling about their stag evening spent aboard the sailboat, but their wives wouldn't believe they had been gone at all.

"Ha!" said Demus. "If you don't believe us, just call Finn. He was with us." That's what they did and found us ready to swear on a stack of bibles that Finn hadn't left the house.

ॐ   ॐ

Summer was a magic time at Havstuen, but we also loved autumn holidays there with the stars in the sky undiminished in brightness by city lights. And we loved to stay there in the winter, with snow all around and not a soul on the beach where we took long walks, kicking frozen sea foam into the wind. We finally got the convenience of hot water and a bathroom and toilet, not because we really needed all that luxury, but because sewer pipes were laid down, and we were obliged to connect. This was a very great change, for until that time, Paps bathed in the sea, even in the winter. However, we never broke down and got a television, and none of us ever missed it.

14

The Welfare State

As a concession to the reader, I'll give notice that this chapter is full of Serious Thinking. Skipping over it will not in any way distract from the rest of the book, and it could always be read afterwards, like one grubs around after the unpopped kernels when having finished a bowl of popcorn.

Copenhagen is a city with lovely old buildings, living history in a country that has enjoyed a long period of relative peace. With a deeper view into the past, however, one realizes that it is rather recent history that is written in these buildings. The more ancient history is written in the character of the Danes. Knowing them tells one something about their forefathers and perhaps explains certain attributes which made them capable of having kept a degree of continuity in their progress towards a modern nation state.

From archaeology, we have learned a lot about the Vikings who lived in these parts so many years ago. The Nordic climate made it necessary early on for them to learn to be well-organized, cooperative, and inventive. Food from the sea was plentiful, and the land was fertile, but skills had to be developed to make it possible to survive the long winters. They lived in close units, developing a strong tradition for tolerance and fairness towards the individual who was willing to carry his or her share of the responsibility. The climate necessitated a sense of orderliness; clothing or food which isn't properly treated and stored would be ruined with the onset of damp weather, and women became important in taking the responsibility for these stores, their men being engaged often in hunting, fishing, plundering, and ambitious seafaring adventures that kept them away for months on end. Though centuries behind Asians and Southern Europeans in finer cultural development, Vikings had developed practical capabilities and admirable personal qualities that enabled them to survive in these less hospitable regions.

The fascinating eye-witness account written by Ahmad ibn Fadlan, an Arab who was the unfortunate kidnap victim of a band of Vikings around the year 900 AD, describes them in a way quite similar to the way Danes are often described by people from southern areas in our day and age. The account is undoubtedly genuine enough as regards actual physical details of things he saw, but, as a very fastidious Arab, he was certain to have been the butt of many a coarse joke which he would not have understood. His contempt for people whom he considered more primitive than himself made him too much of an outsider to judge the merits of their culture, and just as they do today, the Scandinavians would find it more fun to take the mickey out of such an observer than to try to explain their ways.

Years of living in Europe teaches one that there truly are certain characteristics that tend to prevail among people with a common history. The observations made by Tacitus about the Germanic tribes have a ring of truth today, even though the veneer of civilization has glossed over the underlying emotions. The invisible line that divided Belgium when the Romans pushed towards the English Channel is still there, apparent in the differences between those south of it and those north of it. Northern Italians will claim differences to Southern Italians that were described in Michelangelo's times. People are basically the same all over the world, but there is no denying the influences of topography and culture in forming the most characteristic members of a society.

The basic differences between peoples within the Nordic lands surely must have a great deal to do with the geography of these lands, and that part which is Denmark today has been unique in having easily cultivated soil and a juxtaposition closer to the rest of Europe and to England. The most important Nordic settlements grew up where there was easy access to the sea, but for a long period in history, Denmark controlled the sea traffic that had to pass through the narrow straits separating Sweden from Denmark. Although modern economies have erased most of the real differences, the history of each of the Scandinavian countries continues to color the national character, and the exception only proves the rule. Their common heritage from Viking times, however, must be the factor that gives them all a respect for the individual at the same time that there is a deep sense of community, a general feeling that in order to be comfortable with one's prosperity, the rest of society must be well fed, too.

There are other qualities among Danes that make it a country where one can expect fair treatment. I won't claim that Danes are more racially tolerant than other people. In a society as relatively homogeneous as this one, one's tolerance is not put to the test very often. However, they have a tradition for considering tolerance a virtue and for being fair-minded. When the Germans invaded Denmark during World War II, they were quite unprepared for the Danish animosity. The Nazis had singled out the Nordic races as being the chosen ideal, and they had expected the Danes to feel part of a common destiny. When it later was decreed that all Jews should wear the Star of David, the Germans were foiled by King Christian X. This enormously popular king gave courage to his people all through the war years by riding, unguarded, on horseback through the streets of Copenhagen each day, and as soon as the decree was made to wear the yellow star, he appeared on his morning rounds with it on his sleeve. It was clear that all Danes would follow suite, and this means of singling out the Jewish population was rendered useless. (Fortunately, a well-organized rescue effort got most Danish Jews safely over to Sweden, and of those who were rounded up and sent to Treblinka a great many survived because of Scandinavian perseverance in keeping track of them.)

We can probably never erase the potential for hatred among peoples of different races or religions, but it is at least a great step forward when a society has a tradition for not condoning such prejudices.

It was only natural that in a land with traditions for helping each other a welfare state would develop. I've lived here so long that I couldn't conceive of wanting a society without many of the benefits that we take for granted, even though I've been so fortunate as to not have had to make much use of them. However, the welfare state has developed into something too top-heavy. At its worst, it is a cumbersome elephant in an increasingly tacky circus, and, at its best, it is a dear friend. The problem isn't really due to the design of it all. It's due to us human beings.

When observing the changing social patterns and styles of our age, one is reminded of prehistoric creatures that put on a gala exhibition of incredible transformations over millennia, in a spectacular attempt to find a form which could survive the changes in the environment. Bizarre appendages proved to be useless and others appeared, like whimsies of a wizard who couldn't quite make up his mind which dazzling form would do the trick.

While the complexity of the modern world is making mankind feel insecure, we in the West are enjoying a personal freedom which severs us from the sense of security that was assured our parents if they behaved according to certain norms. This breaking away from old patterns is, of course, more noticeable in a country like Denmark where the patterns were the well-established result of hundreds of years of experience. Each generation will notice change, but it really appears to be true that here in this country the changes have been greater in the past thirty years than they were in the preceding hundred years.

A mere eighty years ago, there were still poor houses in Denmark. Those who were unfortunate enough to end up in such a place suffered shame, but not hunger. Everyone did his utmost to somehow avoid such an ignominious fate and loss of identity, even choosing to live under conditions that were considerably worse than those of poor houses. This serves to illustrate how very strong a drive is the need for an identity. But still, it is a luxury need that usually manifests itself when we are well fed, or at least not starving.

With the growth of the welfare state, people have come to take for granted the help they get to fulfill their basic needs. A good many people are now enabled to turn their attention to the more interesting occupation of establishing an identity, but it is an identity in a fantasy world, not one that is an integral part of a functioning society.

This process takes many forms, as one can see when taking a stroll along the Strand in Copenhagen. I sat on a park bench in one of the main squares, waiting for my daughter one spring day, and found myself the odd man out. It seemed to have been the meeting place for two very disparate groups — Punks and motorcycle thugs. I had a lovely time, first talking with some of the punk girls to learn their secrets for making their green and purple hair stand out like spikes, and then talking with a couple of frightening looking leather jacketed blokes about their tattoos. They were reassuringly nice when you got to know them, but they had done all in their power to dress in a way that is guaranteed to alienate them from most of society. While the welfare state provides people like that with the financial freedom to deviate from society's norms, it also deprives them of the challenges that might give them a more meaningful daily life and a sense of identity arising from coping with those challenges.

Before my daughter came and pulled me away from a rather interesting discussion, reprimanding me with just one word: "Mother!" I had developed sympathy for this rather motley group, seeing in their unorthodox behavior an attempt to establish a unique identity in the grey world that was otherwise their lot.

It is only natural that many of the hard-working people who pay some of the highest taxes in the world to support a system that can care for such unappealing dependents are a bit bewildered. We want to give financial aid to the unemployed, but we resent them spending that money on things which we consider unnecessary, like twenty bottles of beer a day. And, when they on top of that dress in a manner that makes them stand out, or when they neglect the appearance of respecting other people's values, resentment builds up.

Even Danish racial tolerance wanes when refugees and foreign workers receive aid from the state which exceeds what the average Dane can hope to earn with hard work. Where there is a democracy like Denmark's, one can solve this problem by changing the system, but I, for one, wouldn't have the foggiest notion of how to go about all this without destroying the system which is so good when it isn't misused.

None of Denmark's thirteen political parties seem to have the answer either, but while they continue to try to work out ways for stopping the deterioration of the welfare system and the spiraling need for more tax money, a shady system is arising on the sidelines. We dutifully pay our taxes while considering it a sport to figure out new ways to fiddle the system, everything from paying "black money" to skilled workers and making trade deals with friends. Each time there is a loophole in the system, a rush is made to take advantage of it, and the politicians show just as much ingenuity in figuring new means of getting revenue.

All this is greatly complicated by Denmark's participation in the European Union. In a country with a population of only five million people, one figures that no matter what sort of a mess we make of things, it can be straightened out, but when one sees the meandering corridors of power within the EEC, the mind boggles. My faith that it will nonetheless all come out in the wash, so to speak, is due to a belief in the Danish heritage, for the now so docile Dane has a proud history of remaining, in spirit, independent of authorities, even when he appears to be complying.

In the 800s, when a few brave missionaries consented to try once more to convert the ferocious Danes to Christianity, their success wasn't so much due to a Nordic denial of past beliefs as it was due to an interest the Normans had for the festivities and baptismal gifts that lay waiting for them when they consented to sail down the Rhine to be christened.

From a description of this practice, written at Saint Gallen's monastery in Switzerland, we learn that Louis I, the pious successor of Charlemagne, offered gifts with his benedictions and lured the Vikings southward in such numbers that on one occasion there weren't enough of the white robes he customarily gave to go around to all who had come. The tailors were ordered to cut the remaining cloth into pieces and sew them together as well as they could. Such a pieced-together robe was given to one of the eldest among the converts, and, after he had inspected it, he said with astonishment, "Well, I never. I've been christened twenty times and have always been given a decent robe, but this time they've given me a sack that would be more suitable for a cattle-driver than a warrior. If I weren't ashamed to go nude, you could give this rag back to your Christ!"

While a more modern Dane has embraced the ideas embodied in the European Union (and while he was at it, cashed in on some of the "gifts" that lured him to Brussels), I feel sure that his lineage back to the old sort of Viking Dane will somehow enable him to retain his identity and his sense of humor.

It is ironic, though, that while the Soviet Union has broken up into dozens of pieces, the rest of Europe is striving to form a power block that would have been an anathema to many of those who lived through World War II. It would seem to be much more farsighted to strive to strengthen a body of international laws, while each country retains the amount of sovereignty necessary for people to feel a sense of identity.

One very important factor in Danish sovereignty is its being a monarchy. Denmark is the oldest kingdom in the world, with a well-documented and intriguing history of the royal line. Once they had lost their absolute power, the royal family in Denmark has had the wisdom to follow the times, making their presence meaningful to each generation within changing eras. King Christian X was a shining light during the dark years of the war, the sort of figure of authority that could allow Danes to feel a sense of self-respect during the humiliating occupation. He was followed by his son, Frederik IX, a very popular, more accessible person who very much suited the less-disciplined population of the fifties and sixties.

When Frederik IX died in 1972, he was loved by everyone, but there still was a smattering of die-hard anti-royalists. Even they forgot themselves, however, in the grips of emotions inspired by the beauty and pageantry surrounding the king's burial rites and the crowning of the new queen.

King Frederik and his queen, Ingrid, had three daughters, and on the eighteenth birthday of the eldest daughter, Margrethe, the constitution was changed, allowing the ascendancy of a female descendant. (In history there was a precedent in having a female ruler: Queen Margrethe I ruled from 1375 to 1412, but her ascendancy to the throne had a different history.) The very moving ceremonies in the days that followed King Frederik's death brought home to the nation the meaning of a monarchy. Politicians come and go, but there is something comforting in seeing a lovely queen step into her role, unsullied by quarrels. The narrow streets of Copenhagen lend a feeling of intimacy to the ancient pageantry that unfolds when a king is taken to his burial place, and everyone had a lump in his throat when the young queen came out on the balcony of Christiansborg Castle. She was tall and regal in an elegant, long black gown, black chiffon veils blowing in the cold wind, with the prime minister proclaiming in three directions: "Frederik IX is dead. Long live Margrethe II."

Queen Margrethe has, in turn, been the perfect monarch for our times. I don't think this is entirely a matter of luck. Obviously, royalty do not possess supernatural powers that make them suited for their roles, but they are the ultimate in the influence of environment. The queen's upbringing in unique surroundings, her early awareness of the sacrifices she would be expected to make, and her constant contact with the touchstones of a long history molded her into a person quite unlike anyone we would be able to find in the population in general. She does have the good luck of being especially gifted in languages and the arts, and in having a keen intelligence, all qualities which instill respect in the demanding times in which we find ourselves. However, even if she were to lack these qualities, only her popularity would be affected, not her usefulness as a well-groomed figurehead.

It would be unrealistic to presume that a monarchy could be created in a country like the United States, but where an old monarchy already exists it must be appreciated for its special attributes. The powers of the Danish queen are merely symbolic, but I think all Danes feel that if everything else failed in the legislative system and they otherwise have a just cause, she could be appealed upon to help out on a personal level. She and other members of the royal family lead very useful lives. No matter which sort of political structure a government leader who is visiting Denmark represents, he or she is bound to be impressed by a meeting with the queen, and her presence transcends ordinary diplomacy. Queen Margrethe would have my vote just for her New Year's speech, a tradition she has of addressing the nation at six p.m. on New Year's Eve, giving us food for thought with a flavor of optimism quite appropriate for such a festive evening.

15

Ice Winter

ce is a thing of beauty and comes in many forms. In California, I associated it with the nice cracking noise it made when dropped in a tall, refreshing drink. That was before I woke up one January morning in Denmark and saw the huge bedroom window totally covered by fantastic flowers that had formed during the night, sparkling like diamonds and aglow with the rosy light of a frosty dawn. Fairy tales prepare us for many of life's wonders, but I had never dreamed that the work of Jack Frost would be of such great beauty. I lay there staring, amazed at the intricacy and variety of design, crystals that fell into patterns of giant ferns and clusters of stylized daisies.

I watched the windows throughout the day, not wanting to miss a moment of this touch of magic. As the sun climbed higher, these formations turned from a deep rose to a burning gold; they sparkled with a cold white light all day and took on a bluish cast as evening approached. They blocked out the view and enclosed us in an ice palace. There were long icicles hanging from the eaves, and those grew longer each day as the powerful February sun melted them, and the frost air caught the drops and froze them into place. The lake was frozen, and skaters moved about among the reeds and whirled gracefully within a circle of lights placed out on the ice for evening skaters.

Most exciting of all, the sea around us was frozen. Where we had frolicked in summer breakers, there was a desolate expanse of frozen sea, with great chunks of aquamarine ice cluttering its surface, as if tossed there by a frost-giant. It was inviting to run out on the ice, this new playground that usually was accessible only by boat. Strange things began to take place. Like a panorama in a surrealistic painting, there appeared people bicycling on the ice, or couples pushing prams for a Sunday stroll with the baby. One family saw an opportunity to make an inexpensive move to Sweden, and they drove over the ice in a truck, just as the Swedish army had used it to launch their invasion of Denmark's capital in 1659.

The ice looked solid and permanent, but it could treacherously shift due to a change in the current, and foolhardy souls could find themselves suddenly adrift in the cold sea. Or one could become a subject for a memorable photograph, like the young man on a bicycle, looking with disbelief at ice-cutters passing on either side of him. Equally unforgettable were the fishermen who found themselves in the open sea on a slab of ice and stubbornly refused to be rescued unless they could bring their catch on board the helicopter.

There was a sense of adventure and excitement about the first ice winter I experienced, and I was disappointed when I realized that years could pass before we had another one. There are many signs that herald the coming of an ice winter, and we watch for them each year when summer sings its swan song, but it is only when we are proved to be right that we remember the signs afterwards, knowingly commenting that the geese had left early or that there was an unusual amount of berries on shrubs or of nuts from trees.

When the next real ice winter finally came, it was sudden and enchanting. We were with friends in their home, a thatched-roof house overlooking a lake, the four of us sitting inside having a cup of afternoon tea, dogs sleeping on the floor and conversation drowsy after a long walk in the sharp, wintry air. The sky was turning that incredible blue that comes in December with really cold weather, and we watched the windows as the room grew darker by candlelight. Suddenly, the air was filled with the sound of musical chimes, unlike anything I had ever heard. This fairy-like music was coming from the lake which was miraculously icing over, sending its sounds out on the clear, frosty air.

With this new awareness of the sound of ice, I discovered the fun of being at a pond just at the right moment, when a thin layer of ice has stretched across the water, and a stone sent skipping over the just freezing surface makes a ringing sound that can be heard all over the forest. It is as if the cold becomes a living thing.

Because of the sea all around, Denmark's weather is erratic, with fresh currents bringing fogs that coat everything with frost or winds that freeze one to the marrow more than a drastic drop in the temperature will do on a still day. With an ice winter, the cold is more stable, and each day is bright and clear with all moisture frozen like diamonds. One can awaken in the morning and find the garden transformed by hoarfrost, coating every twig and sparkling in the sunshine. The snow that falls is allowed to stay and pile deeper, a protective blanket for everything sleeping underground. The steep roof of the house where we lived got a thick layer of snow, and inside we felt the warmth of its insulation. We made pyramids of snowballs and put a candle in their centers to give off a cheery light along our driveway, and the world around us seemed to be more spacious, as snow covered the irregularities of gardens and streets like thick, white house-to-house carpeting.

During mild winters, one knows that a lovely snowfall can be gone in the morning, and we sometimes got the kids out of bed in the middle of the night to go out and romp in it while we could be sure that it was there. However, an ice winter is reliable. The fox and the squirrels and birds are increasingly trusting as it becomes more and more difficult to find food, and a feeding station in the garden serves as the most entertaining feature of winter life. With typical Danish concern, well-organized feeding programs are arranged for over-wintering birds. Thousands of swans and other water birds are imperiled as their feet freeze to their own wastes, and rescue workers go out on the ice daily, to pry them loose and put out feed for them.

During one such ice winter, we had snowfalls unlike any I had seen here, and entire farms disappeared in the flat Lolland landscape, with only chimneys sticking above the snow to show the way to the rescue tanks that the army ordered out. Those farmers who were snowed in dug tunnels in the snow, joining farmhouse and stables, in order to keep the livestock fed and cared for. On one such farm an entire wedding party was marooned for four days, luckily with plenty of food and drink.

We had been invited on a fox hunt, and, although the weather was clear, we didn't know whether we dared risking the long drive down there, for winds were blowing snow across the roads, sometimes burying them within a matter of minutes. However, we were persuaded by our friends on Lolland, who assured us that everything was under control there, and that the scenery was breathtaking.

We had invited Kirsten and Carl Johan to come with us, a couple we can always rely on to be good sports, no matter how uncomfortable the outing turns out to be. We left early in the morning, highly animated and warmly bundled up, with Carl Johan clutching a small shovel like a little kid would a plastic sword, ready to meet any danger. The roads were dry, and we looked forward to a day in the woods at a time of the year when the animals are so approachable, their instincts telling them that the hunting season was closed for all but the fox. Rabies had spread to the peninsula of Jutland, and hunters were appealed upon to shoot a good number of foxes, the chances for the dread disease spreading being less in an area where they are not overpopulated. (The alternative to controlling the problem this way is by gassing their lairs, a method which is quite cruel.)

The going became rough when we turned off the main highway and took the smaller roads heading for our final destination. A stiff northern wind had come up, and snow was drifting swiftly across the roads. Under the deep snow, the landscape around us appeared to be wiped clear of all known landmarks, and we realized that if we got off the road we would be lost. As we slowed to a snail's pace, we could hear the wind howling around us. Driving up a small hill, we missed a bend and landed in a snowdrift too deep to drive out of. While Carl Johan and Finn worked up a sweat to shovel the wheels free, Kirsten and I stood watching, stamping our feet and freezing in the icy wind.

Thinking of keeping warm, I volunteered to run ahead and see if there was a house where I could make a phone call and tell the hunting party that we would be late. Over the top of the rise was a charming cottage, and judging from the type of improvements that had been made, it appeared to be a country house for city dwellers. There was a car out front, but no sign of life inside. I found that snow had drifted up against the front door and decided that before I rang the bell, I would have to shovel the snow away or they would be greeted by an avalanche when they opened their door. Conveniently, there was a snow shovel leaning against the house, and I worked hard to clear a path, a nice exercise for getting warm, but a waste of time since no one answered when I rang. Feeling great contempt for city people who go to the country to sleep late, I plodded back to the car and told the rest that I had had no luck. Just at that moment, Finn succeeded in getting the car free and, not wanting to stop until he got to better ground, he shot up the road with us running behind.

Carl Johan thought that this pause was just as good as any to take the pause that refreshes, and while Kirsten and I went around the bend, he lagged behind to commune with nature. The most convenient place was the front yard of the house where I had just been, and, being a lawyer, he used logic to reach the conclusion that since they hadn't answered the bell, no one was home. Meanwhile, the occupants of the house had roused themselves and went to the window just in time to see a tall man relieving himself in their front yard. Carl Johan spotted them and beat a hasty retreat, but needless to say, after that, we couldn't ask them to use their phone and had to find another farm farther up the road. (The first lot is probably still trying to figure out whether the character out front had first tried to shovel his way into the house.)

At the next farm, Finn made the phone call and arranged to meet the hunting party in the forest, rather than at the sawmill that had been our destination. They assured us that they had no trouble getting around on forest roads; what they didn't remember to tell us was that they were driving Land Rovers. It was ages later, after digging our way out of a number of snowdrifts and ditches that we finally caught up with them.

Although barrels of grain had been put out for the forest animals, and bulldozers had cleared patches after each fresh snowfall for them to find dirt to scratch in, the animals we saw that day were clearly weakened by the hard winter. Deer that ran by us panted and stumbled, their long legs unsuited to the deep snow with its hard crust of ice on the surface. Pheasants took flight and were tossed by the strong wind. The usually so jovial party was quiet — everyone feeling uncomfortable for disturbing the creatures of the forest on such a cruel day.

One pheasant flew right into a tree and fell to the ground, too stunned to move. A hunter gently lifted her up and found her to be bleeding slightly from her beak. It was agreed that with fresh blood on her she wouldn't survive, for the fox would have an easy time finding her. However, her wings looked unharmed, and we knew that if she could be kept safe a few days, she would be right as rain. Finn and I decided to take her home and put her in with our chickens and bring her back to Lolland when the spring thaw set in. I carried her to the car, and she was remarkably calm in my arms, while she kept her bright eyes fixed on me. We put her in a box, and she settled down like birds usually do, in the belief that darkness is safe.

We drove home soon after lunch, not wanting to tackle the roads in the early darkness that descends upon a winter afternoon. My thoughts kept returning to the pheasant hen in the trunk with an uneasy feeling about having a wild animal in captivity, no matter how well-meant our intentions. When we got home, we carried the box out to the hen yard, an enclosure with chicken wire on the top as well as the sides. When we let her out of the box, she battered herself against the wiring in a pathetic attempt to regain her freedom. Our hens had been locked in their house much earlier, and the pheasant finally settled on the snow-covered roof, wary but resigned.

We did what we could to try to improve the conditions of her captivity. We put fir branches in the corner for her to hide under, and we tried to avoid startling her, but as the days went by, it became clear that she was and would remain an entirely wild creature. We still couldn't release her, for her flying against the wiring had damaged her tail feathers, and the cold was so severe that we wanted her in better shape before turning her free.

We didn't realize it then, but it was very foolish to have put her in with the hens. Hens can be ferocious when a new bird enters their territory, but fortunately these left her alone, and she spent much of her time hiding under the branches. In the evening, when the hens were locked in, she came out and perched on top of the roof of the hen house, under the frost clear sky that looked like blue-black velvet studded with brilliants. One longed to be able to explain to her that her captivity was for a limited time, and that we understood how much she suffered, being shut up with a bunch of silly, domesticated birds. The look in her eyes spoke volumes about what she thought of us.

One night, when the patches of snow had begun to diminish in the places most open to the sun, she unexpectedly flew directly into the wiring on top of the pen and miraculously hit an opening where two rolls of netting had been joined together. It was almost like she had been studying the possibility of that being an escape hatch. She was off in a flash, and we watched her swift flight over the snow white ground in the bright moonlight. We were both disappointed that we hadn't been able to return her to her own forest, foolishly thinking that then she might have fathomed our good intentions, but at least we knew she was now well-fed and strong, with a good chance that she would fare well.

Her flight marked the end of that ice winter, and it was many years before we had another one quite like that. Each one brings special memories though, such as the winter when an unprecedented cold spell hit this part of the world right at the time that Poland, our next-door neighbor, was put into the grip of martial law. The fate of Polish men, rounded up in the middle of the night, not given a chance to dress warmly before being interrogated, weighed on our minds as we crept into icy beds at night and stared at the pale moonlight effusing the layer of ice on the inside of our bedroom windows. The time for bravery is in the summertime, not in the middle of the night with a freezing wind.

One such year Finn found a small black and white tufted duck floundering in the snow drifts by the road that follows the Danish Riviera. The cunning little creature was so weak that he couldn't fly, and we brought him home to warm him up. He was a much more willing captive, and we put him in the greenhouse where he thrived until the happy day in the springtime when we could turn him loose for the mating season, sleek and well fed.

Perhaps the most dramatic winter on our street was the one which hit so suddenly that the sea all around was frozen over within three days, a process that normally takes weeks during an ice winter. I felt like a traitor when Finn drove me through a blizzard to the airport. While he and Bjørn were freezing at home, I was lapping up sunshine in Southern California. Of course, as soon as I was out the door, Finn turned off nearly all the heat, thinking it was a marvelous opportunity to save on oil. Bjørn had a college chum staying in the house, and the two of them weren't about to admit that they couldn't take just as much as the governor, so the temperature continued to drop with each cold day.

A house down the street caught on fire, and when neighbors called to tell Finn about it, he couldn't see the five meter high flames because the ice flowers on our windows had totally blocked out all views. It was minus twenty-eight degrees centigrade with the added cooling factor of a good stiff wind. The fire engines arrived promptly, but their hoses were too frozen to draw water. Fire engines arriving from a neighboring community were warmed up enough to get water, but the cascade used to quench the flames froze as it seeped through the big house, forming eerie stalactites from all the ceilings and down the frozen stairwell.

Before most of the world opted for worrying about the greenhouse effect, there was talk of the possibility of a new ice age, one which would be heralded by a severe winter that is not followed up by a normal summer. Thus, a good deal of speculation was kicked about after that very awe-inspiring winter, when we had a summer so miserable that one had to go back exactly nine hundred years to find one like it. That was in 1087, when pious King Knud had been murdered by rebellious landowners while he kneeled before the altar at Saint Albani's Church in Odense. His brother, Oluf, ascended the throne, after having taken the rebels' side at the fateful moment. The following summer was so dreadful, first with drought and then with steady rain, that Denmark experienced a crop failure and famine unparalleled in the history of this usually so fertile land.

Poor Oluf earned the nickname "Oluf Hunger", and he himself was more than willing to accept the blame for the bad weather. Like all kings of that time, he assumed that his power was divine and ill fortune for his land was proof of divine dissatisfaction with his rule. King Knud was promptly declared a saint, and Oluf did his duty and died, clearing the way for Erik "Ejegod" ("good through and through") and the return of good weather and prosperity. Mind you, all this took six years of lousy summers even back in those days when one knew whom to blame and how to rectify the ill deeds that had brought on such bad weather.

In our summer of 1987, however, the only plausible explanation seemed to be that we were getting ready for a *Fimbulwinter*, three of which will set the stage for Ragnarök and the battle of the gods, the Vikings' concept of the end of the world as we know it now.

It is only natural that the Scandinavian climate would inspire a Nordic view of doomsday as a time for the big freeze, just as those prophets who lived in and around the Fertile Crescent would conceive of an end to the world in all-consuming fire. After all, their most uncomfortable weather came from too much heat. With the choice between the threat of a reappearance of an ice age or an atomic holocaust in the Middle East, the mind boggles, and I turn my attention to more immediate problems, like what to make for dinner.

16

My Cup Runneth Over

In these few pages describing our somewhat sedentary life in Copenhagen, I hope that I haven't given the impression that all our waking hours are spent imbibing. Alcohol is, indeed, a very important part of life in Denmark, but it is a stable factor. It is we humans who tend to vary. There are people here who don't drink heavily, but there are very few who don't drink at all.

Psychologists study the whys and wherefores of people's drinking habits, but my private study of Finn has convinced me that the reason he drinks is simply because he loves the stuff. Alcohol is, for him, a life elixir which is necessary for blood circulation, digestion, and being able to stand lesser mortals; furthermore, he is not, by any means, an isolated case. I believe that Danish drinking habits can be traced right back to their Viking roots, and that being such an ancient influence, it is perhaps more deserving of reverence than of understanding.

Many Americans are victims of preventive medicine. A yearly check-up reveals ailments long before they actually appear, and friends of ours have made it to our doorstep, with a crease of worry on their brows, to confide in us that they have been told by their doctors to avoid a long list of foods and all alcoholic beverages. Like many unnaturally fit people, Finn and his father were absolutely terrified of sick people, and while listening politely, they poured themselves an extra shot of ninety-proof bourbon, hoping that with the protection offered by this disinfecting agent, they could refrain from panicking and running pell-mell out of the room.

Much to their relief, closer examination of the subject revealed that the guests weren't actually ill, but merely planning their illnesses, with the aid of technological insights into their medical future. Unsuspectingly, such a poor friend will have by now inspired Finn to start a tireless campaign to drown these dreary portents in a sea of booze, that being, in his mind, a surefire cure for all ills.

With a consistency that prohibits all further discussion, Finn will adamantly refuse any form of painkiller, including ordinary aspirin, to dull a toothache, but he will blindly adhere to the more questionable benefits of a bottle of whiskey. (The only time he won't drink is if he is unhappy, proof that he doesn't consider ills of the mind worthy of alcoholic cure-alls.) Even the meekest Dane will wax quite warm in his faith that one or two shots of snaps are the best panacea for the discomforts of old age.

Other Danes, particularly the ambitious thirty- and forty-year-olds, are more likely to be influenced by American trends and are trying to limit their consumption of alcohol. In order to do this without interfering too much with well-established habits, such Danes start out by insisting on sticking to only one form of drink throughout the course of the evening, usually white wine or red wine. The most impressive example of this Puritanism I have witnessed was in the case of someone my husband has dubbed "Yoyo." Our son, Bjørn, had been asked to help serve the guests at a rather large dinner party at our home, and Yoyo gave instructions to pour the same beverage in his glass all through the dinner. Much to my horror, the one thing he had chosen was gin, and he didn't want to be obvious in his fanaticism, so he had it poured into his red wine glass and drank it as if it were water.

Of course, it would undoubtedly be a better world if all people could be happy without the indisputably harmful props we use, like alcoholic beverages. However, there does seem to be a deep-seated need among many human beings to release the less-inhibited self from the more presentable self, and that need seems to be intensified in a land with changing seasons. The Nordic psyche is "heavier" than the southern one, more susceptible to dark moods. The poignancy of life's changes is more painful where the sharp distinctions of varied seasons constantly remind one of the passage of time, and many and varied are the means Danes use to push these thoughts of mortality out of mind.

In Shakespeare's *As You Like It*, when the character Jaques, with a little pretentious comedy, says all the world is a stage and all its people are players, I think he must have been referring not only to the entertainment in watching life go by, but also to a need we humans have — to want to be a part of the play. Although alcohol will by no means enhance your talents, it does have the effect of making one feel

more talented, allowing one to imagine brief moments of glory before
the curtain falls on each act. The many customs and rituals that are
involved in Danish drinking habits enable those who drink to have an
evening or a day where they feel that their lives are a little bit above
the ordinary. The visual setting in general is very important in this
deception, as is the very quality of the glass from which one drinks.
The mood would be quite shattered for my kind of Dane if he were
served a good red wine in a glass meant for an inferior beverage, and a
good wine will be a bit more special in a very fine old glass.

The importance placed on these material aspects of drinking,
make it possible to actually feel quite intoxicated by the setting,
without having too much in the glass. I have been with Danes on
many an occasion, spending hours singing songs and making toasts
during a lunch with a small glass of snaps, and only when one sees
how little a dent we have put in the bottle is one aware of the fact
that we have all fooled each other into thinking we have drunk deeply
in a splendid feast.

One Christmas, we invited a very old friend of Mums' family to
Christmas Eve dinner. Frøken (Miss) Sauer was in her nineties, and
her parents had been close friends with Finn's grandparents when they
lived in Norway. Her father earned a fortune sending ships to the Far
East and bought a hotel in order to retire. This background, with hotel
service and money, had furnished Frøken Sauer with regal mannerisms
and discerning taste. Being an old maid, she had never had to make any
compromises on either front.

She came up the snow-covered drive that evening, jabbing her cane
with distaste at our cobblestones. Her warm cloak was weighted down
with the old-fashioned furs one used to look at with fascination when
riding trains, the sort with claws hanging down and beady eyes staring
from small heads. The taxi driver had sampled the full volume of the
displeasure she felt at having been subjected to riding in a vehicle as
ungracious as a modern cab, but he gave us a good-natured wink as
he carried the gifts she had brought into the entrée, knowing he could
count on her for a good tip. With no small amount of scoldings for
the steepness of our front steps and the coldness of the weather, she
allowed us to settle her into a comfortable chair, where she sat straight
and queenly, in a long black gown from the thirties, trimmed with rich
black lace, her beautiful silvery hair piled in soft waves and pulled back
into a chignon.

She is a type I have encountered more than once among the older generation. So haughty that it is an absolute treat, too old to worry about the opinions of others and out to get the very last drop of enjoyment out of any moment that presents itself. She had a zest for life unadulterated by any compromises a younger person would make in order to be acceptable to his surroundings. With no patience for fools and not a trace of doubt as to her own status, she was delightfully dominating.

Finn thought he would please her by serving a glass of Rhine wine in some very special antique red goblets. Frøken Sauer had given two of them to Finn when he was just a teenager, telling him that they were English and more than a hundred years old, remnants from her parents' well-equipped home. Browsing in an antique store in Copenhagen, Finn found six more of these lovely glasses and was able to complete a set. Being hand-blown, the stems vary slightly in thickness, but these variations only enhanced their uniqueness.

She was nearly blind, and Finn carefully handed her a goblet filled with wine, waiting to let go of it until he was sure she had a firm grip on the stem. "Do you remember this glass, Frøken Sauer?" he asked, thinking she would be happy that he remembered her as the giver.

Rather than being pleased, she looked puzzled. "This isn't the glass I gave you! Whatever have you done with my goblets?" By bringing the tray within her reach, we soon solved the mystery. After all those years, she still recalled the thickness of the stem on her glasses, and the ones Finn had bought as a supplement had thinner stems. Once she was given one of her own and could weigh it in her hand, her face lit up in pleasure, and she could enjoy the wine.

That, I must admit, can be filed among the "niceties of drinking Danish," but there is the more rowdy, Viking side, too, and, on such occasions, I find myself projected into a role as keeper of a trained bear. He's a bit wild and woolly, but at least I hold the other end of the chain. Such was the case when we were invited to a big party up in Tisvilde. The man who was giving the party was celebrating his sixtieth birthday, and the setting, in a lovely old place on high cliffs overlooking the sea, was perfect for a summer party. The only flaw was in the host's idea of saving a bit of money by having his son, Jan, and his pal, Finn, serve as bartenders.

The two of them made themselves busy right from the start, the first job being to open the bottles of white wine that were earmarked for dinner. Jan couldn't get around his father's liquor supply without falling back into his old habits from the days when he liked to swipe shots of whiskey from the decanter and fill up the void with water. He decided that each bottle of wine should, by rights, be tasted, to control the quality, an impressive undertaking, considering the size of the crowd that had been invited. Dutifully, he and Finn uncorked cases of bottles, sampling each one and pronouncing it satisfactory, until they reached the last one, which Jan declared unfit for anything but chug-a-lugging to the last drop.

Having thus approved the vintage, they proceeded to set up the bar for the welcome drinks. Everyone who has visited Denmark knows how expensive liquor is in this country, and, of course, the best labels are outrageously dear. Unknown to me, Finn had made a trip to a shop for party gags, and his pockets were full of horrible labels and a set of plastic werewolf teeth. Any prospects of impressing these rather distinguished guests by the selection of well-known brands were dashed by the colorful array of ludicrous labels which Finn and Jan slapped onto all the bottles. Fine brands were disguised by pictures with red-nosed clowns, hula girls, and sundry obscenities. If the bottles looked silly, the bartenders looked even sillier, and despite their claims to having had just one little glass of wine, they had definitely aroused the suspicions of Jan's parents.

The guests started to arrive, and we mingled on the terrace, welcome drink in hand, enjoying the view beyond the steep cliffs that ended in a strip of sandy beach, where the water was an inviting blue, clear as a bell over the shoals that ran far out to sea. Jan and Finn had appeared their most contrite and promised they would do a good job of bartending. Finn had even put his werewolf teeth back into his pocket. Judging from the guests reactions, however, they were doing their job too well. Finn has a great respect for the older generation, and could at least have been counted on to be one hundred percent correct towards those of the guests who were past sixty; however, Jan was on his home turf, and the only inhibition he demonstrated was when he belched and turned to blame the noise on Finn. If they had been running a clearance sale on alcohol, I would say their success was colossal. They were supplying each guest with a drink that could be compared to a booster on a rocket. It wasn't long before they were able to close down the bar and join the crowd, and the only mitigating factor was that most of the drinks served had been such stiff ones that there was a chance that no one would even notice the behavior of the two bartenders.

By now there was the beginning of a glorious sunset, like something hired for the occasion. It had captured everyone's attention, but out of the corner of my eye, I had noticed that Finn had taken off most of his clothes and was heading downhill for a dip in the sea.

We were too many for a proper sit-down affair; we filled our plates at a buffet and wandered off to the seating arrangement of our choice. Finn was beyond controlling, and at least I had found a place where I couldn't see what he was doing. Darkness falls late on a summer evening, and it wasn't until after dark that I began to worry about what he might be up to. The moon hadn't risen, and it was pitch black on the terrace where I went to try to peer out over the cliff's edge. From the whoops and hollers down below, I could surmise that he had returned to the watery elements. This made me quite nervous until someone told me that he had taken a very stacked young lady with him. As much as I love Finn, when it comes to accompanying him for an icy dip in the sea, I will gladly step aside for one evening, and this gal had impressed me as being robust enough to keep the two of them afloat if there should be a mishap.

It became an extremely long evening. Finn had the time of his life, which he can't remember, and I was a nervous wreck trying to keep him from taking head-first dives from the cliff or practicing handstands near Chinese vases or getting in arm-wrestling contests guaranteed to spoil his opponents chances of ever again playing the piano or eating with chopsticks.

After an evening like that, a husband is absolute putty in one's hands. He will believe any mortifying thing you tell him he has done, and he will spend at least twelve hours trying to make it up to you. (Don't push it past the twelve hours; at that point he will begin to run down and feel irritable and self-defensive, and you will have lost the initiative.)

The next time we went to a similar party, I was doubly encumbered by having friend Jan along. He was staying with us for a couple of weeks, while his wife was in Jutland. The perils of the party, however, are nothing compared to the problem of getting home. It is probably not necessary to point out that a person who is thoroughly inebriated is not in his right mind, and when Finn reached the stage of thinking he could drive home, I knew he was beyond the pale. Well knowing that Jan was in no better shape, I used reverse psychology and told him that I was counting on his level-headedness to get us into a taxi and on our way home before Finn discovered that we had left the car behind.

Taxi drivers have nerves of steel. While the two men tumbled into the cab, this one remained poker-faced as he tried to sort out what I was saying about our destination and what they were telling him about where they fancied going. I could see his face in the rear view mirror, and his expression was like someone who had found a fly in his soup. It was a long drive home and Finn and Jan had a marvelous time all the way. They sang, belched, smoked cigars, broke wind, and shook their fists whenever we passed a police car, laughing until tears rolled down their cheeks over a whole repertoire of unintelligible babble. When we were halfway home, I realized that I had forgotten my house keys in our car, but I didn't dare say anything that would give them an excuse to go back to the party. Instead, I sat wracking my brain, trying to think of a way to get into the house once we arrived. The kids were staying in the country, and the only prospect seemed to be to climb into an upstairs window.

We pulled up in front of the house at long last, and, much to the driver's disgust, I had as much trouble getting the revelers out of the car as I had had in getting them in. Finn kept telling the disinterested driver that he didn't know who I was but that I had been following him all evening, and Jan kept tumbling back into the cab and saying he wanted to go to Hamburg.

A well-built Danish villa is like a fortress, with double glazing on all windows, but I had recalled that there were two tiny windows open on the north side of the house. Luckily, Finn was in such a state that he didn't find anything odd in my telling him to get me a ladder so I could crawl into one of these windows. He good-naturedly went to the garage and hauled out a very long, very wobbly ladder and put it up against the house.

In all my party finery, I started to climb the rickety steps, while Finn held onto the ladder, unsteady on his feet, but firm in his promise to catch me if I fell. When I got to the top I discovered that the window I had chosen opened into the stairwell, with a long fall on the other side of the sill. I wanted the other window, opening into a guest toilet. I waited until I was down on the ground again before telling Finn that he had to move the ladder, having feared that he otherwise might have done so with me still on top. Up I went again, while Jan, who was on the other side of the garden, with a firm grip on the flagpole, said, "Don't you worry, hic, Judy, I'm holding on, too."

This time I had chosen the right window and started to squeeze my way in, but after I wedged my shoulders through the narrow opening, I found myself stuck, unable to move forward and not daring to move backwards. I started to giggle, thinking how silly I would look if the fire department had to be called, but the thought of Finn and Jan diversifying their activities by calling the fire department was enough to make me pull myself together and, with a supreme effort, pull the last inches of excess bum through the window frame.

Having gotten in, it was an easy matter to go downstairs and open the door for the men. It was however much more difficult to convince them that they should come in, for they were having so much fun frolicking around in the garden. Only the thought of how I would feel in the morning kept me from wishing I were in the same state as they. (Finn is blessed with never having a hangover.) I had to bribe them with food to get them in the house. Jan always could be counted on to respond to what he claimed was needed to counteract drink — "something strong for the organism" — and he came up the front steps on all fours, without bending his knees. The last I saw of them that night was their backs as they sat on two tall stools in the kitchen, eating bacon and eggs smothered in Tabasco sauce. Jan was feeling philosophic and complained about how seldom one had a real night out like that nowadays. Shaking his head sadly, he lamented, "It's the rich who have money." Finn poured him another snaps to cheer him up, and they both said, "Skål!"

Cß   CR

These occasional lapses from being a good husband and father are too funny to cause any consternation on my part, although I have tried hard to have a row with Finn on at least one occasion. I was coming down with a cold just before a weekend when we were having out-of-town guests. Finding me less than entertaining, Finn decided to visit one of the neighbors and invite him on a hunt. I asked that he take his keys, because I planned to go to bed early with a hot toddy. "No need, darling. I'll be back in a jiffy. Remember, I have to get up at six to play tennis tomorrow morning."

Naturally he wasn't home by the time I wanted to go to bed, and I hated to be a harpy and call the neighbors. I waited a couple of hours but finally had to call and say I was putting the keys under the mat. However, once in bed, I couldn't fall asleep. An old house is full of creaks and groans, and I kept imagining a burglar having found the keys and wandering around on the ground floor.

When Finn did come home, hours later, he felt exceedingly pleased with himself for having reached such high levels of communication with a fellow neighbor, over a few bottles of wine, and I was ready to kill him. I sprang out of bed, ran to the top of the stairs, and hurled his duvet at him, snarling that he could blooming well sleep on the sofa.

Poor Finn, who had been so content a moment before, looked bewildered at what he imagined to be the fickleness of women. After all, I loved him when he left just (as he thought) minutes before. Not being in a mood to ponder over the treachery of females, he shrugged his shoulders and shuffled into the dining room, either forgetting where the sofa was or preferring the place with happy memories of past meals.

This passive attitude was most unfair when I had worked up such a healthy rage, and I stormed downstairs, alarm clock in hand, telling him he could get up on his own in the morning, and hurling the poor clock the full length of the dining room, taking care not to hit anything breakable. (The alarm clock was the only thing in the house I felt like smashing, but, as luck would have it, it lay there ticking, just as unperturbed as Finn.)

What really made my cup run over, however, was that Finn still hadn't said anything, but like a great bear had curled up on the parquet floor, not even on one of the carpets, and was already starting to snore. I knew how a general must feel when he stands with superior forces and a well-planned attack, only to see the enemy retreat. Suddenly I realized that if I allowed Finn to sleep there on that hard, cold floor, he would wake up miserable, and that all the fun of being the martyr would be his, not mine.

I poked him in the side, un-gently, with my foot, and told him to wake up so I could fight with him, but the poking made him ticklish and whatever he had been given to drink across the street had rendered him so peaceful, that he just chuckled and mumbled that I was right and resumed his snoring. My only remaining choice was to get him to move upstairs to our nice, comfortable bed and salvage the remnants of being the injured party. Luckily, he was so docile that I succeeded, but it took a lot of sweet-talking and prodding, and who can stay angry with a man at the same time that he's being sweet-talked?

It is like Finn always says, "Something is a problem only if you make it a problem." And as you can clearly see, it was I, not he, who had problems with drinking.

17

Togetherness

When I came to Denmark, I was weighted down with a certain amount of mental baggage, such as the impression created in the fifties by *Ladies Home Journal* that married couples should strive for something called "togetherness." It worried me a great deal that Finn and I were so different, because this naturally makes togetherness impractical. Maybe it was the impracticality of it that enabled me to discover that it can also be fun to watch someone in action who is quite another cup of tea — as the Danish expression goes, "to be a fly on the wall," an innocent form of voyeurism.

There is something very touching about men when they get together with those with whom they share a military past. If they have been in the same regiment at the same time, their conversation is limited to broken bits and pieces sufficient to set them afloat on clouds of reminiscence to a Never Never Land where cold was colder and tired was more tired and men were men, with the exception of the occasional bloke who fell through in boot camp and gave all the rest of his mates a puffed-up feeling of having succeeded beyond their wildest dreams. Such reunions are good clean fun, but like a good film, they are more enjoyable when the onlooker doesn't make his or her presence felt, thereby not shattering the mood that has been created.

Finn was in the Royal Guard for three of the best years of his life, leaving as a first lieutenant, confident that he was thus capable of doing anything and everything. During his stay in America, however, he found that his military record didn't command the same respect, and a job application was rejected with the flat statement, "We don't like war heroes here, buddy." Undaunted, he used his credentials to impress me, and I will admit to being swayed by the thought of him having stood palace guard in the snow under the magnificent shelter of a bearskin busby.

After our marriage, his military career was limited to yearly stints in the reserves, taking part in NATO maneuvers, and although his officer's uniform now would be a very tight squeeze, due to all the "muscles" men get as they age, the clipped accents of the officer are just a drink away when he gets around anyone who shares these military ties. No matter how dilapidated these old officers may become, they have learned a certain posture that makes them rather dashing, a definite hint of class at any gathering.

One of my favorites is Kaj, a handsome man with a great deal of charm and a reputation for being impossible to live with — A reputation, by the way, which I suspect him of having created in order to keep his freedom. Due to his military flair he could, with a devilish wink in his eye, state opinions which no one else dared breathe, and we would all nod vigorously in agreement. I have been spellbound on more than one occasion, listening to a story I had heard before, too intrigued with the man and his voice to interrupt.

To hear him tell about months spent in Finland as a Danish volunteer, during the winter when the Finns fought the Soviets in 1939–40, was to feel the chill of the wind through somber pines, even though we sat in front of a roaring fire, with full brandy snifters in our hands. One could even glean practical advice from the tale, like the trick of heating a small stone in a fire and hanging it by a string from the centre of the tent, in order to create a tiny source of heat that warmed far beyond proportions in the bitter cold of a Finnish winter.

The Danish volunteers spent long months waiting for the chance to go into action, and nostalgic recall of such utter misery usually brought on Kaj's favorite party number — a Finnish song in seventeen verses, the last of which promised to produce a tear that would roll soundlessly down his lean cheek as we sat on the edge of our seats, watching its course. That having been accomplished, he broke out in his disarming grin, clenched his teeth to flex that soldierly muscle right under his temple, giving his jaw the proper military angle, and resumed the stories.

Men of this sort were, needless to say, frustrated by the Danish policy of neutrality during World War II, and they usually made up for this frustration by becoming involved in the resistance. Tales of the resistance never fail to stir up interest among the younger generation, but Kaj had an edge over his peers, for he had actually been captured and scheduled for execution at the end of the war. Like so many other incomprehensible things the Nazis did when their defeat was imminent, they accelerated executions, rather than delaying them. Kaj had been holed up a rum amount of time in their worst prison in Copenhagen and was to be shot the day before the liberation, but on that day, the written orders for his execution had been misplaced. With German fidelity to correct procedure, a message was hurried off to Berlin to renew the missing order. This brief delay was enough to save Kaj's life.

I was, of course, ever so impressed when I asked him what deprivation had been worst during those dark days and was told that the greatest misery was not being able to get a hold of a cigarette. Tough as nails was our Kaj.

Usually, the kids and I got the full benefit of these illustrious personalities when they all piled into a cab and came to our home after a luncheon at Finn's office. On one such occasion, there was an old officer in the party whose nickname can best be translated as "Damn-it-all" Ovesen, a dear man who wanted to finish off the session at our home with a series of fairy tales told to the kids. Kaj had warmed up already with his Finnish song, complete with the inevitable tear, and the two of them launched into their version of the Three Bears, one which graphically stripped Goldilocks of all virtue and could have been used as a handbook in spine-tingling suspense and wicked oaths. I hoped Lani and Bjørn weren't taking in all of it, but I have seldom seen their attention so riveted on the speakers.

Obviously, women were in this company at their own risk, and I felt it wasn't my place to curb their boyish enthusiasm. By the same token, I thought that Finn could have been more understanding on the one and only time I had a ladies' luncheon.

It all came about because I received a phone call inviting me to such an affair, and having reached the point in life where I really had no excuse to stay home, I said yes. As soon as I put down the receiver, I complained to Finn, telling him that I couldn't imagine anything less interesting than spending the greater part of an afternoon with a bunch of females. I liked the hostess, but our friendship had been limited to seeing each other at dinner parties where we were with our husbands. My life in Denmark always having been linked to Finn's with never a dull moment, I hadn't yet reached the stage where I felt I had time to spend with ladies of leisure.

Of course, it turned out to be an extremely entertaining afternoon. I found that the ladies I already knew were definitely not less of personalities for being without their alter egos, and those who were new acquaintances could be judged on their own merits, not in any way affected by the men they had married. We were a party of twelve and, unlike such a party where half would have been men, our conversation revolved around a shared subject. We've come a long way in rethinking the roles of the sexes, but we still haven't changed the nature of people and, by nature, most women like to please the men they are talking with. We try to talk about things which interest them, and since men love the opportunity to show off how interesting they are, the result is often six conversations in a group of twelve people.

Just to illustrate how true this is, I can tell that I recently found myself in the enviable position, for a woman past fifty, of being seated next to a very handsome gynecologist. There I was, with at least three hours to learn all about my plumbing, but I didn't get a word in edgewise. I did, however, learn a great deal about the past twenty years of his life. (It was just as well, of course; ignorance is bliss.)

I had such a good time with the ladies that when it came time to break up, I invited all those who were free to come to lunch the following week. I was still chuckling over one of the stories I had heard that afternoon when Finn and I sat in the kitchen before dinner, having a drink. I told him about these two marvelous sisters whom I had met. They had married two Italian brothers and had gone to live in separate wings of the family castle in Italy.

When the eldest sister was to give birth to her first child, she became the centre of attention, and, of course, everyone expected her to produce a son. When she started labor, she was put into a very large room in the company of an odd little doctor and two very gloomy nuns. In the adjoining room, was an impressive gathering of family and worthy citizens who settled in for a longer siege, playing cards, gossiping, and keeping up their strength with refreshments and cigars.

Being a first birth, labor dragged out endlessly. The mother-to-be was utterly miserable, but at this point, the doctor was in even more of a state, feeling that the responsibility of producing a son was entirely on his shoulders. The nuns appeared to find the whole affair most distasteful and offered no comfort whatsoever. Finally, at the point when a modern hospital would have opted for a caesarean section, the doctor, who was a very round little man, went to the far side of this immense room, lifted himself up on his toes like a ballet dancer, and came charging full speed towards the mother, leaping in the air and landing flat on her poor belly. The baby popped out like a cork from a bottle of champagne, and the doctor discovered that he might just as well have spared himself the exertion — The child was a girl. It was just good luck that both mother and daughter survived the ordeal, but the sisters made a pact never to have any more babies in the lap of the family.

I pointed out to Finn, who had turned quite pale at the very mention of a doctor, that I never hear such a lovely story at our parties, and I added that some of the "girls" were coming to our place the following week. Suddenly, my husband revealed a side I had not yet seen. We had thrown formal dinner parties for thirty people, and he never showed the slightest concern that I would fix something to everyone's liking, but with the mere mention of a ladies' luncheon, he was his mother's son. Mums' favorite pastime was planning the next meal, and when that included her lady friends, she reached an absolute state of frenzy until the whole menu was in place. He wanted to know what I planned to serve.

"I haven't given it a thought," I said in answer to his question. "I'll see what looks good next week."

"Yes, but I have to know. I have to buy the wine. How many are coming? What will you want to drink before lunch? How about after lunch?"

By now, he looked like he was about to rush out the door, and I tried to assure him that, for us women, drink really wasn't important. "Besides, half of them will be watching their weight, and none of them will want to drink any quantity. Don't worry about it. You can bring a couple of bottles up from the wine cellar on Wednesday."

Only eight were coming, and it turned out that Finn bought a whole case of excellent white wine and an equally good case of red wine, in order not to risk any shortage. Then he wanted to know what time he could come home that day. I pointed out to him that Lisbeth's husband, George, didn't show up until we were leaving, but, at that parallel, Finn looked so crestfallen that I relented and said he could come home a bit sooner if he wanted.

When Finn came home from the office, we were still lingering over the dessert, having a very animated conversation about one of the many topics middle-aged men are no longer interested in. Just as I could have predicted, Finn sat down at one end of the table, and two of the ladies turned to a subject that would amuse him, while the rest of us continued our absorbing conversation. For a fleeting moment, I considered the possibility that in old days the ladies weren't really sent out of the room while the men drank their port. It might have been some wise hostess who figured out that system!

CB   CB

Once however, we experienced togetherness in the true Ladies' Home Journal meaning. That was the soccer season when Bjørn was out travelling, and there wasn't the usual crowd of young men to keep Finn company in front of the television while Denmark's team fought their way to glory. I didn't profess to having a clue about soccer, but seeing how dejected Finn looked the day of the first big match, I called our good friend, Sussi, and asked her assistance in creating the right spectator atmosphere. We could always count on Sussi, who is the epitome of everything Danish, to give an event its proper due.

After dinner, when Finn had gone upstairs to turn on the television, there were two short rings on the doorbell, and I knew she had arrived. When I opened the door, there she stood, all dolled up in the Danish red and white colors, with a ridiculous hat on her head, a spare assortment of silly hats for us, and a basket brimming over with bottles of beer, noisemakers, and a roll of toilet paper to throw across the imaginary field.

"You're a peach, Sussi!" (Actually, in Danish, one says "you're a prune," but never mind.) "That ought to make poor Finn happy, and I'm sure you and I can stand a couple of hours of watching soccer."

What we hadn't anticipated was how much fun we would have. It turned out to be the best soccer season Denmark had had in many a year, and we became avid home spectators for every match, thrilled by the acrobatic maneuvers of an imaginative team of brilliant players. We wore our hats, tooted our horns, stamped our feet, and cheered every advance. Finn was so pleased with us that he didn't even object when we occasionally let ourselves be sidetracked by motherly concern over whether or not the Danish centre should be back in the game so soon after that nasty French player butted heads with him.

I will admit, however, that we turned out to be fickle fans. Two seasons later, many of the players we had become personally involved with, so to speak, were off to other pastures, and we found it too exhausting to work up the same enthusiasm year after year. Finn is back on his own, but I think he will tell you that we three had a lot of fun while it lasted.

18

Crises

King Christian IV reigned from 1584–1648 and was called the "builder king." He can take credit for some of the most beautiful buildings in Copenhagen, and for having emptied the state's treasury. Despite the expenses incurred by his grand visions, however, he was personally a very frugal man, supervising in detail the inventory of his castles, and, like my husband, he didn't believe in heating rooms before the first of November. So at least one can say that not all his extravagances went up in smoke, but remained to give pleasure to future generations. Following the grandeur of his reign, Denmark was to endure a long period of hard times, and knowing about this and similar fluctuations can help one to put contemporary periods of prosperity and recession into perspective.

Times of deprivation usually call for greater ingenuity, and the effort entailed in being ingenious is gratifying, to the point that one forgets what it was that was lost. In a young country with lots of space, civilization's failures have room to move on, and I had grown up in America with a vague notion that the slate had been erased clean with each disaster. In a tiny country, like Denmark, recent history is physically superimposed upon ancient history, and the very presence of old buildings and streets are a tangible testimonial to the resilience of human beings. Periodically, we make a right mess of things, but the same people who saw the flood of change wash away the sandcastle help to build it up again, using the same basic building principles.

We Americans have often been accused of being materialists, but moving to Denmark caused me to question that label. On the contrary, the truth of the matter is that our respect for materials could stand on a very tiny place, whereas Danes have always had respect for material goods and preferred them to be of the finest quality so that they could last forever. At the end of the fifties, we Americans were already well into the throw-away trend. In California, at least, nothing was mended, and we were accustomed early on to a wealth of products which made our trash cans bulge by the end of the week.

The person who resisted this tendency came across as being reactionary. Having already then reached a stage where I questioned the wisdom of increasing the gross national product when it meant using up the national resources faster than they could be replaced, I was pleased to come to an orderly little country where people were able to get along with so much less. Purchases at the market were often wrapped in old newspaper, and everyone brought a tote bag to carry his groceries home. Many of the products that were old hat in America hadn't yet made their appearance here, and those that had, such as paper towels, were of such a poor quality and were so expensive that I gladly did without them. I settled into a simpler existence with a better conscience as to what resources I was burning up.

While I slumbered, Denmark woke up to what they refer to as the Happy Sixties, trying with a vengeance to catch up on the American way of life. The consequent problems with pollution and waste have hit them, too. The main difference is that with characteristic sensibility, today's Danes are more willing to comply with government attempts to curb such waste by means of taxes and other legislation.

Unfortunately, the sacrifices involved sound more depressing than they need do. Human memory is short, and for many people who have forgotten or never known the quality of life that used to prevail the current interest in curtailing the present rate of consumption seems like a step backwards to less prosperous times. The specter of a recession becomes a tangible nightmare when we try to imagine being deprived of consumer goods which we have led ourselves to believe are indispensable. It is interesting to see how differently people react to "hard times." The more we have, the more we seem to worry about losing something.

Our present-day sense of security is reinforced with items which were totally unknown to rather recent ancestors and will probably be of no interest to future generations. In cleaning out the cellar of our old house, we found that in the years following the war, Grandfather Julius had hoarded things which were considered totally useless by anyone in the sixties. But they were those items which his generation missed greatly during the war years, even though they were resourceful in finding substitutes.

At some time in life, most of us have wished so badly for something that we have prayed to a sort of Santa Claus god, promising that if only this wish is granted, we will never be unhappy again. If only we could capture that moment and live it the rest of our days, our lives would have so much less clutter.

It always seemed plausible that Cassandra was a woman. With her gut instinct for pending disaster and the fact that no one listened to her, I've found it easy to identify with her, tending to think that disaster is just around the corner. However, because Danish history is so alive, it is possible to keep things in proportion. The intertwined dragons that form the spire of the Copenhagen Stock Exchange have been guarding over that magnificent building since 1625. They are symbolic of the larger framework of the nation, wherein good times and bad times have produced individuals remarkably similar in their ability to get things moving.

In the forests we find large ant hills, some of them man-high. Poking around in them with a stick must be comparable to creating a series of violent earthquakes, and the poor ants frantically scramble to set things right as soon as they are disturbed. In that way, we can be expected to behave like the ants; however, I wonder if they have among their ranks individuals capable of worrying about the next disaster or remembering the last one. Two heavy burdens for the human race are premonitions and memory. It can be soothing to think that when disaster actually does appear on the scene, entirely unexpected elements take on importance, invalidating our premonitions and offering welcome distractions to the pain of memory. Feelings are intensified, but values are in flux.

A drink, like coffee, which is consumed at present in quantities that can be deleterious to the health, was so scarce during the war years that a single cup was an unforgettable experience. A friend of Finn's mother had such a longing for real coffee that she traded an entire rococo dining ensemble for a sack of roasted coffee beans. Rare is the person who will hold onto furnishings or jewels if he has to choose between them and food or warmth, and, as foolish as the coffee lover might seem, who is to know the degree of pleasure she must have gotten from that first brewed pot?

Hard times can force us to look at our desires from a fresh viewpoint. I'm not one for plunging into a cold sea, but if forced to do so, I know that the feeling afterwards is most invigorating. Learning about past hard times in a country whose history is so long serves as a guidebook, a reminder that better times are just around the corner, and what counts is putting on a good front while the times are lean.

One of the best examples of such fortitude was Leonora Christina, a favorite daughter of Christian IV. The king was a devoted father to a wealth of offspring, both those born to Queen Anna Katrine, who died fifteen years after their marriage, and those who were the fruit of two love affairs and a long-standing marriage of sorts with Kirsten Munch. (The children who weren't of royal blood from both sides enjoyed a certain status nonetheless and were given the poetic name, Gyldenløv, which means golden lion.) Leonora was a daughter to non-royal Kirsten Munch, but she grew up in Rosenborg castle and was treated like a real princess.

She became the jewel of the court, gifted and charming, influential and rich, recognized even in the sophisticated court of the young Louis XIV in France as a beauty with great wit. Unfortunately, she was very ambitious, and there seemed to be no end to the amount of wealth she and her Swedish husband, Corfitz Ulfeldt, wanted to amass. As the aged king's health waned, they scandalized the court with their profligacy and schemes, clearly indicating that even the king didn't have all their loyalty.

When King Christian died, he was succeeded by his son, Frederik II, whose young queen, Sophie Amalie, harbored an intense hatred for Leonora Christina. Unwisely, Corfitz Ulfeldt and Leonora continued with their intrigues, flouting the power of the new king and openly plotting against him through an alliance with Swedish forces. The very stormy culmination of their ill deeds was when Corfitz died ignominiously, fleeing from the king's men, while Leonora Christina, who had traveled to England to collect a debt from Charles II, was tricked into Danish captivity on board a ship set for Copenhagen.

Sophie Amalie at last had the opportunity to revenge herself on the woman who had caused her to seethe with envy. (Mind you, the brilliant Leonora had made no bones about making the queen's ego suffer, for they were diametrically opposed personalities.) During a humiliating frisking, Leonora was stripped of all her finery, even her underwear, and furnished with a coarse, linen garment. She was then imprisoned in the Blue Tower, in the courtyard of the royal castle, where Sophie Amalie could receive daily reports of her rival's sufferings. Her cell was rudely furnished with a small table, with one brass candlestick holder furnished with a single candle, a high-backed chair, two smaller chairs, a pine bed, with coarse bedding, and a chamber pot. The men who had been imprisoned there the day she arrived had been moved hastily to another place, and the cell still stank of their wastes. It was cold, dark, and infested with fleas and rats. To add to this misery, the queen had ordered that Leonora should have constant company of one or two other women who were either criminal or insane. She was furthermore denied any means of diverting her attention from these surroundings — no needle or thread, no pen or paper.

Leonora was held prisoner for twenty-two years. She was finally granted certain favors and was allowed to read, write and sew, but before that she had to use her imagination to make her own tools. The pen she wrote with was made from a wing feather from a hen, sharpened with a tool she fashioned from a flint stone, and the ink was a mixture of soot and beer. The reason we know so much about her ordeal is that in 1674 she wrote a remarkable account, entitled "Jammer's Minde" (In Remembrance of Misery).

While one can offer a great deal of speculation trying to understand the psychology of a person who seemed to be incapable of seeing the justice in the fate that struck her, there is no denying the quality behind this impressive document. The mental process by which Leonora reached the conclusion that by inflicting such trials on her, God had singled her out — in order to give her a unique opportunity to gain wisdom — bears witness not only to an amazing strength of character, but also a keen intellect.

When she was finally released, at the age of sixty-four, she had gained the respect of everyone younger than she was and had outlived most of her virulent enemies. She had turned her defeat to triumph, and by choosing to spend the rest of her days in a nunnery, she demonstrated that her transformation was genuine and her worldly ambitions truly were no longer of importance. The details of her fascinating autobiography leave no doubt, however, that her spiritual development had been achieved the hard way.

Other lucky souls are blessed from the start with this indifference to material wealth and status. I think I've run across them more often in Denmark than elsewhere, simply because of the fact that in such a small country, a man can more easily be judged by so many other merits than his material assets, and, if lacking in merit, no amount of wealth will protect him from the scorn of fellow Danes. Such a free spirit was "Uncle" Valdemar, whom I met soon after coming to Denmark.

It was a cold day in February, and Tante Kirsten had literally just blown in, her cheeks aglow and her lovely blue eyes sparkling as she pushed the front door shut against the freezing wind. She was all wrapped in soft furs, and was bubbling over with the sort of good spirits that Mums had liked about her since they were schoolgirls together. Just the sight of her gave the day a festive touch, and we had soon made a pot of tea and lit candles on the tea trolley in the verandah. I loved to hear them talk about old times, Mums in her lilting Norwegian, and Tante Kirsten in low-pitched tones that were ever so upper class.

With the fun of spilling a bit of gossip, Mums suddenly said, "Guess what! Valdemar Lier has invited Judy and me to lunch next week. He wants to introduce us to his American girlfriend!" Uncle Valdemar, I have to tell you, was at that time past ninety, and his girlfriend was a woman who had spent more than forty years in the states and had come home in order to make ends meet with an American Social Security check.

Kirsten chuckled when Valdemar was mentioned, and she turned to me to tell about a dinner party he had attended in Finn's parents' home. It was a black-tie affair, and Mums as usual had made a great fuss about the menu. She had chosen a light vegetable soup for the first course, in order to show off her gold-rimmed bouillon cups and saucers, and at the end of the evening, when the guests were leaving, most of them complimented her on this, along with the rest of the menu — except for Uncle Valdemar. He reached into the pocket of his dinner jacket, and, as he shook hands with Mums, he filled her palm with all the celery bits that had been in his soup. "You know I don't like celery, Lily, but I hate to see it go to waste," was his only comment.

When Finn came home, I was pleased to tell him that I was going to have the opportunity to meet one of the neighborhood characters, and of course Finn had his share of stories to add. Valdemar had a university degree in engineering, and he had a flair for inventing. One of his inventions was the Lier lamp, and word has it that he also developed the first vending machine, but before he had a proper patent his plans were stolen in Paris.

Most of his inventions were more fun than functional, such as a sand machine he had allowed Finn to play with when he was a small boy. Sand, poured into a funnel, set off a series of movements among figures he had cut out of plywood. Not being adept at drawing, he furnished their features with incongruous pictures cut out of the tabloids, creating a plaything that would probably be admired in a museum for modern art in our day and age.

Despite the fact that he had no claim to official recognition, no one doubted his being clever, and the neighborhood's belief in him was merely strengthened by the fact that he had shown no interest in pursuing success by ordinary channels. Indeed, he had only worked once in his life. Following his studies, he had been given a job in a well-established engineering firm, but when the director found Valdemar's work to be very satisfactory, he made the mistake of offering him a raise. Valdemar, squared his shoulders, threw back his chin, and said, in a voice that trembled with indignation, "If you thought I was working for money, I refuse to stay!" And he quit. In little Denmark, one grand gesture of such a magnitude can easily make more conventional achievements seem insignificant.

He lived next door to Finn's parents, sharing a villa with his only daughter and her husband — who was a bit of a thorn in the side of such a conservative community, for he was a true-blue communist. Valdemar had been married three times and had had two silver wedding anniversaries. When his first wife died, he married her younger sister, whom he also outlived, thereby marrying the third and youngest sister. One does get the impression that his idea of a wife was more like a housekeeper, for when his third wife died, he was satisfied with the services of his daughter.

This poor, patient offspring had the sweet temperament necessary to cope with living with a very eccentric father who liked nothing better than teasing her dreadfully serious husband. The husband, despite his political leanings, was set upon inheriting the house they all three lived in. Unfortunately for him, Valdemar showed no signs of ever slowing down, much less dying.

Like many Danish leftists, the husband was a vegetarian, and Valdemar's daughter had made a variety of vegetable dishes for our lunch. As sometimes was the case in old-fashioned households, the seepage of gas from the rubber hoses that connected the gas burners in the kitchen had flavored the food, something to which old Uncle Valdemar seemed oblivious, and he ate with great appetite. The girlfriend from America was a nondescript, rather meek lady, who had never learned English adequately and seemed to have forgotten most of her Danish. On the Q.T., Uncle Valdemar confided in me that he wasn't too keen on her, because she insisted on pulling the blinds when he wanted to kiss her. However, as he put it, he didn't know how to break the relationship off, because he was fond of her parents.

He was a dapper old codger, quick in his movements, his large moustache in constant motion on a very animated face. He took me by the arm and, while patting my hand, told me he had something he wanted to show me in his bedroom. I thought it would seem silly to refuse to follow a man who was more than ninety into his room, but my mind was racing with ideas for gracefully declining any kinky whims he might have.

The room we entered was very large, with a waxed parquet floor, and the only thing in it was a wooden bicycle, leaning against the far wall. He proudly told me that this was one of his latest inventions, and with the energy of a natural born show-off, the old guy mounted it and started pedaling around the room at full speed, casting glances in my direction to check my reaction. I had been warned that he was potty, but I didn't know what sort of expression I should paste on my face. Figuring that age doesn't affect the male ego, I opted for bald admiration and hoped that he had included brakes on this contraption. When the demonstration was through, I was a nervous wreck, having expected him to break every bone in his body if he crashed. He, on the other hand, was so obviously exhilarated by his successful demonstration that when we rejoined the others I wondered whether I needed to offer an explanation of what we had been doing in the other room.

It wasn't too long after that when Finn and I encountered him one fine spring evening, seated on a sofa that he had converted to a gondola of sorts and put on wheels. He was poleing it down the middle of the street, and when he lifted his hat to greet us, he had that same look of satisfaction he had displayed after his bike ride.

Several years passed, and his daughter and son-in-law seemed to age more than Valdemar. He was well aware of their waning hopes to have the house to themselves, for his being a pain in the neck was usually calculated. Grasping a last chance to tease his heirs, he took up with a very attractive, younger woman, someone in her seventies. (The American girlfriend had disappeared from the scene soon after that memorable lunch party.) With a fiendish twinkle in his eye, he talked about marriage, knowing that such a move would tie the house up even longer. Luckily for his long-suffering daughter, the woman he met wasn't interested in his property, and Valdemar finally died without any last-minute pranks.

The last year he lived, Finn and I ran into him in the woods near his home. It was late, a spooky night in November. The wind was whistling through the trees, and black clouds scudded across a stormy sky, casting dark shadows when they passed the moon. Ahead of us, on the narrow, winding path, we saw a stooped figure with a cane, making his way slowly over the uneven terrain. As we caught up with him, the moon was unveiled, and, in its light, we recognized Uncle Valdemar. He had aged, but when Finn addressed him, asking him whether he wasn't afraid, being alone on such a dark and stormy night, his face lit up in the same youthful and mischievous manner. "Hell, yes!" he said. "I'm afraid someone might see an old geezer like me out in the woods and be scared to death!"

Uncle Valdemar was just one of the many people who gave flavor to my first years in Denmark. Were people more individualistic, or did we just have more time to notice one another? Or do we unwittingly become characters ourselves, to be amusing to younger generations whom we find blandly beautiful?

19

Conversations

had used the heavy linen tablecloth with the century-old Russian lace that Mums' father had brought home to Norway in the days of the czar. The table was set with the gold-rimmed plates with hunting scenes and with tall crystal glasses. The linen napkins were folded like fleur-de-lis, and I was trying to pull a creamy cluster of freesia out of the centerpiece to move it higher up in the arrangement when the phone rang. Trying not to drip water from the stem, I lifted the blossom gingerly over the tablecloth and went to the phone.

It was Finn. I absentmindedly answered some question he had about the seating arrangement, while my mind raced over things still to be done. All morning long I had been rushing around, putting rooms in order, keeping an eye on the bread rising on the counter and pots simmering on the back of the stove, and each time the phone jingled I was pulled off the track. Most of the calls had come from Finn, and I could picture him in his office, picturing me at home, longing to be here to arrange logs in the fireplaces and putter around with drink glasses and dance tapes.

Putting down the receiver, I headed for the cellar, to dust the rumpus room where we would be dancing later in the evening. After that, I went into the furnace room to bring up plum blossoms that I had been nurturing into an early bloom to be arranged with crisp bunches of tulips. As soon as I had both hands full of branches, the impatient jangle of the phone again interrupted. I rushed up the stairs, slipped as I hurried over the freshly waxed floors, and landed in a disheveled heap on the chair beside the phone. It was Finn again, just to ask me how things were going.

Trying not to sound cross, I carefully asked him if it was a particularly slow day at the office. "Slow? Hell yes! I'm bored out of my mind."

"Well, isn't there something you can do in there when you're bored?"

"Yeah. I call you." This being by now quite obvious, I chuckled and said, "I know that, but what do you do when you are *really* bored?"

"I hang up," said Finn. And he did.

ೞ   ೞ

If that conversation sounds silly, imagine the one a week later. Finn called from the office and told me that he was bringing a man home who was the foreman for the organization for sharpshooters. He just wanted to prepare me for the fact that this poor fellow had one disability common to people who shoot guns — he was extremely hard of hearing. "You'll have to really talk loudly if you want him to catch what you're saying. He's too vain to wear a hearing aid."

They arrived late in the afternoon, and while Niels and I became acquainted, Finn busied himself with pouring drinks.

I shouted that I understood he was quite a good shot with a pistol, and I wasn't surprised when he shouted back. I've often noticed that people who are nearly deaf tend to talk loudly themselves. At the top of our lungs we discovered a common interest in gardening, and although I found the conversation a bit exhausting, I thought he was very nice. What a pity it was that he was so handicapped by his deafness.

I don't remember how long he and I carried on like this, before we discovered that Finn was doubled over with suppressed laughter. It turned out that he had given Niels the same line, telling him that I was very hard of hearing and that he would have to shout, and we might never have learned the truth, hadn't Finn lost control.

I'll borrow a statement made by a lovely lady who recently had her golden wedding anniversary. An old school chum expressed surprise and asked her how ever she had managed to put up with her husband all those years. "That's easy. We're both in love with the same man."

20

Quieter Times

Looking back, there seems to have been an abundance of details frozen in a life busy with predictable steps, like a minuet. Strict state laws regulated the hours during which shops could be open, and the resulting stillness of Saturday afternoons and entire Sundays furnished a backdrop for a lifestyle that unfolded with the memorable characteristics of those more controlled times. We took long walks together and gathered with the rest of the family at least once a week. On such occasions, the women often busied themselves with needlework while we drank tea and indulged in friendly discussions which were limited, preferably, to topics which could be settled by checking the many reference books found in a surprising amount of homes.

To buy tea, we liked to visit Perk's Tea Shop, which still exists, although the nice old gentleman Mums introduced me to is long gone. He was one of the Perk brothers, and he appeared ancient to my young eyes. I felt like I had stepped into another era when we opened the door to this deliciously fragrant shop with every imaginable tea on stock, and Mr. Perk was perfect for the setting. He was briskly cheerful, his bald head held erect by the stiff removable collar he wore. He spoke English with me, and though his English was flawless, he occasionally lacked a word, whereupon he impatiently tapped his shiny pate with his pencil, a process which always produced an immediate result and a pleased smile.

At least this shop has resisted the changes of time. A wonderfully preserved lady who had been with them for many years was interviewed for a newspaper article about the quality of tea. When asked to compare various brews, she proved to be very knowledgeable and opinionated, but her patience didn't extend to the phenomena of teabags. Her judgment of Twinings teabag version of a Darjeeling blend was one of frosty disgust. She claimed it tasted like paper and disdained to make allowances when the interviewer pointed out to her that she should have removed the bag from its packet before contemptuously dropping it into the pot.

Copenhagen abounded with shops that had been established for many years, and the clerks in these shops prided themselves on knowing their customers. Mums made it her duty to take me to those places she considered most important and give me a proper introduction. One of the first places on the list was the silversmith's.

The shop no longer exists, but I still can picture the dark interior with its quiet air and lustrous stock and recall a winter day when Finn and I stopped by with our firstborn to show her off. Lani was a pretty picture dressed in pale yellow, her cheeks pink from the cold air, and all business was forgotten as the sweet, elderly ladies who were always there to serve a shrinking public dropped their dignified decor to fuss over her and called the shy silversmith from the back of the shop to come out and admire her, too.

It was typical of those trusting times that when I visited the silversmith's to choose a pattern, I was told to take several home and show them to Finn, and no receipt was required.

The selection of ready-made wear was sparse in those days, compared to that of American stores, but there still were exclusive shops where one could have things tailored to one's taste and size. However, with a lack of awareness which I consider rather alarming in retrospect, I dismissed the clothing scene as being hopeless and decided to cope in my own way.

Not being versed in the articles of apparel available for living in a cold climate, I improvised and found my pink flannel pajama bottoms the very ticket for keeping warm when wearing skirts. They were just like old-fashioned bloomers, with a rather dashing flounce at the bottom of each leg. Until the elastic began to get slack, I could keep them in place above my knees, discreetly hitching them up whenever they began to slip. It was only when I once forgot myself and crossed my legs that the puzzled look on the gentleman sitting across from me convinced me that they really wouldn't do.

Not being able to find anything in my size, I decided to sew my own clothes and chose a grand ball to create my first gown. Danes in those days seemed to be baffled by this American tendency towards improvisation. In a land where everyone took pride in only doing things expertly, I found myself the odd one out when I blindly plunged into some new arena; however, I didn't let myself get the least discouraged by polite questions from Mums and Brit as to whether or not I knew how to sew. Instead, I blithely set out to buy some fabric and a pattern.

That the pattern was printed in Swedish was only a momentary setback; the diagrams would help. Neither did I falter when the clerk pointed out to me that I was browsing in the curtain fabric department rather than the dress fabrics. The only clear part of my plan was which color to choose. At least Finn was supportive, as always. He found an old sewing machine for me in the loft.

Somehow a ball gown actually did take shape, and I felt quite pleased with the result. The family breathed a sigh of relief when they saw it, but I think they took it as beginner's luck. They had to endure many other examples of my bizarre faith in myself, such as when the same dress was used to upholster a chair. Basically, however, they preferred to place their faith in the wealth of experts that Denmark could boast of. Do-it-yourself was a much more recent phenomena here, appearing on the scene when the tax system made it too expensive to hire skilled workers to do all the things we like to have done to our homes.

In that respect, Gutte was a link between the older generation and ours. "Need teaches naked ladies to spin cloth," and she could whip up a couturière dress effortlessly. Her inspirations came too quickly to be achieved through the ordinary channels, her creative drives leading her into every imaginable endeavor — sewing, painting, decorating with wallpaper, and creating cunning small figures to use as Christmas decorations. She was a housewife with all the virtues valued in those times: She kept a tidy house, made delicious food, was a whiz at tending potted plants, and could set a magnificent table with whatever means at hand. In short, she furnished the home with an atmosphere of caring.

No detail was too unimportant to be neglected when she planned a dinner party, and her enthusiasm carried her to such extremes that she had to admit to once selling heirloom silver to buy crepe paper and flowers in red, white and blue to celebrate Montgomery's liberation of Denmark from the Germans.

She and her husband, Kjeld, lived just three houses down the street from us, in the house that had been his childhood home. Kjeld was younger than Paps, but he had attended the same school and remembered evenings in Julius's and Emma's home, when his parents joined them to play chamber music and drink rum toddies so potent that the smell of rum saturated the heavy drapes for days afterwards.

He vas one of the kindest men I've ever known and a most welcome addition to any gathering, always ready with a humorous remark, with never a thoughtless word to anyone. Gutte was ten years younger and bubbling over with fun, and their home was a magnet for an endless stream of good friends.

An American living abroad will miss the practice, so common in the states, of neighbors just dropping in on one another. Gutte was the rare exception who made me feel welcome any time of the night or day, and I turned to her often for a bit of expert advice or a comforting word. One reason that most Danes are not that hospitable to the unexpected visitor is that they all feel obliged to serve some refreshment to whoever crosses their doorstep. But Gutte loved to make a cup of tea or coffee and always had ready a home-baked sweet or a glass of sherry, despite the fact that her generosity had forced Kjeld to parcel out her house-holding money by the week rather than monthly.

Our acquaintance with Gutte and Kjeld was triggered off by their son, Stephan, one night when he and a group of neighborhood youngsters were out ringing doorbells and bolting. We decided it would be fun to catch them, make them think they would be in for a bollocking and then treat them to cookies and soft drinks.

Once we became friends with Kjeld and Gutte, it was more fun to play pranks on them and wait with anticipation for their revenge. One of the many opportunities for this pleasant diversion presented itself when Yuri Kapralov, a Russian artist friend of ours from New York, came to visit one summer, and we were invited to bring him over for a cup of afternoon tea served in the shelter of their overgrown hedge.

Yuri had arrived sporting a floppy hat which concealed his bald head. He had a thick, black beard, and wore appropriately artistic smock-like shirts with a peculiar piece of jewelry hanging around his neck. When Kjeld and Gutte had exhausted their stock English phrases about the weather and his being welcome, they asked Finn, in Danish, whether the medallion our friend was wearing had any special significance. Without cracking a smile, Finn discreetly informed them that a medallion of that sort was the American equivalent to the yellow armband with black spots that is worn in Europe by handicapped persons. Yuri spent the afternoon basking in their sympathetic concern, and they politely refrained from asking what his particular handicap was. Taking pity on them, I set the record straight just as we were leaving.

Such a trick had to be repaid, and a few days later, we opened the door to a total stranger who wanted to buy eggs. Since we seemed to be surprised, he pointed to a sign in our driveway, advertising fresh country eggs for sale, and asked why we had put that up if we didn't intend to sell any.

One of Finn's more elaborate inspirations took place one dark, December evening, when Stephan came over to let us hear his new record. Just as he was leaving, Finn told him we had planned a surprise for his father's birthday the next morning. "We've noticed that your parents' rose-bed isn't looking too hot, and we have some special organic material that will do wonders for the rose bushes if you spread it out now and let it stand over the winter. What I'm going to ask you to do is to take it home tonight, empty it out among the roses, and watch how happy your dad will be when he sees the garden in the morning!"

Poor unsuspecting Stephan bought this hook, line, and sinker, knowing that his parents' garden left much to be desired. They preferred relaxing in it, rather than worrying about what was growing there. He lugged home a very large bag of dead leaves that we had raked together, and dutifully dumped them all out in Kjeld's carefully raked rose bed. It was too dark to see what it really was, but he did a fine job of spreading the leaves in among all the bushes.

His good-natured father was touched by the amount of planning that had paved the way for such a splendid trick, but he immediately began to devise the counterattack. Finn was flattered when they asked him for help in making rice wine, and he not only gave them his recipe, but spent a good deal of time checking to make sure that they followed his instructions carefully.

The big day arrived when the concoction was to be tapped off the original bottle with all its sediment, into a clean wine flask, where it was to age. It was a rather worried Kjeld who called to ask Finn if he would mind very much coming over to taste the wine and tell them whether there might be something wrong with it. Finn hurried over and found Kjeld, Gutte and Stephan in an uncharacteristically solemn mood. This home brew might have been meant as a money-saving experiment, but the ingredients made it a rather expensive one if it should fail. Four glasses were placed on the table, and a pitcher of the new wine was standing ready for tasting. They all three watched intently as Finn carefully sipped the wine, and nodded in agreement when they saw the horrified look on his face. It was all he could do to refrain from spitting it out on the carpet.

Finn was devastated; it tasted just like vinegar. Breaking out in a sweat, he tried to go over the process they had used, hoping that the mistake had been in something they had done and not in his instructions. They insisted that he shouldn't feel too badly. It was, after all, only money, and of course a lot of work.

After leaving him to squirm an adequate length of time, they brought out a pitcher of the real stuff, admitting that what they had given him to taste really was vinegar.

CrossCross

Not only did we have many happy hours with various neighbors, we could always rely on Købmand Christensen for entertainment. *Købmand* is the Danish term for the merchant who deals in groceries, and Købmand Christensen ran what could best be described as a general store, located in a small villa a few blocks away. It was just the right distance for a walk with the children, before they were old enough to start school and a walk was one of the highlights of the day.

There was only one door to enter the small room that was furnished with a wooden counter and stacks all the way to the ceiling of every possible canned good. There were bins of apples and other fruits of the season. One could buy potatoes, onions, and carrots, tins of meat or fish, coffee, tea and soap powder, everything needed for scraping through the week. However, Købmand Christensen's pride and joy and real interest lay in the multitude of exotic goods that he liked to keep on stock, such as palm hearts from Brazil or squid from Asia.

To compete with the supermarkets that were beginning to appear on the scene, he called his tiny niche a mini-market, and he sent out periodic letters, advertising tempting delicacies and special offers, with well-worded suggestions as to how to prepare them or how to brighten one's day in general. One letter, in particular, was priceless: Keeping in mind the Danish penchant for holidays of all sorts, he proposed a national holiday to commemorate sewing on buttons. His plan was that all stores and businesses were to be closed on the appointed day, devoting it to sewing buttons on all the clothes which were undoubtedly in need of such an operation. Naturally, a national holiday would require a celebration in the evening, and eventually, the eve prior to said holiday would also be celebrated and could be called Little Button-Sewing-On Eve. This imaginative suggestion was followed up by a recommended menu which relied, of course, on the large variety of goods available at Købmand Christensen's.

Long philosophic discourses took place in the pleasantly cramped space of his dark, little shop, where the smells of household goods had the soothing effect produced by familiar sensations. We were a fiercely loyal group of customers, and Christensen, in turn, defended in no meek terms our right to the time we needed to restore our souls while stocking our shelves, telling hurried customers to bug off if they tried to interrupt our discourses. The misguided person who was impatient for his turn soon learned not to stop by — or if he did, to stay calm.

I liked to go there in the early part of the day, with Lani and Bjørn skipping ahead of me on the sidewalk. On warm summer days, they often ran in and out of the open door of the shop, chasing white butterflies attracted to a lavender bush or exploring the small garden. On winter days, they could amuse themselves by looking at the collection of old prints with which he had papered the ceiling. While they were contentedly distracted, I could have long conversations with Købmand Christensen, learning about bygone times from his childhood in Copenhagen or other fascinating periods in history. His interests were catholic, and he could recommend good reading material about everything from growing tobacco to Egyptian archaeology.

As with most experiences, certain quaint bits of information stand out in my memory, like bright pins dropped on a patterned carpet. One was an account of a recurrent dream Christensen had wherein he was taken back in time to what could have been the 1600s. In the dream, he was a young man carrying a heavy sack of grain on his back and walking up a ramp into a storeroom, the interior of which lay in darkness. Just as he bent to enter the low doorway, he received a blow on the head and was killed. After having experienced this dream vividly more than once, he visited an open-air museum in Jutland where he found himself looking at the very same setting, and it was a købmand's place from ancient times.

Such a good story was a marvelous diversion on a bright spring day, giving me something other than household duties to contemplate while walking home.

A new owner of the house where the store was located decided to raise the rent, and Købmand Christensen and his very attractive wife decided to close up shop. The large, motley group that consisted of his most loyal customers gathered on the evening of the last day of business, and with torches in hand, we gave them a proper sendoff. For us, it was the end of an epoch, rather than just a change of shopping habits. I squirreled away his best newsletters in old, leather-bound classics, with a thought to future generations who will find them and wonder at bygone business practices.

The local supermarket suited the changed lifestyle that was making its appearance. It replaced an array of small shops on an old street — six bakers, five butchers, two fish stores, two dairy shops, a cheese store, and four greengrocers, plus two grocery stores much like Købmand Christensen's. In each of these small shops, there had been owners who knew their clientele, and daily shopping was an important event in the early years of most children and a wide-open door for me to enter the Danish way of life. These small shopkeepers had patiently allowed me to practice my Danish, politely refraining from creasing up when I asked for things they had never before heard called such ridiculous names. Unless Finn happened to be along and overheard my rather eccentric vocabulary, I could get by for years with the most outrageous substitute names for things. (In Copenhagen, clerks were less kindly disposed, and I was given a rather curt reply, when I once shopped in a toy store. Not knowing the word for "toxic," I asked whether the modeling clay I wanted to buy for the children was edible. Looking me over as if she found me quite mad, the young lady who was helping me said, "It might very well be, but here in Denmark we prefer not to eat it.")

When I lamented the loss of these quaint shops, Paps shook his head and said, "Oh Judy, think of the changes I've seen!" And he told me of his young days, when the train conductor used to hold back the morning train to Copenhagen if Julius hadn't yet arrived at the station.

It was more fun to complain to Lauersen, our wine dealer, because he could readily share our views and join us in bemoaning more recent changes. Through the keg-shaped doorway of his shop, we could find the same friendly atmosphere as we had at Christensen's, but with a more expensive stock. There, too, we could count on a warm reception, and a sample of some select bottle of wine.

Mille was another of his regulars. She was a classically beautiful woman, even when she was in her seventies, with a nonchalant elegance that set her apart. She was quick to catch on to Finn's sense of humor and loved to join in on a chance to have some fun when an unsuspecting victim happened into their charmed circle. One day, this happened to be a very serious young man who was clutching a long shopping list and was clearly the timid sort who agonizes over every purchase.

When Mille and Finn stepped aside, with filled port wine glasses in hand, and let him come forth to the counter with his order, Mille recognized him as the fellow whose wife had been in the day before to cash in an empty snaps bottle and get the crown piece that is the deposit.

He now stood carefully reviewing his list, his eyebrows knitted together in concentration, and Mille took advantage of the delay. With a wink to Lauersen, she reached down into her basket, took up an empty snaps bottle, and said, "Excuse me, Lauersen, I keep forgetting this. Could you give me the five-crown deposit?"

The tense young man looked up, startled, and said, "My wife says that there is only one crown in deposit money!" It was written all over his worried face that he was counting up all the crowns he had imagined them to have lost out on over the years.

"And how long has this been going on, may I ask?" said Mille indignantly.

As soon as he was out of the shop, Finn, Mille, and Lauersen laughed until they cried, but Lauersen finally sniffed and said, "It's fine for you two, but I'm the one who has to face his wife when she comes in tomorrow to demand to know why some customers get five crowns, and she only gets one."

Quieter times they were, but there seemed to be a cheerful sound of a gurgling brook running through our lives. It's still there. Only the noises of a more dynamic society drown it out.

21

Milestones

Marriage is like a tapestry. You start by mounting a very large cloth on a frame and then comes the monumental task of filling in the design. Certain modern works are handsome abstract designs, soothing in their well-integrated colors, but a bit boring in their execution. I prefer the old style — vivid colors and a multitude of scenes, everything from battles to births and banquets.

While working on a tapestry, one directs one's thoughts to the thread in hand, be it silk, gold or coarse linen. Hours pass by in a pleasant concentration on some minute part of the work, but the reward comes when one steps back every now and then and views the progress of the design as a whole. In large modern designs, I suppose there is a satisfaction in seeing the entire tapestry completed, but in the more traditional types, there is a feeling of accomplishment with the completion of each integral part.

With the freedom offered by a society such as ours, one isn't usually allowed the relatively easy task of filling out a pattern dictated by tradition, and for many people it must be far easier to make a lot of small tapestries, keeping each one tidy, rather than taking the risk of committing oneself to a big project, with no promise of its becoming a work of art.

While the Denmark I've loved seems to be ebbing out on the tides of change, the bold strokes for the design of my tapestry were established in advance. Like milestones, they crop up in most lives in this part of the world, and they become touchstones for contemplating the passage of all other events. It is very Danish, to mark these occasions with a celebration, and although that entails a great deal of work, one is able to look back at a scene that seems larger by the presence of so many sharp details.

The first twelve years of marriage prepare one for the obligations that come in the next twelve years, and a big party is planned to celebrate the copper wedding anniversary, the twelve-and-a-half-year juncture when dancing is still on the program, and no one goes home early. After that, it seemed to be one long series of unforgettable festivities: Confirmation parties for the children, when they each reached the age of fourteen; roaring celebrations for fortieth birthdays (to prove that we really still felt like roaring); graduation parties, as the youngsters advanced in school; interspersed with formal dinner parties to celebrate "round" birthdays of those who are dear to us; the golden wedding anniversary of Finn's parents; their eightieth birthdays; and finally, the party of all parties, our daughter's wedding.

The feelings one has about a daughter's marriage must be much the same all over the world. One is overjoyed at seeing her so happy, and one tries hard not to think about how dreadful it will be when she leaves home. The only way to get through the months that follow the announcement of an engagement is to plunge into preparations for the wedding, and, in our case this was to be very therapeutic, because we had to make up in work what we lacked in money.

Daughters have a way of turning one's quiet life upside down at the most unexpected times. Having never had a moment's displeasure with Lani, we were defenseless when she suddenly took charge of her own life in a way that revealed far more imagination than we had suspected lurked under a very reliable surface. None of us was surprised when she graduated from college at the top of her class, but having done that so well, she felt she had paid her dues and wanted to start living. This involved not only plans for her future, but seemed to entail redecorating the house and revamping her parents. While we were trying to catch our breath between some of her projects, we all went to England to attend a couple of grand parties thrown by our friends, Gil and Joanne.

Lani had such a good time that she decided to toss aside her studies at the university and stay in London to work. Because she had been a paragon of virtue all her young life, there was absolutely no reason in the world to argue with her about such a whim, and we travelled back home thinking that a little fling was well-deserved.

By Christmas she was in love, and by February she was engaged and took a flying trip home with her fiancé, so we could throw a party to celebrate their engagement. It was at this point that her father went into a state of shock, and the rest of the world doesn't know it, but he hasn't totally recovered yet. Preparations for a black-tie dinner took my mind off the sadness of contemplating the fact that our only daughter would be married and living in England, and it was a grand party. Peter, the future groom, was immediately popular with all our friends and with our small family, and Lani was radiant with happiness. They came home Friday evening, and in the fog of the morning after the night before, we used Saturday and Sunday to plan the wedding which was to take place in August.

Now came Finn's second shock. His idea of a wedding was an affair for the immediate family, where the number of guests was determined by the amount of place settings that could be done up with our best china and our own silver, with a dignified amount of elbow room in our own dining room. True to his unique, but archaic, romantic notions, he confessed to certain ideas which sounded more like an occasion to measure a father's worth than to merely celebrate a marriage. We could accommodate thirty in our dining room, but that number would be exceeded if just the English contingent came over, and our family was so small that we would have to invite some of our liveliest friends in order to hold our own at all.

Even so, I didn't need to protest; our equally strong-minded daughter had already made plans. It was decided that a marquee was to be pitched on the front lawn and that the very shortest guest list would include fifty people. In a one-day whirl of activity, Lani made arrangements with the vicar, wrote a guest list, and chose the fabric for her wedding gown, with vague instructions as to how she would like it to take form. When we put the happy couple on a flight back to London Sunday evening, we shook our heads in dazed confusion. It seemed we had been given leading roles in an action film. Lani would be coming home in June, and the wedding was to take place at the end of August. All I could do very much in advance was to sew my own dress and make long lists of things to do later.

That spring and summer we watched Mums slip away from us, and everything else that happened was a welcome distraction to the sadness of losing her. From a hospital bed she struggled bravely, trying to recover enough to take part in the wedding. During my daily visits, she followed each event, and, with her love for festivities, she felt increasingly frustrated over missing out. She had a zest for life that could hardly be matched by many a younger person.

Bjørn's graduation, in May, was the usual rousing scene that has unfolded in Denmark for more than a century. Those who pass the exams in *gymnasium* have achieved a level of education similar to a bachelor of arts and qualify to call themselves "student," being eligible to enter the university. They receive a smart white cap with black bill and a wine-red sweatband, an official mark of recognition introduced in 1856, which gives them entry to an uninterrupted round of festivities. It starts with a boisterous day spent in a horse-drawn wagon, going from house to house to be congratulated by the students' parents, after first having made the trip into Copenhagen to dance around the statue in the King's New Square.

One of the many jubilant signs of a Danish summer is to hear singing, accompanied by the patient plodding of horse hooves, and to catch sight of a festive wagon full of white-clad students with their jaunty caps and high spirits. At a time of year when the sun barely bothers to set, they put notches in the brim of their caps for each night that they come home after sunrise, in what could be mistaken as an attempt to blast all their recently acquired knowledge out of their poor, tired heads. The first few days after graduation, they conspicuously fill the streets of Copenhagen and are met with good will wherever they go.

What Bjørn might have lacked in grades he made up for in popularity, and the weeks when he wore his hat went by in a blur. The young people he knew seemed to form a network so thickly woven that we didn't worry about him, knowing that he and an unlimited amount of friends looked out for each other. By the time the notches on his hat were nearly all around the rim, I was sufficiently blasé to stop keeping track of the comings and goings of these charmed creatures. Bjørn was going out with four of his chums, and I absentmindedly said, "That's nice dear," and reminded him to take his keys.

When I came downstairs in the morning I noticed a room key to the Hotel Plaza lying alongside of Bjørn's keys on the hallway table; his shoes were at the bottom of the stairs so I knew he had tip-toed up to his room, but I began to wonder what he had been doing all the rest of that previous night.

While he slept on, the phone calls started coming in, from amused friends whose daughters had come home with funny accounts of Bjørn's painting the old town red. One flock of girls had spotted him astride an equestrian statue of Bishop Absalom in the heart of Copenhagen, dressed in his pajamas and robe, with his student cap firmly anchored on his head. From this excellent vantage point, he

could communicate with the seemingly unlimited amount of young people he knew in the city that evening. When laughingly asked what in the world he was doing up there dressed like he was, he grinned from ear to ear and replied, "My mom said that if I would put on my pajamas, I could stay up as late as I want!" (I had to confess that I did use this line of reasoning, but that had been when he was four years old — which proves that he had learned something when he was little.)

With that story and a good many more about a very eventful night, including a hilarious episode at the Plaza Hotel, I could count myself lucky that Copenhagen was such a safe place. (Safe, that is except for intoxicated Swedes whom Danes love to chuck into the canals.) George Bernard Shaw's statement that youth is wasted on young people has certainly never applied to Bjørn.

When Lani arrived home from England, all distractions were put aside and work began. With a touching faith in my abilities, she had chosen a very difficult pattern for the bridesmaids' dresses. For days I struggled with miles of pink taffeta, until the finished results could be hung aside, waiting for a final fitting when the bridesmaids could come. For her dress, she had selected a rich duchesse satin; a single stitch out of place would ruin the flow of fabric, making the gown look like a satin-coated plaster cast. However, if I was lucky and could "keep my tongue straight in my mouth," as they say in Danish, I could see that the dress could be a dream.

A call to the confectioner's made it clear that if Lani was to have the tiered wedding cake she desired I was going to have to make it. Fashions have changed now, but in those days there was no tradition in Denmark for that sort of cake, and the baker would charge ten dollars per portion to create what we wanted. "Don't worry," I blithely reassured the nervous bride. "It will be a cinch to make," and I started baking building blocks of delicious orange-carrot cake, thinking that for once it would be a wedding cake that tasted good.

The marquis on the lawn had been ruled out when we learned that a pre-fab party house with wooden floor could be rented for the same amount and would be far better if it rained. We made arrangements for that to be built four days before the wedding, in order to give us plenty of time to set up all the rentals and organize the decorations. Once the wedding dinner was cleared out, there could be dancing in the rented house, keeping our house tidy for the more sedate guests.

The trouble with a wedding is that the more you plan, the more inspired you become. I shudder to think what might have happened if we had decided to do it all on borrowed money; the sky would have been the limit, for never had we planned a party that lent itself to so many niceties. It was a splendid summer, and we spent hours in the garden, working out an increasing amount of details for the big day. Soon we were talking about live music, and before Finn could gather his thoughts enough to object, I had gone inside to call a former schoolmate of Lani's who was a successful musician. He said he wouldn't be able to make it for that date, but he recommended some pals of his. I called their number, and learning that they were free, I hired them, no questions asked.

Feeling pleased with myself, I went outside to tell the family about our good luck, and Finn was so unkind as to point out to me the possibility that this unknown band might not boast the sort of people one invites home to dinner, and he asked me whether I had told them what to wear. While defensively arguing that in this day and age one can't tell people what to wear, I suddenly had visions of a dodgy lot who looked like something from the Muppet show, playing punk rock. Despite all our protests, Finn marched inside, dialed their number and put on his military voice to inform these poor musicians that he expected them to meet up dressed uniformly. "Ah well," thought I, "if worse comes to worse, we can always pay them to go home again."

A thorough spring cleaning, polishing of all silver and brass and copper while Finn busily painted woodwork freshly white and the stone steps of the stairway leading to the terrace a pearly grey, made for weeks of toil, culminating in a few frenzied days of tending dozens of last minute details. I was making almost daily alterations on the wedding dress as our darling daughter developed her notions of what the dream dress should be, elaborating on her original design. We decided the severe lines of the satin dress should be softened, and this was achieved by using manicure scissors to cut thirty meters of lace out of my wedding gown and appliqué it onto hers, a task that I would have loved doing, had I been given a summer of isolation in a castle tower.

The wedding was to take place Saturday at five in the evening, and the promised house and rentals didn't show until two days before the event, adding an element of confusion to the general chaos. While making food for the fifty some odd guests and the ten people who were going to help serving, I had to make decorations for home and church, and finish making the bridal cake.

At the crack of dawn on Thursday morning, one of the supervisors who worked for Finn drove me to the greengrocers' market, where he knew enough owners of stalls to wheel and deal for all the prime vegetables, fruit and flowers I needed. As I hopped into his van, Kurt looked me over to see whether or not I was showing any signs of cracking up. Seeming to be satisfied that I would survive, he offered me a piece of candy for extra energy. It was a big, red jawbreaker, and it tasted like something made out of pure cayenne pepper. I wondered how I could take it out of my mouth without him noticing and getting hurt feelings. It was too big to swallow whole, too hard to crack, and too sticky to hide in my hand. This became a bigger problem than all the shopping and distracted me from the usual pleasure of seeing so many prime flowers and delicious groceries displayed in such abundance in one place.

By the time we got back to the house with a van-load of goods, I was ready to crawl back into bed. Instead, I set up shop in the kitchen, surrounded by pails brimming over with the flowers I was using to make the score of arrangements needed for the dining tables and the altar at the church, and the dozens of small bouquets to use up the aisle, plus posies for the bridesmaids. The night before, I had taken all the "building blocks" of cake out of the freezer. They were stacked up and glued together with a lemon and coconut cake filling and had begun to resemble a three-tiered cake. I decided that before I started fussing with flowers, it would be fun to begin frosting the cake.

I've never liked icing, and really didn't have a clue as to how to frost the cake, but I figured that a quick call to my friend, Joanne, in England, would sort that one out. After listening to her explicit instructions, I proceeded to do everything wrong, and the result was a nondescript mound with icky white frosting running down the sides. Lani came floating downstairs on a cloud, entered the kitchen smiling, and stopped short when she saw the pathetic heap of cake. Anticipating her question, I looked her square in the eye and lied, telling her that frosted cakes always look like that in the beginning phases.

Usually, I could count on Lani to be an absolute brick to help out in a pinch, but I had noticed that not only did she seem reluctant to descend from her pink cloud these days, but she was likely to be irritated with the rest of us mortals when she was jarred into consciousness. She hadn't even been the least bit amused when Bjørn toyed with the idea of furnishing the church pews with poopy pillows. I sized up the situation and ended by encouraging her to spend the day shopping for the dress she needed for the blessing Peter's parents were giving in England. She gave me a hug and a peck on the cheek, wrapped herself in her cloud, and floated out of the kitchen, wreathed in smiles.

By Friday, I could no longer tell myself that I had plenty of time to get everything in place. All day long, I made swipes at the cake with fresh batches of gooey icing while attending a million other details. It began to resemble Moby Dick, minus the fins. We were having the closest thing to a heat wave that Denmark ever produces, and most of the food couldn't be made in advance, for fear that it would spoil. The refrigerator was crammed with all the sauces and garnishes that could be made ready, and the house became more and more chaotic as plans progressed. I have a most unfortunate knack for looking totally unstressed, and as friends came around to see if they could lend a hand or deliver a present, they were quickly lulled into thinking there was no need for panic. Everyone was having a wonderful time, confident that I knew what I was doing.

As usual, Finn had proceeded single-mindedly with what he considered most important: the bar. He had constructed an eye-catching structure out on the terrace, decorated it with all sorts of props borrowed from our favorite wine merchant, and equipped it with every imaginable beverage, including a couple of kegs of Carlsberg's best beer. The bar was flanked by two poles and, with a great deal of difficulty, he had acquired a Union Jack to fly alongside the Danish flag, making the whole setup look impressively official. Here he set up shop, feeling rather inadequate in the other arenas. Every time I went out to the wooden house on the lawn, I found a crowd of potential helpers gathered around this miniature pub, with Finn standing behind the counter, keeping them happy. Out of the corner of my eye, I could tell that his contribution was a great success, and I wondered whether the party would break up in time for the wedding.

Actually, he couldn't have found a better way to help, for he held my work pool captive, making sure that they were enjoying themselves. Except for the fact that I had developed a splitting headache, it was fun — like a country fair. Luckily, some of our friends had years of experience in resisting Finn's hospitality and were industriously helping me with setting the tables and decorating the party house. Bjørn and his pal, Jesper, had put chairs in the sun and were getting a tan and having water fights, while scrubbing the small almond potatoes we use for special occasions. I made an effort to tell myself silly people can also be of help, and since Lani had left to meet Peter at the airport, I didn't have to worry about convincing her.

In the general confusion, I gathered that all was well in the outside world, and that many of the guests from England had arrived safely and had checked into their hotels, ready to enjoy wonderful Copenhagen at its summer best. When I had reached my most frazzled state, Gil and Joanne swept in to see how things were going. Joanne was a sight for sore eyes, and I pulled her into the kitchen, pointing at the vast bulk of wedding cake. "If anyone can save that mess, you can Joanne. Where should I go from here!"

She looked at it askance, but being a true friend, she gave me a hug and told me "Not to worry. I'm sure it can be rescued." All I had to do was to get a few yards of white satin ribbon, a lot of pins, and something to plop on the top. She had made a gorgeous bridal veil for Lani, and she had spare white silk roses that could be used on the cake.

Somehow, it all got into place. The food, the wine, the tables set with antique lace tablecloths, pink satin ribbon, tall rose candles and pastel flowers, the bridesmaids in pink, the bride a picture in satin and old lace, the groom handsome and doting, all the guests a treat in their finery, the rich interior of the lovely old church, with alternately creamy candles and pastel bouquets in the holders all along the rows

of pews, the church singers a musical delight, and the cheerful crowd
of friends who couldn't be included in the wedding party, but came to
lend their support on such a happy day.

The usually fickle Danish weather had opted for showing Denmark
at its very best. The sky was a bright, summer blue, and there was the
look of a pageant unfolding when the wedding party left the church
and walked along the hedge-lined lane through the churchyard to our
house. Acting on an inspiration of her own, Lani and Peter lingered
behind while she placed her wedding bouquet on her grandmother's
grave, with a thought for how much Mums would have loved such a
festive scene.

We started with champagne in the garden, the ladies long dresses
gracefully sweeping the lawn, the men handsome in their tuxedos and,
in the case of two, their full-dress uniforms. A spanking new Danish
flag gently fluttered in the slight breeze that comes up just before
sundown, but the air remained balmy even after the sun had set in a
sky tinted red. Seldom is a day so late in August quite like that day.
Twilight came without the heavy dew characteristic for that time of
year, and except for the pattern of the stars, we could have been in
the tropics.

In the rustic party house, the tables had been arranged in a
horseshoe, and the spell cast by candlelight created an atmosphere like
that of an old Danish painting. With all the fun of such a dinner, the
smiling faces with healthy tans from the exceptional summer, and the
joviality and toasts, one image in particular stands out in my memory,
that of my father-in-law making his speech.

With his usual sense of duty, he had called me weeks before to ask
me to come over and help him with a speech in English. I bicycled
over to his place in the late afternoon, and, as always with any family
member, he greeted me like I was the most important event of the
day. He insisted on getting out a decanter of whiskey, and there was no
arguing with him about having a glass together. Finally, we got down
to business, and I read a speech he had toiled over for several days.
I decided not to point out the faults; they were insignificant and did
nothing to change the meaning, and the meaning of his words was
beautiful. The minor flaws merely served as a reminder of what work
and love had gone into the making of the speech. I can still picture him
in the glow of candlelight at the wedding dinner, standing tall at the
head table, handsome in his starched shirt front and black tie, telling

what a very happy man he was, to listeners so attentive that you could hear a pin drop.

While the dinner things were being cleared for dancing, we all went inside for coffee and cutting of the cake, which by now stood magnificently transformed by Joanne's artistic talents. With candlelight glowing warmly on the high oak panels of the dining room and lending its soft aura to all the happy faces, Peter and Lani cut the cake with her father's officer's sword, while colored confetti brought over from England rained down on the scene. Everything seemed touched with magic that evening, and when we went out to the house in the garden for the bridal waltz, I could breathe a sigh of relief: the musicians were in place — a handsome group, all dressed in white with good summer tans. They turned out to be one of the best jazz bands we could have wished for, and they also did well with the lilting strains of the traditional Danish bridal waltz.

With the guests in a circle, clapping hands in tact to the music, the bride and groom set off in a waltz, and the circle closed in on them as the waltz gained speed. The tradition is that the women join hands and crowd the couple until they can snatch the veil from the bride and tear it to pieces, but we chose to jump over that custom and save the beautiful veil Joanne had so lovingly made.

Soon after that, Lani and Peter left in a shower of rice, and we were kept from tears because the guests stayed. The musicians switched to Louis Armstrong-style jazz, and the party carried on, far into the warm night. Candles were lit inside the freshly painted mullioned windows, casting cheerful patches of light into the garden, augmented by tall torches in the flower beds. Their flames picked up the bright hues of late summer blooms, while garden candles lit a path across the lawn. From a window in the garden house, a bright spot of light illuminated the scarlet sweet peas climbing up a white wall. White baskets filled with red coral-top plants were spaced atop the parapets of the verandah stairs.

The well-stocked bar was most popular for its Carlsberg golden brew, the strong beer in the keg. At some late point in the evening, I noticed that our son had a slap-happy grin pasted all over his face and seemed to think that he was holding up the ceiling of the garden house, while the dancers moved around him. "How are you doing, Bjørn?" I asked as a test question.

Without letting go of the ceiling, he sang out, "Fine, Mom! This

is the best party I've ever been to!" I decided he definitely needed
supervision, and I found his friend, Jesper, who had been helping out
all through the evening, asking him to keep an eye on Bjørn so he
wouldn't do something daft, like trying to dive into the bird bath.

"Sure, Judy," said Jesper, as he turned to me with a silly grin exactly
matching Bjørn's.

Hours later, when closing up the house, I found the two of them
still smiling, fast asleep with all their clothes on, lying flat on their
backs on the cold floor of the rumpus room in the cellar. I had to leave
them there, Bjørn's room having been taken over by English guests. All
the younger guests from England had been told that they could move
into our home the night of the wedding, and they were a welcome
presence in the morning. The sad moment when the party would end
was postponed, and seeing so many cheerful faces around the breakfast
table in the morning kept our minds off the fact that Lani was gone.

The following evening, we had planned a buffet dinner for the
English crowd and one pair of good Danish friends who couldn't be
among the wedding guests. The party house was still on the lawn, and
in it we set up one long table for the thirty or so people. After all the
logistics of the wedding, this event was duck soup, and Finn and I
could relax completely. With the mood of the night before still hanging
in the air, it only took slight remarks to set off gales of laughter among
our guests. After a boisterous dinner, we ended the evening by moving
into the house for coffee and port, the young crowd settling in the
dining room, and the "wrinklies," as they dubbed us, comfortably
crowded in the living room.

English people have a wonderful tradition of singing, and they
also have lovely voices. Before long, we were joining together in old
favorites, with the young crowd in the adjacent room belting out
echoes. Peter's Uncle Brian surprised us all with a very competent solo,
and the youngsters felt challenged to file in, line up, and sing a song
demanding more port. Finn is never one to begrudge a guest all he can
hold, but keeping in mind that this lot was going to be spending the
night, he was aware of them having had plenty already.

"All right," he said, "you're on. That is, if Jeremy can pass the
sobriety test." Jeremy was quick to reply that he could easily pass any
test, and Finn left the room and returned with a bottle full of water.
The bottle had an old-fashioned, hinged stopper to close it tightly. Our
young friend was instructed to stick the bottle in the left pocket of

his trousers. With his right hand, he was to reach behind his back and release the lock on the bottle, without spilling any water.

Feeling very cocky, Jeremy claimed that that would be a cinch, and he quickly complied. What he didn't know was that Finn had drilled a tiny hole in the bottom of the bottle. While the bottle was full and closed, the water stayed in, due to pressure, but once the top was released, the water ran out into Jeremy's pocket, thoroughly drenching his trousers. Of course, this rude sort of Danish parlor trick occasioned giant guffaws, and we wrinklies felt we had gained the upper hand.

A few of the young crowd stayed on the following day also, there being a bank holiday in England, and we sat in the sun on the terrace. Reluctant to start the chore of clearing the shambles, we swapped stories and prolonged the festivities. On the fourth day, they had all gone, the house was quiet, and we could detect a subtle change in the weather. Morning mists were chilly, and the afternoons were hazy as the cooler late-summer air met the sun-warm ground. Two days later, Bjorn left for his stint with the Royal Guard, and Finn and I had our first taste of quiet in more than twenty years. It's a feeling we have all experienced, after a great deal of work has been swept away in a whirlwind of events. It is a sweet sort of sadness and a restlessness in one's soul, where it helps to have someone to share that odd space in time.

22

Change

Change is exhilarating when one rides on the crest of it, but for those of us who are treading water, it is rather disconcerting. No matter how quiet one's life, change is an inevitable factor, and even when it is for the better, it is disturbing. The autumn days that followed that memorable summer were stepping stones in unexplored terrain, and they stretched luxuriously ahead of us, uncharted and unsettling. With unaccustomed leisure hours, I tended the house in a more orderly fashion, dressed more carefully, and enjoyed a welcome but unfamiliar feeling of control.

Our small dachshund had died and was replaced with a large, good-natured mixture that needed exercising, and daily walks in the nearby woods revealed clearly the changes that had taken place all around us. The neighborhood was not the same. Some of the largest of the villas had been demolished and replaced with uniformly boring modern bungalows, and some of the expansive gardens had been reduced to accommodate similar small houses. While the general prosperity had quite clearly improved, and homes were handsome in their fresh paint and restored grandeur, the gardens had been transformed into uniformly planned appendages, easily tended by a busy, working couple. Gone were the ambitious garden schemes of former times, the mixed borders that demanded both a broad knowledge of flowers, plus a willingness to tend them or to spend part of one's income to hire a gardener.

During daytime walks around the lake and in the woods and park, I no longer encountered strolling families or young mothers pushing prams, but harassed-looking joggers, tuned into a walkman and too concentrated to smile or nod, or the idle unemployed, sitting sideways on park benches, one arm slung over the back, a vacant look in their eyes. In the very dullness of the scene, one sensed an undercurrent of tension, the invisible riptide of a more mercantile society.

Home-going housewives were as rare as fleas on fish, but I had no desire to seek a career, and I soon began to enjoy the luxury of having only Finn to consider. On the spur of the moment, I could take the train into Copenhagen and wander around the charming old streets, enjoying the atmosphere of the many recently renovated old buildings and the never-ending surprises one discovers when taking the time to stop up and enjoy the many architectural pearls.

When in Copenhagen, I have never been able to resist the temptation to follow the Royal Guard when they march through the old city on their way to the palace for the changing of the guard. Just seeing them in their magnificent uniforms with the tall bearskin busbies has always made me happy, and whether they march to the parade music furnished by their music corps or just to the fife and drums, I find myself quickening my pace and following them through the winding streets. The following year, when Bjørn had finished his basic training, I could have the additional thrill of seeing one of them wink and flash me an un-regimental smile.

I felt privileged. While never having had to sacrifice our ideals, we had reached the point when one reaps the harvest of one's efforts — A full larder, no real worries, and a life busy with pleasant events. To top it off, with her usual sense of direction, Lani decided to have a family, and not much more than a year after the wedding, she was expecting twins.

In epic literature or even

in Danish history, one often encounters the description of wind or weather or any unusual phenomenon occurring at the time of an event and underlining the importance of the occasion. I used to attribute this to poetic license, but the truth is that people who notice the whims of nature tend to take note of anything atypical at the time of a significant happening. If there is a violent storm, or if a migrant bird makes its appearance earlier than expected, it is only natural to connect this to one's personal experience and remember that experience more clearly for having done so.

In old days these were considered omens. I am no longer skeptical when I read that in 1577 Queen Sophia of Denmark gave birth to the future King Christian IV under a hawthorn tree, which was in full bloom a month too early. And, having said that, I will ask you to believe me when I tell you that one summer day Finn and I witnessed no less than five rainbows at one brilliant moment, the first three luminously clear, and the others in diminishing brightness, all piled above one another against a silver-grey sky, a portent of appropriate magnitude for the birth of our first grandchildren.

While I was in England for more than two months to be of help to Lani, Finn managed to cope on his own, with a great deal of help from friends who could always count on a good meal. The most faithful, Sussi, warned me that everyone had gained ten pounds and our wine dealer was getting rich, but upon returning, what I found most interesting was to discover those aspects which Finn seemed to have considered the most important in running a household. In a zealous attempt to match my standards, he made sure there always was freshly baked bread and a well-stocked refrigerator. Potted plants were well tended. Pets, friends, and Bjørn were well-fed. The garden's vegetables were diligently harvested and frozen, and he saw to his own pet priority: the toaster was highly polished. He even spent countless hours nursing a sick cat, though he claims he detests cats.

Cleaning and weeding were obviously not on his list, and as a lesson for me, no one seemed to have noticed their having been discontinued. It was rather fun to come home and be able to vacuum stripes on the parquet floors. To mark each day of my absences, he has always put matchsticks in a potato, and this particular potato animal joined his collection, with so many matchsticks that it looked like a porcupine.

Another pleasant dimension of my life in Denmark was tied up with

Finn's work. He has always had a knack of making any commitment
a personal one, even while maintaining the lines of authority, and
employees under his management responded with a loyalty that isn't
all that common. For me it meant a wealth of extra friendships, and
a good many laughs shared with people from all different walks of
life. The firm he managed was a window-cleaning outfit, and the
window cleaners themselves were a very special breed. Most of them
were skilled workers who opted out for a job under Finn, because they
could earn good money and have more personal freedom. They were
a proud lot, capable, reliable, and full of initiative.

Rather than recruiting outside management, Finn believed in
trying to find people among the workers who were capable of filling
supervisory posts, and these diamonds in the rough demonstrated an
uncanny ability to cope with difficult customers. They were gems as
long as they were managed by someone with eyes in the back of his
head and a sixth sense for reading their minds. It was the military all over
again, making best use of human raw material at hand. Consequently,
when I look back and picture them all, each one stands out clearly with
endearing quirks. There were real rascals, old charmers, eager-beavers,
and protected softies.

The window cleaners worked mostly in teams and were paid piece
rates. A good team could earn a considerable amount of money while
keeping a protective hand over the man among them who wasn't as
efficient. As long as they kept the customer satisfied, Finn could only
be amused by their brainstorms for cutting corners. One team met up
to do their job at the police headquarters one hot spring day when the
fishing was good. The lot of them was polite and presentable, and no
suspicions were aroused when they sympathized with the office staff
for having to work in the unbearable heat.

"I'll tell you what," said the leader of the team, "we aren't supposed
to do any heavy lifting, but you folks are always so nice that if you like,
we'll take down all your double glazing and store it in the cellar. That
sure would make things cooler." The office staff was ever so grateful,
and no one objected when he added, "Of course, that won't leave us
time to do the windows today."

The windows looked cleaner anyway, when the double glazing came
down, and having done that in less than an hour, the team could take
off the rest of the day for fishing. The office staff wouldn't dream of
complaining, for they figured the window cleaners had gone beyond

the line of duty to help them out, and they were more pleased than ever with the service.

Then there was Carlo. Carlo was what Danes term a *liv's kunstner*, directly translated, a "life artist." Like a white Eddie Murphy, he could always con his way through the most dodgy situation, coming out ahead and leaving everyone happy or too confused to know what had hit them. He turned out to be one of Finn's most valuable employees, with the largest portfolio of customers and an incredible flair for keeping them satisfied. When sent out to bid on an especially big contract, Finn was surprised to note how quickly Carlo had arrived at a large figure to present to the customer, and how readily they had accepted it. Though very pleased, Finn couldn't help but ask just the same, "Tell me, Carlo, how did you arrive at that figure?"

"Oh, that's easy," said Carlo, looking deceptively modest, "I was in the boss's office. You wouldn't believe how thick that carpet was, and the curtains! They must have cost a mint." And, shaking his head in wonder, he figured that question had been answered. He had a flair for stringing together a whole lot of sentences which made absolutely no sense, but left his listener with the feeling of having been told something important which shouldn't need repeating.

But Finn was persistent. "Yes, but Carlo, what's that got to do with the amount of windows to be cleaned!"

Though he seemed puzzled that his boss could be so dense, he patiently replied, "Well, of course, with those furnishings, I knew they could afford a lot for window cleaning." And, as usual, he was right.

Finn's policy with his help was, as long as the customer was happy and the books were in order, they could have a free hand. He combined an old-fashioned patriarchal pattern with a modern informality, and the result was that they respected him as their boss and felt motivated to work hard, knowing it meant more freedom on the job. The most striking result was that they seemed to have such a lot of fun at work, yet the profits were the highest in the concern, a very ambitious conglomerate that furnished cleaning services for every walk of life.

While the firm at large was well into modern times, with a great deal of organized waste for the sake of efficiency, Finn continued to take a pride in keeping the office overhead low and the workers well paid. The offices he rented were cozy, but not posh, his own least of all. Instead, he tried to create an atmosphere that appealed to the workers, a place where they loved to pop in for a cup of coffee or a game of ping-pong. Once a year he planned a grand party for them at a really good restaurant to reward them for the invariably excellent results, and restaurant owners vied to have them because of their nice behavior, a token of their respect for a boss who looked the part. How they behaved after they parted with Finn, with an excellent meal in their bellies, three sheets to the wind, and headed for a night on the town, was a different kettle of fish, but that second part of the evening provided entertaining stories for the rest of the year.

While the rest of the firm conformed to a strict uniformity both in office facilities and company policy, Finn ran an outfit which was quaintly original and homelike. The practice in other districts was to use the company's cleaners to clean the office facilities, and those cleaners followed a routine that was dictated across the lines. Such regimented cleaners stuck fiercely to their rights while being obliged to avoid doing anything that wasn't specifically demanded by the cleaning contract. To organize all this, directives were issued frequently to insure that all offices could be treated as a uniform quantity. Thus, for the sake of efficiency, disposable beverage cups were made an ultimatum.

Always the nonconformist, Finn banned plastic utensils from the premises, and he found a jewel of a cleaning lady who took pride in keeping the place tidy. "Curly" as Finn dubbed her, was a whole different story from the company-issue cleaner. She was given a key to the place, and like any good housewife, could keep her own schedule, as long as the place was spic and span. Like the rest of the people employed by Finn, the resulting sense of responsibility meant that she took pride in doing a good job and used her own good judgment to decide what was most important in the daily routine. She became part of the team and gladly joined the other ladies in adding the feminine touch to each morning meeting that was called to celebrate a special event, even when that meant voluntarily meeting early to set a festive table. There was an atmosphere of home and a feeling of family. I know, because they liked to call me and ask me to join them.

Finn also had a talent for spotting quality inside a person and wasn't distracted by the usual criteria for employment. From his early experience in the military, he had developed the strong belief that there is no such thing as a poor soldier, but only an inadequate officer. An alcoholic who could be honest about his problem and try to control it was certain of being given a fair chance, and anyone who had been employed for many years could be sure of keeping his job, even if his health failed and he couldn't perform as well.

If they seemed like a family, the mother hen was Ebba, the eldest office lady. She was a case herself, having been hired with a broken leg. Her last employer had sacked her when she had to extend her sick leave because of complications with her leg, and there she was — too old to find a job and not old enough to qualify for a state pension. Finn picked her out for the good penmanship on her application and called her in for an interview. When she left his office, she had landed a job, he had an employee who would have gone on the barricades for him, and we had made a new friend for life. As for the window cleaners, they had acquired a loyal champion who lovingly kept them in line, while lending an ear to their problems or raking them over the coals, whichever she thought was needed.

Finn was a maverick in a concern where conformity was in the high seat. Because he ran his part of the outfit so successfully and profitably, with very good relations with the union and his own personnel, he was able to stay virtually independent of the mother company for many years, but he presented a problem to a large concern where everything was done so differently and without always the same degree of success. And, typically for him, he considered it beneath his dignity to try to win the people who opposed him over to his camp. He consistently refused to socialize with his peers in the concern unless they had won his respect on their own, and he thereby alienated himself from the very people who might have been helpful to him later on. He was playing with fire, for it was a company notorious for firing its old employees within the administration and replacing them with slick young hopefuls. Under the new director, this was usually done just before the twenty-fifth anniversary of one's employment — a date that released a nice bonus.

I think his real Waterloo was the fact that he ran things too well. Like with most things that always run smoothly, it eventually looked easy. There was a steady stream of new people at the top of the hierarchy, and without the memory of how poor a record the window-cleaning department had when Finn took over, they got the idea that his success was due to the nature of the operation, not his personal style. They decided to turn this prize plum over to one of their own lads, moving him into Finn's office, with jurisdiction over Finn.

The poor little man turned out to be someone who lacked real leadership abilities and couldn't win over Finn's fiercely loyal people. Of course, Finn himself quickly sized him up as a total nincompoop and by meticulously following his orders made him look even more incompetent. The only solution left was to make the window-cleaning department move into the head office quarters and force them to relinquish the independent image they had built up over so many years. It was equivalent to making a squadron of leatherneck marines comply to the leadership of the boy scouts. What followed was a total transformation of the outfit, with a good many people quitting, and all of them longing for the good old days — plus a drastic decline in profits.

Through all this, Finn conformed to the letter of the law, but not the spirit of it; he was seething with rage, watching such a good operation being destroyed and seeing the team of real characters whom he had cultivated lose their bearings under poor leadership. Of course, from the head office point of view, there was no way back. It was obvious that he was the misfit in a system such as theirs.

He would come home thoroughly exasperated over very basic differences in a service company's goals. He had, for example, set aside an amount in the budget for a well-deserved pay hike for the workers, one which was being negotiated and that he wanted to see made retroactive. It was used instead on smart new furnishings for the sterile office space the staff had been moved into. Naturally, I saw everything from Finn's side, and I wanted him to quit, but he reminded me that the prospects look bleak for a man past fifty looking for a new job.

The wonderful thing about life is that many things happen for us. Just as I was beginning to worry that the stress Finn was facing would ruin his health, he came home one day, his face a mask over his emotions, threw his briefcase down in the hallway and said, "They sacked me. After twenty-one years, I'm out." Behind the facade of a modern man, a Viking stood before me, bursting with unspent fury. I was reminded of Gulliver and the irritating Lilliputians.

Knowing he wasn't in the mood for me to sound flippant, I resisted the urge to shout, "Congratulations!" and, instead, let him tell me just what had happened. It was actually rather funny. The poor little man who had been placed over Finn had, as usual, been trying to make new rules without having really understood the old ones, and one of Finn's more outspoken staff members had called him something rather rude that was too close to the mark and left the meeting in disgust. The collectively suppressed laughter was almost palpable. It became quite clear that as long as the new man was compared to Finn, he was going to fall short and be laughed at, and he was left no choice but to fire Finn.

Call me irresponsible, but I thought it was tremendous good luck. I knew Finn was far too conscientious and careful about our economy to have quit, but with our kids out of the nest, and us still young enough to go off in new directions, this couldn't have come at a better time. Finn morosely pointed out to me that it takes a lot of money to live on in this day and age, and it would be nearly ten years before we could dip into our savings, but then he remembered to tell me that the firm had been obliged to give him a year and a half's salary. By now I was starting to get excited. "Take it as a paid vacation! This is great. We have scads of time to figure out what to do." I felt like we were on the crest of the wave, and it felt good.

Lucky for Finn, my attitude turned out to be a minority opinion, and at least all our friends and Finn's father could be counted on to share his distress. They urged him to get right out and find a new job, but he didn't even want to try, knowing that it would be the same story all over again, unless he owned his own firm. Like so many people his age, he was experiencing the bewilderment of being kicked out of a plane at high altitudes, just when he felt he had achieved a competence that made flying the plane so easy.

Interestingly enough, we learned that Denmark, which is otherwise so advanced as regards workers' rights, was in those days unique in its neglect of executives' rights. In most of the Western world, a person who is fired without grounds after so many years of loyal service would be able to sue for damages when his former position with the firm continues to exist. Over the years, Finn had many times been approached by competitors who saw in him a chance to make big profits, and out of a sense of misplaced loyalty, he had refused. Now, he felt burnt out, unmotivated to contact anyone and refusing to believe all of us who claimed that a man of his talents would easily find something else.

Real frustration and anger cannot be wiped away by well-meaning loved ones. I could only stand by and watch, ready with a comforting word or a soothing cup of tea, feeling all the while that this was a heck of a way to spend what looked like our last paid vacation. We spent hours talking about how we would manage when the year and

a half had passed by; I felt we were lucky to have so much time, but
Finn felt bitter that his well-formulated plans for security should go
up in smoke.

Meanwhile, I was irritatingly cheerful, my mind buzzing with
helpful suggestions. These brilliant schemes had so far not appealed
to Finn. I had proposed everything, from the idea of me going to
work for a change to turning our home into a first-class restaurant
for a very rich and exclusive clientele of Americans who would find it
quaint. Feeling generous, I even told Finn that he could use this period
without obligations to take off on an adventure in the wilderness or
sign up as a crew member on a sailing trip. Some days I went so far as
to say I was willing to go out on a limb, turn our home into an office
and start up for ourselves, just for the sake of cornering the customers
and ruining all prospects of his old firm ever straightening up the mess
they had made. This latter suggestion was reinforced by the frequent
ringing of the phone, as people from Finn's old outfit called, unhappy
with their new situation and wanting to work for Finn once more. In
order to start up on his own, however, Finn would have had to borrow
money with our house as collateral. Borrowing money was not his idea
of a sound idea.

Finally, I got an idea that hit home, with the help of the Danish
tax department. Here in Denmark, we almost have taxes on taxes,
and the government shows considerable ingenuity in finding new
means of paying for the incredibly high standards of such a small
country. (Imagine, for example, what it costs each individual Dane to
help maintain embassies all over the world, to send even one corvette
to the Persian Gulf, and to enforce some of the most stringent
environmental measures passed, when there are only five and a half
million inhabitants. One can hardly blame the government for the high
taxes, but we do constantly try to find ways to avoid them.) Although
Finn had been assiduously saving for our old age, we both knew that
when the time came for our savings to be released and counted in on
what is termed our "fortune," we would face a serious tax problem.
That money, combined with the evaluation of our house, would all
count as "fortune," even though bricks aren't money until they are
sold, and the resulting fortune tax would be so great that nearly all our
income would go to paying our taxes.

"Why don't we sell the house now, buy something much cheaper in
the country, and live off the capital gained until we get our pensions?

We will not only have squeaked by, but we will have a less valuable place to count in on our fortune."

As soon as the words were over my lips, I felt the enormity of what I had said. Finn had always sworn he would have to be carried out of our home feet first, and I could imagine the air around me vibrating with alarm emitted from the ghosts of Finn's ancestors. I felt as if I had hurt the house's feelings by the mere mention of something so treacherous. One look at Finn, and I knew he shared these thoughts.

However, in the days to come, we kept circling around the same idea, and, finally, it was clear that it was the best solution. We knew we couldn't enjoy living in such a demanding dwelling without sufficient means to maintain it, and we had seen often enough how depressing it is to go on living in a large house and have to let it deteriorate. We could also foresee that the city would continue to encroach on our quiet neighborhood, and there would be no future in trying to fight against the changes that would follow. Of course, any decision we made would have to be acceptable to both Finn's father and Lani and Bjørn, but I knew in advance what they would say.

Cʒ   Cʁ

Finn's family was always an important part of our lives, but it was a very small family. We lost his sister, Brit, when she was much too young, and not long afterwards, Faster Eli. When Mums died, those few of us left had drawn together in an even tighter group, and Paps was like the tall oak, sheltering the rest of us.

Since the first time I met Paps, he had generously bestowed on me the same undemanding love that he unflaggingly gave his own children. To people who didn't know him, he could appear formidable — a large man of unusual physical strength, never hesitant to form an opinion, and willing to put forth his opinions with authority, his dark eyes flashing under thick black eyebrows.

From a succession of old photographs, one can follow the molding of a real gentleman of his time: The beautiful baby in monogrammed batiste snugly tucked into an elaborate pram, the good-looking boy in his sailor suit, standing straight for a family portrait, taken with all of them in their spring finery for an outing in the woods, the jaunty student wearing his white cap and gaily waving from a horse-drawn wagon, the dashing young champion of a fencing duel, and the slightly dazed bridegroom with his vivacious bride. All of his upbringing and his place in society had molded him into a person with high ideals and an unwavering loyalty to king and family.

As a widower, he tried to keep up the home, but it proved too much for him, and much to our relief, he decided to sell the villa and buy a flat. However, he really hadn't come to feel at home in the new surroundings, and when we talked to him of moving with us to a place in the country, he was very keen on the idea. He had been very pleased when we bought his childhood home and had so loved the many happy hours we all spent together in those familiar surroundings. I know it must have been difficult for him to think about us leaving it, but meanwhile life went on as usual, lulling him into vague dreams about a new life with all of us together in the country.

We no longer had a car — that having been the firm's, but without a word of complaint Finn accepted that inconvenience and rediscovered the fun of bicycling. For once he had to let me be the expert, as I introduced him to the convenience of public transportation, which was very convenient, indeed, here in Denmark. He did at least introduce a touching element of nostalgia to the scene at the train station, innocently asking where he could buy a ticket to go onto the platform, a surcharge which had been discontinued more than twenty years previously.

Fortunately, we have always kept our private life separate from business, and that went on as usual, with good friends, having good times. In fact, just by chance, it proved to be an especially busy year socially; we made many new friends and felt rather trendy, being able to shock people with our new non-status.

Now that most people have joined the workforce, the weather is no longer the prime mover for starting a conversation. Most people ask politely what "you do," and what they mean is what do you do for money? For years I've gotten a hoot out of watching their discomfort when I tell them I do nothing at all. I thereby put myself in an unknown category, something which makes people insecure. They usually regained their bearings by following that question up with, "Oh, what does your husband do?" thinking that he surely must be so important that it can make up for my lack of ambition. Finn definitely has the appearance of someone in command, and while they sized him up across the room, I could now innocently reply, "He doesn't do anything either."

This invariably caused them to be intrigued and probe further, expecting to discover by what means a man of his age, looking so prosperous, could retire so early. That's when I felt trendy when I said, "He got sacked."

Finn and I would bicycle home from such affairs and sit in the kitchen having night food, laughing 'til our sides hurt as we compared notes. Once Finn ran into a man whom he had known when they both were officers in the Royal Guard. They were delighted to see each other, and remembering the fellow as a bit of a bon vivant, Finn asked what he was doing now. He was a good-looking bloke, full of fun, and Finn thought he was taking the mickey out of him when he answered that he was a vicar. I saw them laughing so hard they had to hold each other up, because Finn then informed his friend that he was in the ranks of the unemployed. Neither one of them believed what the other one was saying, but they were certainly enjoying the reunion.

We could see that we needed to invent a new title for Finn. In Danish, to call yourself "unemployed" is to say that you are on the dole, but to call yourself "retired" is to make people think you are past sixty or stinking rich.

Still, Finn was uncomfortable with this period of uncertainty. As luck would have it, the real estate market went into a slump unparalleled in our times. We wouldn't even consider looking for anything else until we had sold our house, as our future income depended on what we got for our house and had to pay for our new home. Being the sort that not only worries about my security but also about the unborn generations of the family, Finn couldn't relax until all the pieces of our plan were in place.

23

Adrift

In these unsettled times, our circumstances were not all that unique, but people we knew who had been through similarly trying periods had chosen to more or less disappear from the scene until they could step back on the stage in an acceptable role. Life is too short for lying low, and if Finn felt gloomy, I knew at least that he would never let our friends feel it. He kept busy with activities that have to do with being on one tennis board and being foreman for another, and we continued to have a steady stream of guests.

One good diversion was furnished when our friend, Carl, who had a sawmill on Lolland, complained that it was unfair that Finn knew so many good-looking women from our neck of the woods. Finn said that he was willing to share them with Carl, if Carl would plan a shoot and invite them along as beaters. We got together most of our Easter crowd, the ones who come to the party that has taken place since I gave up my hopes for work projects during Easter, friends who are always ready for the worst.

Only one other among this crowd was a hunter, and the rest of us were to be beaters. They met at our place a drizzly November morning, six men who were like boys playing hooky from school, and eight very attractive women. Finn and I piled into separate cars to direct the caravan on the two-hour drive to Lolland. We were to meet with Carl in a place called Fagersted Skov, meaning "place of beauty woods," a truly enchanting forest where the terrain is full of brambles, undergrowth, bogs, and bracken, all of which lends itself to a day guaranteed to shake all propriety out of the beaters who have to force their way through it.

Our breath was steaming in the cold air, and the woods were saturated with the rain that had been falling all during the night. While the three real hunters took their posts, I was entrusted with the job of

lining up the rest of us so that we could move systematically through
the forest. This was made rather difficult by Niels, Carl Johan, and
Gokke, who used every opportunity to fool around, jostling each other
for the best positions, pulling Gokke's hat down over his eyes, and
generally showing off for the ladies.

Carl had been all starry-eyed at the sight of so many gorgeous
creatures, but I knew that neither he nor Finn would take any frailties
into account, once the signal had been sounded to start the shoot.
Those who had been along previously were prepared for the beating
one's clothing and footwear take in rain-soaked woods, but Lisbeth
and Jeaneal looked like they had been sent on a photo assignment for
Vogue, and Julie, in a smart Burberry cloak, with her long, dark hair
flowing loosely beneath a matching hat, was brandishing a long walking
stick, as if she imagined her path would be uncluttered by obstacles. I
could count on Sus to get the other end of the line organized, because
she has a managerial position and is a redhead to boot, but down on my
end I had to rely on George, who is a crazy Belgian, intent on telling me
how many Walloons he had killed that morning. I knew that as soon
as we had pushed our way through the first five hundred meters, our
line would be chaos anyway, and when Carl gave the signal to start, we
all forged forward, looking most disorganized, jovial remarks ringing
through the air, rather than just the usual sounds made by beaters, such
as clapping hands and grunts.

We soon came within the vicinity of an ancient oak that stands alone
in a small meadow, its branches spreading unhindered in all directions.
It is one of my favorite spots, partly for the tree and also for an idyllic
thatch-roofed house that is beside a small pond, within a stone's throw
of the tree. Unfortunately, this picturesque house was inhabited for
years by one of the few Danish families who live like pigs. The lovely
setting was always cluttered with refuse, and the people themselves
looked like they were found at the dump.

The forest is part of a much larger estate, and the baron who owns
it decided to try to help these people out of their morose condition
by offering to install a nice bathroom in their cottage. The work was
done, all nicely tiled, and the baron stopped by one day when he was
out riding, to ask if they were quite satisfied with the results.

"Oh, yes sir!" said the man of the house, his dirty old cap clutched
respectfully in his hand.

"Well, if you don't mind, I'd like to see it," said the baron. It had cost him a pretty penny, and he wanted the pleasure of seeing what an improvement it must have been for these poor people.

The battered cap was back on the chap's head, but he still seemed a bit overwhelmed by such an important visit, and he shuffled his wooden clogs uncomfortably in the dirt in front of his stoop. Being unable to find a reason to stall, he hesitatingly stepped aside, and the baron entered the cluttered cottage, ducking his head to pass under the low doorway. One look at the bathroom, and he understood the man's discomfort. The brand-new bathtub was filled with water and swimming around happily was a flock of ducklings. The sides of the tub and the tiled floor were streaked with droppings.

"It's only temp'ry, gov'nor — We really plan to put them out on the pond. But it's a bit nippy out there now, you see, and look how happy the little blighters are."

This family had finally moved on, and the cottage was deserted. The ducks and noisy geese were gone, and the litter in the yard had eventually disappeared as the neglected garden swallowed it in its dense growth. In following my route along the lines we had set up, I found myself on the edge of this garden, face to face with an immense blackcurrant bush. Going around the bush would signal a change in direction to those to the right and the left of me, and I found it simpler to crawl under its branches. In the deep layer of leaves that lay on the ground, my hand grazed what seemed to be the top of an old crock with a handle. Much to my amazement, when I pulled it up, an unbroken crock followed, without a chip or a crack. It was an antique water jug, and under a layer of dirt, it appeared to be a lovely shade of aqua marine, with a rose gracefully adorning its side. I lugged it around with me the remainder of the day, eager to take it home and wash it off to see what lay under the years of grime.

There wasn't much game sighted that day. We were too busy keeping track of the antics of our unruly numbers. But seldom have we had more fun. Many similar occasions had paved the way for a shortcut to a riotous day, and the lunch that followed in the conference room of the sawmill was an especially rowdy affair. Everyone present had been to exotic places and lived a comfortable life, but we could always rely on them to be a barrel of fun on a cold, wet day, and when we drove home late in the afternoon, tired and happy, we didn't have a care in the world.

The next morning, I awakened eager to clean up the jug I had found in the forest, wondering if its color was burned into the glaze or merely a residue of moss. I was delighted when I found that it was really a beauty, and I carried it from room to room, trying to find a suitable place to have it standing.

There are moments in a long life when the most obvious things come as a revelation, and standing with this simple jug in my hands, it dawned on me that Finn and I had changed our style over the years. The rustic ceramic jug clashed with the furnishings of the rooms on the ground floor. With a thought dedicated to Hans Christian Andersen, I imagined the indignation of the finer pieces, if I placed such a simple country beauty in their midst. I finally put it in the upstairs sitting room, where its color blended so nicely with the greens of that room to make style unimportant. But it served as a reminder of the love we always have had for Danish farm furniture with its honest simplicity and how far we had moved from our early dreams, a thought that strengthened my belief that we could find happiness in another setting.

CB CR

Christmas was coming, and we tried not to think that this would be the last Christmas in such well-established surroundings. More disturbing was the fact that this Christmas Paps wasn't strong enough for his annual outing with me. When Mums died, Paps had turned to me for help with his Christmas shopping. He was perfectly capable of choosing gifts, but it soon became obvious that this was just a ploy he had dreamed up in order to give me a treat. The shopping was a necessary duty, quickly accomplished, to allow plenty of time for his main purpose, the lunch afterwards. I made it a habit to go to Copenhagen a day prior to our outing and look around for appropriate gifts; we could then zip around picking them up and not have to waste too much time before lunch.

When we met in Copenhagen, Paps was always very grand, in a fine silk tie, elegant gold cufflinks on French cuffs, a nicely tailored, dark-blue suit, an overcoat and bowler hat, carrying a silver-handled cane, which he tapped on the pavement with an air of authority as he walked briskly along. With characteristic thoroughness, he would first have consulted with his friend François, to learn where to go for the best meal.

François' name was really Franz, but he had the unique distinction of having been brought up in a French monastery, and this qualified him to use the French version of his name and to pride himself on being a gourmet. His mother had been a devout Catholic and had produced enough sons to dream of one of them becoming a priest. Poor François was chosen, packed off to France at a very young age, and while receiving an excellent education, the threat of a celibate future turned him into a very dapper man who had a clear idea of that which he didn't want to renounce. Following his expert advice, we headed for a different restaurant each year, and while I worried about how much money Paps was throwing away on me, he relished his role as benefactor.

No corners were cut as we made our way through a series of courses and the accompanying beverages. Waiters seemed to take pride in waiting on Paps's table, for he was a paragon of good breeding, and there were never any unpleasant hitches in their performance. Paps and I always loved talking about everything under the sun, and as the busy bustle of the lunchtime crowd of business people petered out, we still lingered over the last bite of food, thoroughly engrossed in squeezing the final drop of enjoyment out of this rare treat.

By then we were both a bit tipsy and had reached the reminiscing stage. Coffee was ordered with a sweet, and having lost all compunction, I would say yes to a brandy, savoring the atmosphere of being surrounded with the imaginary presences of all the loved ones we had called forth by remembering them. When we got into a cab at the end of the day, we felt more peace on Earth and good will towards mankind than all the Christmas season put together.

But this season was different, and our outing was postponed. Paps had aged rather suddenly. He slept a great deal, and when he dozed off, he dreamed of the dead . . . pleasant dreams that took more and more of his time. He became less aware of the distinction between sleeping and waking hours and could easily slide from one state to the next, until one day he slipped away from us, quietly and peacefully. He had been our most loyal champion, our last real link to the past and this world seemed a poorer place after his parting.

He lived to be eighty-six, and proof that he had lived a good life was the large amount of people who came to his funeral. It was a brilliant frost day, with a high blue sky. The white casket was magnificently covered with red poinsettias, and the beauty of the day seemed a fitting farewell to a man who had maintained so much dignity in the long journey through life.

With the help of many good friends, we got through that Christmas, and the dismal chore of closing down his flat kept Finn too busy to spend too much time thinking. The period of waiting for our villa to be sold had the unsettling, rather exciting feeling of breaking camp — considerably complicated by the fact that "camp" consisted of four floors filled with antiques and mementos. Finn and I agonized over each plant we would be abandoning, each brass door-handle, and every part of the paneling his great-grandfather Bernhard had carefully fitted into the dining room. But if we had our doubts, mine at least were settled when we went up to the summer place for a few days.

In that rustic little cottage by the sea, one regains a sense of balance. Sitting at the scrubbed wooden table, looking past the golden tufts of ripe grass and the soft mauves of heather, to watch seagulls glide in the wind and land on the bright blue surf on a sunny day or the rain beat the sea grey-green and make the rose hips glisten like rubies on a stormy one, I was reminded of how really little it takes to make one happy.

24

A New Harbor

With the luck of the Irish, we finally managed to sell our house, despite the slump, and, much to our relief, it was bought by a very nice couple who would love it the way we had. As soon as the place was sold, we felt free to look for a new home. Ignoring the advice of all of our friends, who had resigned themselves to our move but having done that, wanted us to be practical, we turned our attention to the rural areas that are far from the beaten path.

Many thought the smartest thing would be to move to England and benefit from the resulting ease in taxes. As much as we love England and miss our daughter and her new family, we knew what it takes to put down the sort of deep roots we like to have. Besides, that would have left Bjørn behind. The rest of our friends thought the only sensible thing to do (and, of course, they were right) was to get rid of most of our things and move into something easy to manage, a step in the right direction for one's old age.

However, if you leave a place that you love very much, you will only be happy if you move somewhere that can make you just as happy. We felt a need to recreate the atmosphere that had enveloped us in the family home. I thought that would entail looking for weeks or even months for just the right place in the country, and we had plenty of time, for the new owners wouldn't be taking over for more than a half a year.

I was in England when the sale went in order, and when Finn called with the good news, I urged him to start looking right away. When he picked me up at the airport, he excitedly told me about a place he had seen that he thought was just the ticket. Well aware of which features he might have considered unimportant in our new home, like whether or not the place had central heating, I was unimpressed and insisted that we had to check out dozens of places.

By now we had bought a small, used car, and we set out for countryside that was far from the mundane area where we have the summer place. After a couple of days of looking at dismal ruins in our price bracket, Finn cunningly arranged a trip in the neighborhood of the place he had seen. My skepticism didn't diminish, though the countryside all around was lovely, but when he turned into the drive, he could see I was just as enchanted as he was. There in the middle of nowhere was a comfortably restored, thatched-roof, half-timbered cottage, nestled in an overgrown garden, where it had been for hundreds of years. It was April, and sunlight flooded the rooms as the owner showed us through the house. Finn gave me a look that told me to hide my enthusiasm, but once back in the car, we both agreed. There was no point in looking anywhere else. That was Wednesday. On Friday, we invited the owners to dinner to close the deal.

Not wanting to have time for regrets, Finn ordered the movers for July, just as soon as our new home could be vacated. After that, he went into a "coma," reviving only to be sociable whenever the occasion presented itself. While trying to enjoy the last bittersweet months of living near Copenhagen in a house that lent itself so well to entertaining, I was trying to get everything ready to be packed and moved. For days I sat with floor plans of the new house, figuring out where to place each piece of furniture and whether we could keep it all. Luckily, Finn gave me free hands, for like most men, he hates to see the home changed and would have made the task impossible by trying to put it all together exactly the same as it had been in a much different setting, like putting square pegs in round holes.

I tried to keep the household as normal as possible while all this was taking place, but finally the point was reached where it had to be confusing. With moving boxes filling up the entire downstairs and a seemingly unending amount of things still to be packed, I tactfully suggested to my usually-so-dynamic husband that he could at least try to sort out the things in his desk, but I was too busy to notice when he sneaked out of the house and was stretched out in a lounge chair, feigning sleep. I thought I had had an inspiration when I filled a cardboard box with things from his desk and carried it out in the sun. Plopping that in front of him and a large bin beside it, I suggested that he sort out the things worth keeping and discard the rest.

An hour later, Lisbeth came by and found me in the kitchen, busily packing china into crates. Lisbeth is one of these clever creatures who has given her husband an upbringing and still is adored. "What's Finn doing while you're packing away all the household goods?" she demanded, her tone oozing with criticism.

"Oh, he's busy, too," I said defensively. "He's sorting out the things he wants to keep from his desk." Lisbeth wasn't satisfied with my word for it, and we went out in the garden to see how things were going. Finn was brown as a berry, and sweat trickled down his chest, not from hard work, but from the noonday sun. Before him was an impressive heap of memorabilia that had been stuffed into his desk during nearly three decades of serious squirreling.

"See?" I said proudly to Lisbeth, "just like I said, Finn's getting rid of junk." But then I noticed the almost empty bin and said, "But, honey . . . you were supposed to throw it in there."

Finn scowled at me for thinking I needed to meddle and corrected me, pointing to the bin, "No, that is for trash . . . These are things I want to save," and he indicated the enormous pile, which included his Cub Scout cap, sundry parts of dead animals shot on his hunt, every birthday card he has ever received, brochures of things we once considered buying but were probably no longer on the market, old receipts and letters, wooden cigar boxes filled with an indiscriminate blend of dippydoots, gadgets that might prove to be handy if he ever found himself afloat at sea and wanted to patch the lifeboat, and yellowed newspaper articles about obscure subjects.

Somehow though, the moving day came and we survived it. A crew of nine movers worked from early morning until late in the evening and demonstrated the patience of saints. The only hint of exasperation was when one of them had just loaded the sandstone birdbath in the last van and asked whether Finn wouldn't like for him to roll up the lawn. After eleven hours of hard work, 250 crates and all the rest of the lot were loaded into three huge vans. I felt I had done all I could to cushion the shock of moving Finn to new surroundings. The only problem was that it would all be arriving at our new address the following morning, and we had to face putting it into place.

We were too tired to be sad when we drove off that evening. The fine weather had held all day, but by now it was quietly raining, and the monotonous swishing of the windshield wipers was the only sound in our little car. As we approached the rolling countryside of our new neighborhood, the rain disappeared, and the moon appeared from behind silver and gold nighttime clouds. Our spirits lifted at the sight of the moonlit scenery, and when we arrived at the cottage, it looked inviting and friendly.

With one last effort for the day, Finn bent his tired back and picked me up to carry me over our second threshold. The empty rooms smelled clean, and moonlight streamed through the small-paned windows, spilling onto the tile floor of the hall where there stood a hibiscus plant with large yellow blossoms, an unexpected gift sent by Lani and Peter to welcome us home.

25

New Beginnings

I had given our old home one final cleaning and was waiting for Finn to pick me up for the long drive back to our new place. It was the first time in ninety years that the villa had been empty, and there was a stark beauty in the vacant rooms. I left the comforting sameness of the kitchen, where the thick slab of oak that Finn had brought home from Lolland to make a breakfast nook lent a cheery warmth.

The dining room still had a naked splendor, with its tall oak paneling and the doors and window casings that had been painted at the beginning of the century when a technique was mastered to make them look like mahogany. The pentagon-shaped verandah that extended the room was ablaze with the autumn foliage just outside the many windows. The oak floors with their herring bone pattern, coated with decades of wax, gave the rooms an elegance independent of furnishings. I shut my eyes and flooded my mind with memories of evenings when the air was sweet with perfume and flowers, with laughter, toasts and the rustling of gowns. I recalled summer evenings scented with honeysuckle, when we dined in the verandah, the door open to the stairway down to the garden.

My own memories superimposed upon those told me by the family, of older days when Finn's grandparents hosted dinner parties on a grander scale, with servants and silver bud vases for each lady to take home with the roses they contained and stories of the war years, when heavy, velvet curtains were hung in the archway to the verandah, the family crowding together to enjoy the only oven that was stoked and to listen to forbidden broadcasts by BBC, ironically enough, with the help of a German device to counteract the Nazi radio interference.

My heels clicked on the bare floors as I went into the living room. The half wall that divided the room made me think of Julius, whose study used to be a small room on the other side of the partition. One day the sliding doors had stuck, and Emma had expressed a wish for the space to be opened up, leaving the mahogany trimmed partitions as a point of interest. Where once Julius had retired with the gentlemen for a glass of cognac, and where Faster Eli had played chamber music with her friends, there now was the corner fireplace we had added. How proud we had been when that fireplace was completed, and how very many happy hours we had spent in front of it, watching the flames lick at the logs, casting shadows on the cast iron impressions of the troll and the billygoat from Grimm's Fairy Tales, a dark scene in the warm glow of the fire. The usually-so-cheery fireplace was swept clean, the bricked hearth scrubbed, and in the bare interior, the bas relief figures in cast iron didn't weave the same spell, deprived as they were of the charred remains of wood. They were like a statue of Pan, removed from a garden and put in a museum.

I hurried out into the hallway, and climbing the stairs, I remembered the sight of Lani in her wedding dress, one hand on the banister, and the other holding her long train, her face lit up with happiness and Finn standing at the bottom, smiling with pride. The dog followed me, settling patiently by my feet in each room, her brass tag making a hollow sound on the bare floors and her brown eyes fixed on my face, unable to fathom what this domestic odyssey was supposed to mean.

The upstairs rooms were flooded with afternoon sun, the lovely white paneling and filled doors with their antique brass handles enough adornment to make them inviting. The empty hearth of the first fireplace Benny had built for us so many years ago again reminded me of how much life there had been in these rooms. I ran my hand over the rough oak beam forming the mantelpiece and remembered the day Finn had found it. It was from a ruin of a farmhouse on Lolland, and like much of the thick oak from such an old house, it showed signs of having been part of a ship.

I comforted myself with the thought that the whole place needed a going-over, and that someone else would have to do it. That really wasn't much comfort, though, for the vacated rooms made the task look easy. I had always liked the views from each side of the house and took one last opportunity to enjoy each one, first running up to the attic where one could catch a tiny glimpse of the sea on a clear day. A flood of memories of all the guests we had lodged up there made me wonder how many would find their way to our place now that we would be living so far from Copenhagen.

Descending the attic stairs to the rooms below, I looked out over the churchyard, remembering the Christmas when I stood in a dark room, spellbound by the full moon suspended in the night-blue sky to the right of the church tower. Just at that moment the doors to the tower opened and the huge bell began to peal, the light in the tower turning the bronze bell golden to match the golden sphere of the moon, a magic moment that might never before have occurred and would surely not happen again. The bell was automated now, and the doors no longer opened.

I looked out the windows where I used to watch for the children, waiting for them to come home from school, and I smiled, thinking of a night when I stood waiting to see Bjørn come home. Like most small boys, he was intrigued when he read about the adventures of Tom Sawyer. He wasn't more than nine or ten when he confided in me that he and his friend Hans had agreed to have a nighttime adventure, like Tom Sawyer and Huckleberry Finn. "What sort of adventure?" I asked, wishing he wouldn't always involve me by being so honest about such pranks.

"We're going to meet on the corner, by the bicycle shop, at two o'clock in the morning," he said excitedly. "Is that alright with you, Mom?" Of course, any responsible parent would think it was a bad idea, but my mind raced back to the days when my brother and I had such adventures, and I didn't want to say no. The only difference was that we didn't involve any adults in our escapades.

"All right," I said, "but I won't wake you up. If you and Hans are going to meet, you're on your own. Just one thing," I added as an extra precaution, "promise to wake me up and tell me if you leave the house."

"I promise, Mom. Boy, are we going to have fun!" and he went happily to bed, while I felt pretty clever, having given him permission to do something which I was sure he wouldn't be able to pull off. He didn't have an alarm clock, and without me to wake him up, I knew he would be fast asleep at the appointed hour. Finn was a bit alarmed when I told him, but I reassured him, reminding him of how soundly Bjørn slept.

At a quarter to two, I was awakened by a little voice in the dark. Bjørn was standing by my bed, all dressed and clutching a flashlight. "Bye, Mom — I gotta hurry to meet Hans." And he was off before I could even get dressed and shadow him.

The next hour was a nightmare; I got up and put on my robe, to stand by the window and watch for Bjørn to come home. I kept telling myself there was no need to worry, but I pictured Bjørn, standing on an empty street corner at two a.m., and wondered what people who were coming home late would think of the mother who let her boy go out at that hour. Finally, I could stand it no more. An hour had passed, and he still wasn't home. I hurriedly put my coat over my robe, pulled on some boots, and quietly left the house. Our driveway was dark and spooky, and an owl hooted in the big walnut tree. I looked down the street, in both directions. It was autumn, and the wind swept dead leaves down the tree-lined street. Much to my relief, I spotted a tiny figure in the bend of the road, his head down, walking in the middle of the street, kicking the leaves and making them swirl in his path.

"Hi, honey. Did you have fun?" I asked, trying to look unconcerned. He was too wrapped up in his thoughts to wonder why I was out there waiting for him.

"No! Hans didn't show up. I waited on that stupid old street corner for a really long time, and I even went to his house, but he didn't even come out when I threw rocks at the window. Boy, is that irritating!"

Pleased that he was home safe and sound, and that the outing had been a fiasco not likely to be tried again, I still was curious about one thing. "Well, don't be too angry with Hans. He just didn't wake up. But tell me, how ever did you manage to wake up and to know when it was the right time to leave?"

"That's easy," he said, obviously less impressed than I was. "I went to bed with my tongue sticking out, and every time I fell asleep, my mouth shut and I bit my tongue and woke up. See, I couldn't count the church bells if I was asleep."

The street had been empty that night, so long ago. Now it was lined with cars owned by people we didn't know as well, and I don't think I could have said yes to a small boy's wish to be like Tom Sawyer. With that thought in mind, I went back downstairs to gather my things for the drive home, wondering whether memories could stay as fresh without the familiar setting to trigger them off.

While waiting for Finn, I wearily thought of all the goodbyes we have during a lifetime, and I puzzled over man's eternal search for immortality, his hopes at least for staying young forever. There are so many things to care about in the course of a full life, and even in the midst of happy moments one is aware of their passing. It is difficult to understand a person whose soul would never tire of this endless parade of feelings.

At times like this I like to recall a dream I once had, one conjured up by a brain that was cluttered with too much caring — caring about loved ones and caring about all the damage that mankind is doing to this poor Earth. In my dream, I was a large white bird that settled on a rock in the sea, and like birds do, I shifted weight from one leg to the other while quietly enjoying the scene.

All around me was emptiness, and I possessed an instinctive knowledge that the trees, the flowers, and all fauna had been destroyed by man. Left indestructible was the light of the sunrise, delicate pinks against pale blue, the soft colors of early morning, before the sun has risen high and bleached them or the heat of the day has clouded them with mists. The crystal clear, empty water of the sea, lapping quietly at the rock, stretched inland among barren prominences.

It must have been much the way the world looked in the beginning of time, and the pristine beauty of this empty scene filled me with a happiness that transcended the feeling of loss over all that was missing. The Earthly beauties I treasure, the people I love, and the very concept of the individual had dissolved and melted into the pure loveliness of the two remaining elements, light and water. I awakened filled with joy over what seemed to be a promise that no matter what course the passage of man takes through eternity, we cannot destroy the beauty of the universe.

But it was only the promise in a dream. I couldn't stop the caring, and I don't think we are meant to cease to care. The dog jumped up and ran whining to the door, and I knew it must be Finn. I grabbed my coat, anxious to leave and break the spell of nostalgia. I hurried out to the car, making an effort not to look back. The dog jumped in, wagging her tail, happy to be going wherever we were going, and as soon as we were on the way, my spirits soared as I thought of the excitement of starting a whole new life. Home is where the heart is, I said to myself, but Finn had another concept: Putting his hand affectionately on my knee, he asked, "So, what have you planned for dinner?"

The Author

Judy Falck-Madsen was born in the Hawaiian Islands in 1938. Adventurous parents gave her a nomadic youth in the islands, California, and Las Vegas — in the days before tourism— which she developed into the American saga told in *Life Line*, published in 2005. She is a graduate of the University of California at Santa Barbara. The author currently lives in Denmark.

www.ingramcontent.com/pod-product-compliance
Lightning Source LLC
Chambersburg PA
CBHW022005090426
42741CB00007B/901